Between Two Worlds

Between Two Worlds

The Inner Lives of Children of Divorce

Elizabeth Marquardt

THREE RIVERS PRESS

NEW YORK

Published in the United States by Three Rivers Press, an imprint of the
Crown Publishing Group, a division of Random House, Inc., New York.
www.crownpublishing.com

THREE RIVERS PRESS and the Tugboat design are registered trademarks
of Random House, Inc.

Originally published in hardcover in the United States by Crown Publishers,
an imprint of the Crown Publishing Group, a division of Random House, Inc.,
New York, in 2005.

Library of Congress Cataloging-in-Publication Data
    Marquardt, Elizabeth.
        Between two worlds : the inner lives of children of divorce / Elizabeth
    Marquardt.
        Includes bibliographical references and index.
    1. Children of divorced parents — Psychology.   I. Title.
    HQ777.5.M3746 2005
    306.89 — dc22   2005008032

ISBN-10: 0-307-23711-7
ISBN-13: 978-0-307-23711-8

Printed in the United States of America

Design by Joseph Rutt

10 9 8 7 6 5 4 3 2 1

First Paperback Edition

For Jim, for everything

Contents

Author's Note

With two exceptions noted in the text, the men and women quoted in these pages were participants in the study reported in this book. Although the names and identifying details of study participants have been changed to protect their confidentiality, all quotations are drawn directly from interview transcripts. Details about the interview setting were altered in some cases.

In order not to overload the text with numbers I have typically written about survey data in proportions (i.e., "one-fifth," "more than half"), although at times I have used percentages when a proportion would be unclear. Percentages greater than 1 percent have been rounded off. Any reader wishing to know the exact percentages can find the full survey data at the end of this book.

Foreword

by Judith Wallerstein

This eloquent, achingly honest story of a young woman's growing up with divorced parents carries an important message for America. It is a powerful cry from the heart that touches us all. Drawing on a new national study of young men and women raised in divorced families, who today make up one quarter of the adult population, the author speaks for herself and her generation.

Hers is emphatically not a story of failure. On the contrary, the author today is a beloved young wife and a happy mother of two lovely children. She is also a college graduate. She grew up feeling loved by her parents, who separated when she was two years old and divorced the next year. Her parents remained civil with each other and tried their level best to work together on her behalf, and she continued to reside in both of their homes and to maintain close contact with each throughout her childhood.

Nevertheless—and this is the startling message of this book— along with many young adults she looks back with deep sorrow on a difficult childhood and a bewildering adolescence. These young adults recall how strange their childhoods seemed as they tried to remain connected with two homes, two parents who presented them with sharply different ideas and divergent values, and eventually, as parents remarried, two new families. The author speaks of how often she felt cut in half as she tried to bridge two worlds that spun further away from each other with each advancing year. Despite her eventual successes, she remains haunted to this day by memories of how hard she had to work to keep her balance in life and how lonely she so often felt. Like several children in my studies who told me poignantly, "The day they divorced was the day my childhood ended," she envied those lucky children whose parents lived together. Her two homes, however loving, never enabled her to feel central to her parents' lives or even really secure in their separate worlds.

Thus, no matter how impressive their achievements in adulthood, we learn that the self-image of adults raised in divorced families is still shaped by how burdened they felt as children. The author tells us poignantly how her search to feel "whole" occupied her energies for many years. She describes how adapting to the different lifestyles and values within her parents' second families required her to become a chameleon, to keep secrets from each parent, to be extra discreet, to be hypersensitive to her parents' moods, to "play the game" in ways that left her perpetually wondering about her own true identity. As one of the college students whom she interviewed in her study told her, "It was just very hard to interact with my parents when I was growing up because they were separate. They were two different people, two different places, two different ideas." Nearly all of the young people describe long periods of loneliness while both parents were preoccupied with rebuilding their own lives. Many report the countless times they felt responsible for taking care of a distressed parent. And hardest of all, they describe how they had to figure out for themselves what was right and what was wrong. Because the moral guidelines from each parent conflicted, they had to create their own values and find within themselves the courage and the capacity to trust their own judgment and to make their own way in the world. As one of the young men in my studies told me, "I had to become my own parent."

The study Elizabeth Marquardt conducted included extended face-to-face interviews with more than seventy college graduates between the ages of eighteen and thirty-five. She chose to focus on college graduates because she wanted to report the experiences of young people who were reasonably successful like herself. Half of the people she interviewed in person came from divorced families and half from intact homes. She spoke with each for several hours, asking a wide range of questions about their families, their experiences as children and as young adults, their relationships, their beliefs, and their values. All of the interviewees from divorced families had maintained contact with both parents and had experienced parental divorce before age fourteen. Some hailed from divorces where the parents were locked in conflict. Others were raised in "good divorces" like her own, where the parents were friendly and cooperated in their child rearing. Similarly, some of the intact families were harmonious, and in others the parents were in low or high conflict with each other.

Additionally, Elizabeth Marquardt's book is based on questionnaire interviews with a random sample of fifteen hundred adults between the ages of eighteen and thirty-five, chosen from a national population. The questions were based on what Marquardt had learned from the personal interviews. Here, too, half of the sample was from divorced families and half was raised in intact families. The differences in the lives and responses of those who came from divorced families and those raised in intact families were striking even though some of those in intact families reported that their parents were unhappily married. As in my own work, Marquardt's findings do not support the argument that the children will necessarily be unhappy in families where the adults are unhappy. And my own research showed clearly that children are often content in troubled families and are unaware of their parents' marital disappointments if the parenting is sustained.

One interesting set of new observations she brings to our attention is that the young adults' beliefs in God and in religious teachings and their affiliation with religious institutions were strongly affected by their parents' divorce. Generally speaking, she tells us, adults from divorced families are less religious than those reared in intact homes. Fewer children of divorce belonged to religious institutions or attended services with their families. Many of the adolescents who did seek a religious connection went to services on their own. They described how they sat alone in the back pews, eyeing the intact families with children sitting in the front rows. And they reported sadly how rarely religious leaders approached them or responded to their troubled questions. We learn in this book that attitudes toward God often reflect a young adult's feeling toward his or her parents and that parental divorce affects the way young people feel about religion. Many among those Marquardt interviewed connected their disapproval of one or both parents directly to their rejection of religious beliefs. Some described how their bitter anger at their parents led them to deny the existence of a caring God. For many, their search for a religious affiliation was associated with their longing for the stability and sense of safety that had eluded them in their divorced family.

Divorced fathers, these young adults reported with real disappointment, were rarely moral teachers. Indeed, adolescents in divorced families were often preoccupied with the behavior of their parents and concerned about their parents' morality, or lack of it. They were distressed by their parents' infidelities, past or present. I have reported their exasperation with parents who dated a much younger person or adopted a new or offbeat lifestyle. The traditional commandment about honoring one's parents was baffling to many of these young people. They surely honored the parents who made sacrifices on their behalf, but not parents in general and not unconditionally.

Elizabeth Marquardt's book is important for many reasons. Divorce affects all of society. It is a shared experience in our culture because it shapes the lives of so many children and adults and reflects our collective values. In sheer numbers, divorce in this country has involved at least a million children each year since 1973. As we enter the twenty-first century, we have outpaced the rest of the Western world.

Marquardt's personal experience, along with that of the many young adults whom she interviewed, directly challenges the popular wisdom of our day and the advice that is commonly offered to divorcing parents. It directly contravenes what we, as a society, believe and want so much to keep on believing: that divorce has a time-limited and basically mild to moderate impact on most children. Courts, attorneys, and mental health experts who work in the shadow of the courts regularly tell parents that if they will only refrain from fighting and cooperate in their parenting, and if the child is encouraged to maintain contact with both parents, then the child's upset will be short-lived and he or she will be freed from the stresses of the troubled marriage and able to enjoy a happier though divided family. The implication is that if the parents will only heed this good advice, then divorce is no big deal.

Elizabeth Marquardt's experience, along with that of the young adults she interviewed, does not support this optimistic view. Contrary to the advice offered to divorcing parents by courts and mental health experts, going back and forth frequently between two parental homes did not bring her or her peers greater comfort or relief. In fact, she avers, locating the divorced parents' homes very near to one another does little to ease the child's burden and may even increase it, as the hapless child is forced to worry about hurting one parent's feelings each time she decides to leave in order to be with the other parent. This all-too-common belief in American society—that divorce is no big deal—is regularly reinforced by cheerful reports from academics, who assure us all that because most children of divorce do not end up with psychiatric diagnoses, they are therefore fine. Most of these academic studies are conducted by strangers over the telephone. They fail to explore the young person's feelings and perceptions during their long years in the divorced family. Therefore, the author maintains, they miss what is at the core of the child's experience.

Marquardt wants us all to understand that what she wryly calls the "happy talk" so many legal and psychological advisors dispense is based on denial and wishful thinking. The love she felt from both parents was treasured, but it was not enough. Nor was the absence of parental conflict, although this is the mantra of mental health experts, attorneys, mediators, and the courts. Nor was her sustained contact with both mother and father. None of these supposedly ameliorative conditions took away the pain of the divorce and the extra burdens it imposed on her growing-up years.

She takes issue not only with the advice offered to divorcing parents but also with the whole raft of books written for children presumably to help ease the child's adjustment to the new, divorced family. All these books, with their cheerful illustrations, describe the pleasure and ease for the child of going back and forth from one parent's home to the other's and how each home supplements the other, especially if Dad lives in the country and Mom lives in the city, or other such idyllic arrangements. This is nonsense. The "happy talk" she describes, which bears no relationship to the child's actual experience, serves only to convince the child that she dare not confess to feeling pain, because the grown-ups don't want to hear of any negative feelings about their divorce or that they lack understanding. It only makes things harder for the child, who learns very quickly to keep her true feelings well concealed and to follow the program.

Whom is this book for? It is for those thoughtful people throughout our society who don't need to be falsely reassured by "happy talk" and who have the courage to toss out precut programs and prescriptions that don't fit the real experiences and feelings and needs of real children. This book is designed for the millions of parents who are already divorced and for those who are considering divorce, today or tomorrow; for the judges who sit on family court benches and gravely try to figure out how to protect the best interests of children they rarely see and can barely visualize; for the attorneys who line up on either side to aggressively promote the agenda of their clients; and for the legions of mental health experts and mediators who undertake to advise parents and courts how to thread their way through the thickets of sorrows and conflicting claims that surround divorce. It is, then, for all of us.

All that Elizabeth Marquardt writes rings true. Our failure as parents and as a society to listen to our children, our denial of their pain and anger, and our eagerness to fit them into cookie-cutter programs greatly contribute to their loneliness and isolation. Elizabeth Marquardt has rendered us all a great service by recounting in vivid detail how hard she tried and how much she suffered, while her parents who loved her but no longer loved each other worked to rebuild their separate lives. Her plea to all of us is for honesty and an unflinching look at how divorce changes the lives of children.

This book goes to the heart of the child's experience when a family breaks in two. It accords with all that I have written, from my thirty years of working with children and adults in thousands of divorced and remarried families. It is not, as some will label it, a book against divorce, nor is it designed to make parents who divorce feel guilty for imposing suffering on their children. The author is not arguing against divorce. She and I are both pleading for an honest recognition of the experience of children so that we can begin to really help them. If we can bear to listen to them, we can take the first step. Then and only then can we help. Once they can believe that they are not alone and that we do understand their inner experience, we can help them to manage the breakup of their family. That is the message of this eloquent and moving book.

JUDITH WALLERSTEIN pioneered the study of children of divorce in this country and is the author of the best-selling *The Unexpected Legacy of Divorce: A 25 Year Landmark Study* and other key works on divorce.

Foreword

by Norval Glenn

Several books about the children of divorce have been published in recent years, including books co-authored by each of the two most prominent authorities on the topic and books by persons whose parents divorced, among them a collection of writings by college students. Dozens of academic and journalistic articles on the topic have also been published in the past decade. One might well wonder what is left to be said on the topic.

A great deal, as it turns out. This new book by Elizabeth Marquardt breaks new ground, being the first book, and probably the first major publication of any kind, to deal with the moral and spiritual development of the children of divorce. It combines the insights derived from Marquardt's personal experience as a child of divorce with the results of a systematic comparison of young adults whose parents did and did not experience a parental divorce before they reached adulthood. The study included in-depth interviews with more than seventy young adults in the age range of eighteen to thirty-five and a national telephone survey of fifteen hundred persons in the same age range, half of whom had experienced a parental divorce. The result is an extraordinary book that is must reading for all scholars and researchers interested in the effects of divorce on children and that should be read by all parents considering divorce. Aided by perspectives derived from theology,

psychology, and social science, but unfettered by the jargon of
those disciplines, Marquardt has produced a beautifully written,
moving, and intellectually sophisticated treatment of an immensely
important topic.

An example of an important finding from Marquardt's research
is that apparently many of the consequences of divorce for children are inherent in the divided lives of these children and cannot
be prevented by the efforts of the parents to have a "good divorce."
Certainly it is better for children if the parents do not involve them
in their conflicts, do not ask the children to keep secrets from the
other parent, protect the children from parental worries, and avoid
other obviously destructive behaviors and situations. Still, in some
respects, the childhood experiences of children whose parents had
"good divorces" were not as favorable as even those of the children
whose parents had an intact but not happy marriage. A related
finding not discussed in this book is that whether the parents had
a "good" or "bad divorce" seemed to make no difference in regard
to their offspring's educational attainments and degree of marital
success—two dimensions on which the children of divorce, as a
whole, lag well behind persons who grew up in intact families.

Marquardt does not challenge the statement, made by Mavis
Hetherington among others, that most children of divorce develop
into well-adjusted, successful adults. (Marquardt is a child of
divorce who turned out very well indeed.) She does, however,
object when the fact that a majority of the children of divorce are
clinically normal is used to downplay the seriousness of parental
divorces. Quite aside from the fact that the proportion of emotionally troubled adults is around three times as great among those
whose parents divorced as among those from intact families, no
amount of success in adulthood can compensate for an unhappy
childhood or erase the memory of the pain and confusion of the
divided world of the child of divorce. The shift of emphasis in
research a couple of decades ago from the short-term to the enduring effects of parental divorce was an important and needed development, but an unfortunate consequence was the emergence of

the view that only the enduring effects matter. Marquardt's book reminds us that the quality of life during childhood and adolescence is important in and of itself.

"Happy talk" about parental divorce is well intended, whether it be in children's books about the pleasures of having two homes or in college textbooks about the resilience of the children of divorce. Much of this cheery discussion is meant (at least ostensibly) to avoid making children of divorce feel that they are "damaged goods," in the words of one author. But does it have its intended effect? Marquardt does not think so, nor do I. I first began to change my once sanguine view of the effects of divorce on children when students in my sociology of the family classes whose parents had divorced objected to the statements in the textbook that the effects of a parental divorce on children are temporary and unimportant. These students felt that their own experiences and feelings were being discounted, or that they were unusual and inadequate because of the pain and trauma they had experienced as a result of their parents' divorces. "Happy talk" about the effects of divorce on children may be comforting to divorced parents (and that may be the main reason for it), but I doubt that it is often comforting to the children of divorce of any age.

Marquardt calls for honesty in facing the effects of divorce on children, but her purpose is not to make divorced parents feel guilty. Many divorced parents ended their marriages for good reasons, and others divorced at a time when expert opinion told them that whatever was best for them was also best for their children. Furthermore, there are moral dilemmas involved in weighing the interests of children against the interests of their parents. An emerging view, supported by a great deal of evidence, is that parents in a "good enough marriage" devoid of violence and extreme conflict can best serve the interests of their children by waiting until the children are grown before divorcing. Such sacrifice by parents would seem to be warranted for the sake of children they chose to bring into the world. A moral complication derives, though, from the fact that the sacrifice of the mother is likely to be considerably greater than that of the father because, as the years go by, the chances for remarriage of the mother typically decline, while the chances of remarriage of the father increase. How much should the mother be expected to sacrifice for her children? There is no easy or obvious answer to that question.

Of course, this moral dilemma exists only when there is no doubt that the marriage will eventually end. Often (probably usually) the decision facing parents in a troubled marriage is whether to keep trying to make the marriage work or to resign themselves to divorce. If there is any reasonable prospect that the marriage can be saved (in the sense of being both intact and satisfactory), the interests of the mother and the children usually coincide. Divorce typically hurts women financially more than it hurts men, and even at ages as young as the late thirties, the prospects for remarriage (or recoupling outside of marriage) are better for ex-husbands than for ex-wives, especially if the ex-wife has custody of a child or children. Some observers of American marriage claim that married couples do not usually divorce until they have tried very hard to save the marriage, but persons who have divorced seem generally not to agree with that position. For instance, only about a third of the ever-divorced respondents to a recent national survey conducted by the Office of Survey Research at the University of Texas at Austin said that both they and their ex-spouses worked hard enough to try to save the marriage. And when these respondents were asked to give reasons for their divorces, "lack of commitment on the part of one or both spouses" was the most frequently selected reason. One effect of Marquardt's book should be to motivate parents in troubled marriages to try harder to make their marriages satisfactory.

The most important effect of the book, however, should be to encourage frank and unapologetic acknowledgment of the consequences of divorce for children. Avoiding unnecessary parental guilt is a worthwhile goal, as is avoiding making the children of divorce feel that they are "damaged goods," but these goals should not be attained at the expense of honest, straightforward discussion. Ignoring or denying a problem is rarely if ever a good solution to it. Critics may, of course, disagree with some of Marquardt's interpretations of the evidence, but the discussion the book elicits should be conducted on logical and empirical grounds and should not be inhibited by misguided concerns about feelings of guilt among parents and discouragement among the children of divorce.

NORVAL GLENN is one of our nation's leading family scholars and the author of numerous books, articles, and op-eds. He is the Ashbel Smith Professor of Sociology and Stiles Professor in American Studies at the University of Texas at Austin and is co-investigator, with Elizabeth Marquardt, of the *National Survey on the Moral and Spiritual Lives of Children of Divorce,* the results of which are presented for the first time in this book.

Between Two Worlds

Introduction

What Is Not Known About Our Generation

I am seven years old and climbing the jungle gym outside my school when I overhear two mothers, standing nearby. One says, "Kids with divorced parents are kicked back and forth like a football." The image grabs me. In this small, rural community, I had never heard anyone talk about divorce, even though my own parents had separated when I was two years old and divorced a year later. The divorce was a silent fact of my life, unnoticed by other kids, mentioned by adults only when they asked me how my father was doing when I came back from visiting him.

Kicked back and forth like a football. Even a seven-year-old could sense that this was bad; no one likes to be kicked. But it sounded playful as well. I could see me—the football—flying end over end against a blue sky. It was the kick and the thud on the other end that imparted a vague sense of threat.

Sometime later, while visiting my father, I tried out the idea, mentioning lightly that I was kicked back and forth like a football between him and my mother. His face turned a deep purplish red, his lips tightened, he sputtered. He looked the same way whenever he was angry—this time at the person who had said such a thing to me. He sought to regain control and assured me, sternly, that this image did not apply to me. He and my mother loved me, he said. That saying about the football was about kids whose parents didn't love them.

I had to admit, at the time and over the years, that I didn't feel as if my parents were trying to pass me off to each other. I never felt a rough kick at the airport or at the beginning of the long car ride. On the contrary, my parents were always sad to see me go, and we hugged excitedly when I ran to one of them after a long separation.

Still, there was something about that football. I could see it spinning in its arc, flying freely, even beautifully, from the one who launched it to the one who caught it. But it flew with a freedom that put a catch in my throat. It seemed almost too high, too free; it belonged neither to the place it had left nor to the place where it was going. Maybe it belonged in that space in between. And what a conditional space that was.

I am still thinking about the football and about the deeper implications of that metaphor. This book seeks to answer the question that as a child I was unable to put into words: If your parents love you and they get along reasonably well with each other, why is their divorce still so wrenching for the child?

A New Survey of Young Adults from Divorced Families

It was that question that led me to undertake the Project on the Moral and Spiritual Lives of Children of Divorce, a three-year study I directed with the help of an advisory committee of senior family scholars, and with funding from the Lilly Endowment.

As part of the study, I co-directed with Dr. Norval Glenn, a sociologist and leading family scholar at the University of Texas at Austin, the first nationally representative survey of young adults from divorced families. This survey involved fifteen hundred randomly selected young men and women from around the country between the ages of eighteen and thirty-five years old. Half of them experienced their parents' divorce before they were fourteen years old and the other half grew up in intact families. Those from divorced families continued to see both parents in the years after the divorce.

The questions were inspired by seventy-one in-person interviews I conducted with young adults in the same age group. Again, half experienced their parents' divorce before they were fourteen years old and the other half grew up in intact families. Like the fifteen hundred young adults we surveyed by telephone, the young people I met with in person did not lose touch with a parent after the divorce. The only difference was that while the national survey included young adults with varying levels of educational attainment, the seventy-one young people I met with in person were all college graduates. The fact that they had completed college made it less likely that they were struggling with serious social or emotional problems, which allowed us to see the effects of divorce on those who had proven especially resilient. This indicator was important because I had always felt it was too simple to say that divorce "ruined" children's lives; I was more interested in the long-term difficulties it caused even for those who seemed to have weathered it well.

Almost all of the questions posed in this study have never before been asked of children of divorce. The new questions were fueled not only by the comments of those I interviewed in person but also by a lifetime of experience as a child of divorce.

Because I too am a child of divorce, I decided to write this book in the first person ("I" and "we"), but this book is not a memoir. It includes statistics (all drawn from the study unless otherwise noted) as well as substantial stories and quotations from the many young adults I interviewed in person. Their stories give faces and voices to the numbers and, together with the nationally representative survey data, allow me to speak with confidence for my generation.

What This Book Is *Not* About

There are a couple of things this book is *not* about. First, this book does not argue that no one should ever get divorced. Divorce is a vital option for ending very bad marriages. In homes where there is abuse, violence, serial infidelity, chronic addiction, or other serious problems, the best way to protect members of the family, especially the children, may be to end those marriages.

One major national study has turned up an important finding that helps clarify the question of when divorce is necessary. The researchers found that one-third of divorces end high-conflict marriages, in which the parents report physical abuse or serious and frequent quarreling. Not surprisingly, the children do better after these high-conflict marriages end. However, two-thirds of divorces end low-conflict marriages, in which the parents divorce because they are unhappy or unfulfilled, or have other problems that are not seriously threatening. The children of low-conflict couples fare *worse* after divorce because the divorce marks their first exposure to a serious problem. One day, without much warning, their world just falls apart.

Most parents take the decision to divorce quite seriously, but I urge parents to think harder still. For those who wish to save and improve their marriages there are resources they may not know about. But in the end it is not my place to tell any particular couple whether or not they should divorce; only they can look at all the evidence, get the help they need, and decide for themselves whether divorce is warranted.

Second, this book does *not* argue that divorced parents are bad people. Many people who mean the world to me are divorced, including my own parents. I firmly believe that no one besides the couple knows the full extent of what goes on in someone else's marriage and that some marriages have failed miserably long before the couple begins to think of divorce. It is also the case that most marriages with children are ended by only one of the parents, leaving the other parent to cope with a fate he or she did not want or imagine.

Yet as much as I believe we should support and understand the needs of divorced and single parents, I feel even more strongly that we should not let our concern for them prevent us from looking unflinchingly at the experience of children of divorce. Children are voiceless: they don't write books, they don't vote, they don't usually get interviewed on television. We learn about their experience by sensitively observing their lives and later, when they are grown up, asking them what it was like. For too long the debate about divorce in this country has been dominated by the adult perspective on divorce, with some adults charging that divorce is unjustifiably rampant and others retorting that divorce is a right that no one can question.

We have begun to look at divorce from the child's point of view, but it is only that—just a beginning. We must be sensitive to the experience of divorced adults, but for the sake of the children—those of us who are the first generation to come of age with wide-spread divorce, and the current generation of young children—we need to confront the truth of their lives as well.

Growing Up in a Different Culture

Among the people I met while writing this book was Jennifer, a thirty-one-year-old scientist whose parents have been married for thirty-five years. She is currently dating a guy she loves who happens to be from a divorced family. He wants to get married and Jennifer does too, but she is afraid. Jennifer wants a long, happy marriage like her parents had, and she fears that maybe she and her boyfriend are just too different to make it work.

Jennifer told me that when she was growing up, "a lot of the children from divorced families that I knew were really independent. They did a lot of things on their own that I would never have dreamed of doing, because they didn't grow up with this protective nest around them. They had Mom's house and they had Dad's house and they were kind of in between, taking care of themselves." Her boyfriend being a child of divorce, she said, "makes me a little nervous, quite honestly. It's almost like coming from a different culture."

I hope the fact that her boyfriend's parents divorced will not dissuade Jennifer from marrying him if they really love each other. But Jennifer is right—children of divorce often do seem to float between their mother's and father's homes, having to take care of themselves at a much earlier age than other children do. Growing up in a divorced family *is* like growing up in a different culture.

There is something unique going on with children of divorce, something Jennifer and many others have difficulty putting their finger on. That inexplicable "something" is what this book is about.

1

Growing Up Divorced

When I was growing up, divorce was an all-but-nonexistent topic of conversation. Beyond my own siblings I knew few other children of divorce; much less did I have any sense that I was part of a brand-new cohort, a generation of children marked by the first era of widespread divorce. I did, however, always feel "different" as a child; in the lingo of the seventies I thought of myself as a "weirdo." But I assumed my weirdness was part of who I was. Sometimes I took pride in it, but more often I felt lonely because of it.

It was only in my early twenties that I began to understand how common the experience of having divorced parents was. Only then did I begin to wonder how divorce might have shaped me as a person. I was born in 1970, just as the no-fault divorce revolution started sweeping the country. California was the first state to pass such legislation, in 1969, and virtually all the other states followed. My own parents, high-school sweethearts who were among the top graduates of their class in a small town in North Carolina, married in their first year of college, had me in their sophomore year, and separated when I was two years old.

In the very early pictures of our family my dad has a shaggy haircut, barely covering his ears, that scandalized his father. My mother wears her hair differently in nearly every photo and is clad in hippie regalia—pretty, homemade crocheted vests and snug-fitting shirts and jeans. I am usually dressed in overalls or, for special occasions, in dresses that she and her mother and grandmother sewed for me.

I'm fascinated by those early pictures because I have no memory of that time. I don't remember my parents living together, sharing a home, or hugging, let alone arguing. In one home movie from that brief era — I think my dad's younger brother was holding the camera — my parents give each other a long, deep kiss. They're hamming for the camera but there is unmistakable youthful passion there too. It's the only time I've ever seen them kiss, and I watch it a little embarrassed but also entranced. That's where I came from.

My first memories are of my parents apart. I remember my mother and first stepfather as the parents I called out to when I was scared in the middle of the night. I remember living with my dad, a bachelor getting his master's degree, for a long summer vacation at his apartment. I've learned since that his friends were impressed that a young man could feed, clothe, house, and love a little girl by himself for an entire summer, every summer. When I look at men in their early twenties around me, it seems hard to imagine. But even though I knew that my parents were young, they seemed larger than life, and capable of anything.

In some ways I was a fortunate child of divorce: I could take both parents' love for granted. So many like me lose a warm relationship with their father or lose that relationship entirely. The trouble was that I missed my mother and father terribly when I was separated from one of them — and I was always separated from one of them.

As a result of my parents' divorce, my childhood was filled with constant movement. I traveled often between my parents, spending school years with my mother and long summers, holiday breaks, and occasional weekends with my father. Even when I stayed in one place, other people did not. My childhood was routinely peopled with new faces — parents' boyfriends and girlfriends, new spouses, step- and half-siblings — that came and too often went.

The two people I loved the most and looked to as the rocks on which my own identity was built, my mother and my father, lived completely separate lives a six-hour drive apart. As I entered young adulthood I began to sense that growing up with parents in two different worlds, with me traveling between them, had shaped me in profound ways. I started to read avidly about divorce, looking for an explanation.

What We *Do* Know About Children of Divorce

I learned a lot from the studies I read about children of divorce, but there always seemed to be something missing. Most books and articles focus on the social or economic consequences of divorce, often showing the links between divorce and serious childhood problems such as poverty, dropping out of school, juvenile delinquency, early sexual activity, and teen pregnancy. For example, a recently published study by a major researcher, E. Mavis Hetherington, examined more than a thousand divorced families over three decades and found that 20 to 25 percent of young adults from divorced families experience "long-term damage"—serious social and emotional problems—compared to 10 percent of young people from intact families.

These kinds of studies are valuable. Learning how many children of divorce struggle with truly debilitating problems ought to make us question our society's high rate of divorce. I know some of these young people, and my heart goes out to them. Yet studies such as these are something of a blunt instrument; they capture only the most dramatic negative effects of divorce on children. As far as I could tell, I was not struggling with those kinds of problems, yet I suspected that divorce had still deeply influenced who I was.

Among all the researchers, Judith Wallerstein has been a pioneer in examining the more subtle psychological effects of divorce in children and young people. By getting to know a sample of children of divorce extremely well and returning again and again over the years to talk with them, Wallerstein has painted a detailed and sensitive portrait of the way divorce shapes the inner lives of many children, whether or not they end up with severe, diagnosable symptoms. For instance, her most recent book shows that experiencing parental divorce during childhood has a "sleeper effect": its worst symptoms often appear when children of divorce leave home and attempt to form intimate relationships and families of their own, but do so with much less ability to trust and little idea of what a lasting marriage looks like.

But there is an enormous story left untold. Although the number of divorces stabilized in this country in the early 1980s, close to half of first marriages still end in divorce. Today, one-quarter of all young adults in this country between the ages of eighteen and thirty-five have experienced the divorce of their parents. Many people look around and see plenty of young people from divorced families who seem just fine. These children of divorce graduate from high school and even college or beyond, get jobs, get married, have kids of their own. They are everywhere. If divorce causes such serious problems, then how do we explain these young people?

Some in my generation have noticed and written about this seeming contradiction. Several decided to write about their parents' divorce because of the disconnect between the studies that focus on the tragic consequences of divorce for some children and their own experience of building lives that were outwardly successful but still, they were certain, deeply marked by divorce. Among those accounts are *Split: Stories of a Generation Raised on Divorce,* edited by Ava Chin; *The Love They Lost: Living with the Legacy of Our Parents' Divorce,* by Stephanie Staal; and *Generation Ex: Adult Children of Divorce and the Healing of Our Pain,* by Jen Abbas.

Perhaps the most intriguing book by a Gen X-er about her parents' divorce is one that does not even mention divorce in the title. Rebecca Walker was born in 1969, the daughter of author Alice Walker and attorney Mel Leventhal. She tells the story of her parents' divorce in *Black, White, and Jewish: Autobiography of a Shifting Self.* Although most reviewers focused on Walker's story of growing up biracial, the overriding division in Walker's family life appears to be not race but divorce.

For Walker, whose parents divorced when she was in third grade, *Black, White, and Jewish* is an attempt to make sense of her own history, to locate and describe her own "shifting self." The book opens with the words "I don't remember things." She writes, "Without a memory that can remind me at all times of who I definitely am, I feel amorphous, missing the unbroken black line around my body that everybody else seems to have." Walker locates the roots of her shifting, ambiguous sense of self in her own early, shifting experience of home. Only a child of divorce could write about home as she does: "I remember airports. . . . I am more comfortable in airports than I am in either of the houses I call, with undeserved nostalgia, Home. I am more comfortable in airports than I was in any of the eight different schools where I learned all of the things I now cannot remember. . . . I remember coming and going, going and coming. That, for me, was home."

These books are important additions to what we know about children of divorce, amplifying and extending the story told by impersonal statistics. As far as I can tell, none of these young authors ended up with a psychiatric diagnosis, an arrest record, or a teen pregnancy, but the effects of divorce, and the specific ways it played out in each of their families, influenced by race, religion, or class, were so important and persistent they felt moved to tell their stories.

When I told people I was writing this book, I sensed that some of them thought it would be easy, that it must be a relief to hold my divorced parents up to a critical light, spill my guts, and feel vindicated. But this book is not meant to be triumphant or vindictive, and neither, I believe, are the books by these other young authors. Our voices are searching, reflective, and if anything overly tentative. As I confirmed in my own study, we children of divorce often feel extremely protective of our parents, especially when we are young, and for that reason alone it can be hard for us to speak truthfully about our childhoods. But if our culture is to understand the real impact of divorce and if we are to understand our own lives, we must try to put the experience into words. The love we share with our parents—us for them and them for us—is strong enough to withstand the whole, complex truth.

The individual stories of children of divorce point to the lingering loss and pain that result from divorce even when the children look "fine." The long-term studies point to some of the obvious and troubling differences we possess as a group. But no one has stepped back and explained how divorce changes childhood itself. The new study reported in this book explains how divorce reshuffles many core features of middle-class childhood that our society takes for granted and, in the process, shapes children's identities well into young adulthood.

This larger story must be told because, as a society, we still have not grasped just how radical divorce really is. Too many people imagine that modern divorce has become just a variation of ordinary family life, like growing up in a large family, perhaps, or in a military family that moves a lot. Sure, there may be some discomfort, and some of the kids may end up with big problems, but doesn't childhood as we know it stay basically the same? Most people assume the answer is yes.

They are wrong. In reality, divorce powerfully changes the structure of childhood itself.

Why a "Good Divorce" Is No Solution

The national debate about divorce has generally focused on the worst outcomes, with many assuming there is no need to worry about the children of divorce who appear to be fine. But I can think of few other significant childhood experiences that our society treats in the same way. Many people survive wrenching childhood traumas—child abuse, war, an alcoholic or drug-addicted parent—and nevertheless manage to become productive members of society. Yet no one would suggest that because they have survived the ordeal and now look "fine," their experience of child abuse, war, or addiction was apparently not that bad. On the contrary, our society sympathizes with these young people. It takes active steps to try to help them and to prevent other children, whenever possible, from growing up the same way.

Further, when our society asks only if a child has been hurt, and nothing more, it sets a very low bar for its expectations about children's lives. I'm a mother now. When I first held my daughter did I hope only that she would grow up and not be damaged? Of course not. Like all parents, my husband and I want to protect our children from suffering, but we also want them to thrive, to enjoy rich, loving relationships and have happy, successful futures. Parents do not set a low bar for their children, and neither should our society. Our society must do more than ask whether divorce causes clear and lasting damage to some children. It should also ask probing questions about how divorce shapes the lives of many children who experience it.

Just as most debates about children of divorce focus on the gravest and most obvious outcomes, most discussions about life in divorced families focus on the hot-button issue of conflict. When researchers examine how children fare in divorced families, many of them want to know how well or how poorly the divorced parents get along. Do they battle over custody of the child? Can they be in the same room together without getting into a fight? Are they able to stick to agreements on visitation and child support?

Learning more about the conflicts between divorced parents is undeniably important. But an overriding emphasis on the issue of conflict has led to a troubling idea that has quickly gained credibility in our culture. In recent years, some experts have speculated that if couples divorce amicably and if both parents continue to share in raising the child, then perhaps the negative effects of divorce can be avoided. Experts urge parents, for the sake of their children, to aim for what some call a "good divorce."

The idea of the "good divorce" is attractive to many. Some divorced parents are reassured because it suggests steps they can take to try to protect their children if they must end a very bad marriage. Other parents like the idea of a "good divorce" because it suggests they can end a marriage that may be okay but not completely satisfying and still do right by their children. Family court judges welcome it because they want to make arrangements that, whenever possible, keep both parents in the child's life, and they want to minimize conflict between those parents. Some therapists like the idea because they want to help these families and a "good divorce" gives them a role in teaching parents how to divorce. In addition, many social observers, including journalists, academics, and opinion leaders, like the idea of the "good divorce" because it promises to alleviate much of the anxiety our society has about divorce. What really matters, the experts assure us, is how the parents get along after the divorce, not the divorce itself.

References to the "good divorce"—and the idea behind it, that the quality of the divorce matters as much as if not more than the divorce itself—are everywhere. A therapist is quoted in the *Christian Science Monitor*, "A lot of times it's not the divorce itself that bothers children, but the level of conflict, or being caught in the middle." An academic expert opines, "Rather than discourage divorce per se, we, as a society, need to encourage more humane divorce." Another expert writes in a book review, "The problem is not so much with divorce itself but with the different ways men, women and children experience divorce and react to it." A holiday article in *Newsweek*, titled "Happy Divorce," features divorced families who put their conflicts aside in order to spend Christmas together as a family. It says that researchers "have known for years that *how* parents divorce matters even more than the divorce itself."

A November 2002 cover story in the *Washington Post Magazine* is titled "The Good Divorce: One Couple's Attempt to Split Up Without Tearing the Kids Apart." The cover photograph features a handsome, smiling, divorced family with three girls. Inside we learn about Debbie and Eli. Although their marriage was, according to Debbie, "all in all, an incredibly functional marriage," they divorced when she became troubled by their "lack of connection." The journalist is impressed that Eli, who Debbie agrees is a great father, still comes to Debbie's house each school morning to get the girls ready after she's left for work, as he has since they split three years previously. Eli says he shows up every morning to reassure his kids "that even though Mommy and Daddy aren't married, we're still your parents, we're still there for you and we still love you." Readers of the story might easily assume that the present arrangement will last until the girls leave home.

Yet as any child who has lived it will tell you, an arrangement like that of Eli and Debbie is inherently unstable and any number of events could spell its demise What will happen when Eli or Debbie remarries? Will the new spouse feel happy about Eli showing up at Debbie's house every morning to get the girls ready for school? What happens when one of them begins dating? Will they still want their girls to pop in unannounced? What happens if Debbie gets a great job offer on the West Coast? Will she turn it down so that her ex-husband can continue dropping by for breakfast every morning?

Another genre of "good divorce" news articles features tips and tools to help parents manage their divorce. Several recent articles trumpeted a new website—OurFamilyWizard.com—that is supposed to help divorced parents improve the quality of their communication. At the website each parent can make entries on a shared calendar, message board, data bank, and expense account. The site was created by one divorced dad to help deal with the "chaos" of managing multiple children's schedules in two families. But one journalist says, "Those involved in family law immediately recognized it for its value in the truly nasty cases—the ones where the parents can't get on the phone without the conversation devolving into a screaming match." The tone of articles such as these is always upbeat, with those interviewed expressing great confidence that if the adults will simply get better organized and play by the rules, then the children's pain following their parents' divorce will be greatly reduced.

Each time the "good divorce" is featured in a news article, it is greeted with fanfare and treated as a brand-new idea, one that gives no quarter to moralistic worrywarts who fret about the effects of divorce on children. Yet the idea of the "good divorce" has actually been around for more than a decade. The term was first coined by Constance Ahrons in 1994 when she published *The Good Divorce: Keeping Your Family Together When Your Marriage Comes Apart*. In that book Ahrons says that it is possible for couples to achieve a "good divorce" by setting clear rules governing postdivorce interactions. These rules prevent unnecessary conflict and allow both divorced parents to stay actively involved in the children's lives. If parents can achieve a "good divorce" they will have not a damaged divorced family but rather a thriving "binu-clear" family—another term that Ahrons coins —and the children will be fine.

The premise of the "good divorce" sounds logical. Surely, if divorce does happen, it is better for children not to lose significant relationships entirely, nor to be drawn into bitter, unending fights. However, when you talk to the children themselves you find that the popular idea behind the "good divorce"—that the quality of the divorce matters more than the divorce itself—is actually an adult-centered vision that does not reflect their true experiences.

While a "good divorce" is better than a bad divorce, it is still not *good*. For no matter how amicable divorced parents might be and how much they each love and care for the child, their willingness to do these things does absolutely *nothing* to diminish the radical restructuring of the child's universe.

When Dr. Norval Glenn and I compared young adult children of divorce with their peers from intact families, we found that for chil-dren a "good divorce" often compares poorly even to an unhappy marriage, so long as that marriage is low-conflict (as approximately two-thirds of marriages that end in divorce are). Increasingly, too, many people think that a "good divorce" and a happy intact mar-riage are about the same for kids. As one observer reflected, "A good divorce, a good marriage, it matters not." But our research demonstrates strongly that, without question, a "good divorce" is far worse for children than a happy marriage. Of course, any child could tell you the same thing. No child thinks a "good divorce" is as good as the happy marriage of his or her own two parents.

How Divorce Changes Childhood

To grasp the reality of the lives of children of divorce we could not simply ask, as so many other researchers have, how many children of divorce end up with severe, tragic problems. We had to ask: How do children of divorce make sense of their parents' different beliefs, values, and ways of living when their parents no longer must confront these differences themselves? How do the feelings of loss and loneliness, so widespread in the lives of children of divorce, affect their spiritual journeys? How might divorce divide and shape the inner lives of many children, even those who appear to be successful later in life?

These questions may sound utterly natural but they are entirely new. Even the great works on children's moral and spiritual development either were written before divorce was widespread or ignore the fact of divorce and assume that all children still grow up with their own, married parents.

This study yields a new portrait of children of divorce. For those of us from divorced families, a deep and enduring moral drama was ignited the moment our parents parted. After their parting we spent our childhoods crossing a widening chasm as their divided worlds grew more different every year. Our constant journeys between their worlds had lasting consequences.

Most children cannot conceive of keeping important secrets for their parents, but divorce required us to keep secrets routinely, even when our parents did not ask us to. Most children observe their parents confronting each other about their conflicting values and beliefs; sometimes these confrontations end in fights, sometimes in agreement, sometimes in stalemate. But the majority of those from divorced families say that as the years passed, our divorced parents did *not* have a lot of conflicts. Instead, we experienced something much deeper and more pernicious. The divorce left us with a permanent inner conflict between our parents' worlds. This was a conflict for which we could imagine no resolution, a conflict for which many of us thought we had only ourselves to blame.

For children of divorce, the idea that childhood is an important, protected time of spiritual growth is thrown into question as well. Many, if not most, parents feel that handing core religious or spiritual values on to their children is important. Yet children of divorce more often say that if we have strong spiritual beliefs it is something we came to *alone*, as a reaction to what was missing in our family life rather than an affirmation of it. We love our parents, but the idea that, for instance, God could be like a parent can be as foreboding as it is enticing, beckoning us to a spiritual life or alienating us from faith and spirituality for years to come. And this is only the beginning.

2
Divided Selves

How Divorce Divides the Inner Lives of Children

I am browsing through a bookstore when I stumble across a charmingly illustrated children's book. A young girl with silky black hair, dark button eyes, and an impenetrable gaze stares out from the cover. Her arms and legs are outstretched, like a child about to make a snow angel. To her right is an urban scene—tall apartment buildings clustered together, one topped with a water tower, a spindly green tree in front of another, all framed by a narrow swath of blue sky. To her left are lush green hills, mounded one on top of the other like scoops of ice cream, adorned with towering trees, a little house, a white barn with a red door. The young girl appears to be stretched, quite literally, between two very different worlds.

The book, *To & Fro, Fast & Slow,* is written for young children whose parents are divorced. The unnamed girl in the story travels regularly between her father's apartment in the city and her mother's house in the country. Her parents—and their separate worlds—stand in stark contrast to each other, but the book is about fun and adventure. The little girl enjoys the contrasts. She gets the best of both worlds: the city and the country, a loving mommy and a loving daddy.

From the title to the split images throughout, division and opposites are the overriding theme. The book's cover, featuring the opposite pairing of city and country, also has a dog leaping into the picture on the left and a cat leaping out of the picture on the right. Even the T-shirt the girl wears pictures both a sun and a moon. The motif is clear: Everything this little girl knows, every aspect of her life, is divided down the center. Like the cute sun and moon on her T-shirt, the two halves of her life are as different as night and day. Yet, the author seems intent on assuring us, the little girl loves it. The child's parents may be divorced but this is no nasty divorce. She spends lots of time with her mom and her dad and they both shower her with love. Isn't this, on the whole, just as good as growing up with two parents who are together?

Many people assume the answer is yes. Even when I was growing up I could not have explained what troubled me about my parents' divorce. I loved them and they loved me. I missed each of them desperately when I was away from them, and when they remarried I sometimes struggled to get along with new family members. But if anyone had raised questions about my parents when I was a child, I would have leaped to their defense. It's even possible that I would have liked a book like *To & Fro, Fast & Slow*. I might have been intrigued at seeing my unusual experience depicted in its pages.

As a child I didn't have the ability to be a critic. Growing up in two worlds was all I knew. When I reached my early twenties, though, and could observe more closely the experience of my friends from intact families, I began to wonder if my identity might have been shaped by my experience of always traveling between my parents' worlds, never quite sure who I was or where I belonged. Perhaps this burden I had long felt—this sense of having to figure out everything in life alone, expecting no help from anyone else—was not simply the result of my own inability to deal with life and be happy. Hesitantly, because I did not want to blame my parents or make them feel bad, I began to explore whether this burden I felt might have something to do with the consequences of my parents' divorce.

Later, when I entered graduate school in my mid-twenties, I realized that the private debate that had long raged inside me—

whether my parents' divorce had significant effects on me—was part of a fierce public debate about the effects of divorce on children, and that the American public was as sharply divided on the question as I was.

Divorce Is the Beginning, Not the End

Many people imagine that the hardest time for children of divorce is the moment when their parents first part. That moment *is* hard, but it is only the beginning. The division and restructuring of childhood that immediately follow, and which continue up to and beyond the point the child leaves home, throw into question aspects of childhood that were once taken for granted and keep the divorce very much alive for years to come.

In our national survey, we found that almost two-thirds of children of divorce who stay in contact with both parents say they felt like they grew up in two families, not one. Many changes occur in the wake of divorce. But from the child's point of view the essential change is this: The child suddenly inherits two distinct worlds in which to grow up.

Growing up in two worlds creates endless and often painful complications for a child. But one of the first and most troubling consequences is that resembling a parent is no longer the mark of being an insider, a part of a larger family to which the child and other family members belong. Quite the opposite. Suddenly, resembling a parent, or sharing any kind of experience with a parent, can also mark the child as an outsider.

As children of divorce, we became insiders *and* outsiders in each of our parents' worlds. We were outsiders when we looked or acted like our other parent or when we shared experiences in one world that people in the other knew little or nothing about. And, in a powerful piece of symbolism, we also could have a different last name. By contrast, we were marked as insiders by whatever traits we shared with the family members in one world—physical characteristics, personality, and name—as well as the experiences we shared with that family. We always had at least some traits and experiences in common with the family in each world. Yet because we grew up living in two worlds we never fully belonged in either place. At any moment, without warning, one of our distinguishing traits could mark us as an outsider.

This business of growing up in two worlds is relatively new. Only in recent decades have large numbers of children grown up commuting between their parents' households. No adult advised us on how we should pull this off because the adults themselves did not know. Even a relatively conflict-free divorce left us, with little explanation, on utterly mysterious terrain.

Some still might ask why the *structure* of divorce—the fact that it causes a child to grow up in two worlds—matters as much, if not more, than the *quality* of the divorce. Even when both parents love their child dearly, why does their divorce still present their child with a painful and arduous way of growing up?

What Marriage Does for Children

To understand why divorce itself is the primary problem—to understand what divorce really does to children—I have to explain first what marriage does for children. Most books about children of divorce spend little or no time talking about marriage. They take divorce as their starting point. But this approach is like reading a mystery novel by starting with Chapter 10. When I probed the inner lives of children of divorce I found that our experience actually begins with, and says an awful lot about, marriage.

Think about a deceptively simple word: *parents*. *Parents* is plural, but in common usage it refers to the singular unit of a mother and father. A child knows that his married parents are two separate people, of course, but quite often he thinks of them as a unit, especially when he is young.

A primary challenge of marriage is for two separate people to become one couple, to reconcile their needs and experiences in ways that allow them to care for each other and to avoid unnecessary strife. Couples wish to meet this challenge even if they do not have children because they know they will both be happier if they can live together in relative harmony. But the stakes are higher when they have children, because now they are raising a new person who will be strongly shaped by the environment they create.

Married couples try their best to make sense of their different sets of values, beliefs, and ways of living. Often the work of bringing together their two worlds sparks conflict. Experts usually focus on conflict between husbands and wives, in part because conflict can hurt people, but also because conflict is easier than concord to see and study.

Yet conflict in a marriage can also be seen as a subplot in the couple's larger attempt to bring together two worlds. Husbands and wives conflict because they have common interests at stake but cannot see eye to eye on them. Their mutual interest in trying to reconcile their differences is what keeps them engaged in conflict. As long as a couple is married they will at times experience conflict between their worlds, and no couple will ever be able to, or even want to, get rid of all their differences. In a marriage, therefore, the work of bringing together two worlds often looks and feels like conflict.

It is easy to see the frowns and tense shoulders of two parents who cannot agree whether their child is old enough to go to the park alone with a friend. But when they agree that their child is ready for such a step and one takes her to the door while the other goes back to making dinner, it may look as though nothing has happened. In fact, something has. One parent may be more protective than the other, but on this point they have found agreement. The child can go the park and may never realize that her parents had different opinions about it. If instead they argue about it, their child may observe (if she is paying attention) that they have a difference of opinion. She—and we—may see the conflict, but the larger attempt to bring together their worlds is also visible.

When married parents are successful in their attempts at bringing together their two worlds the results are apparent as they resolve differences, back each other up in front of the child, or try to understand and adapt to each other's quirks. When they are less successful their attempts at making sense of their different ways of living may be expressed by fighting, criticizing the other parent in front of the child, or trying to change each other's irritating habits. Yet however well or poorly they handle the challenge of negotiating their differences, an important but often ignored feature of married life is this: *The work of making sense of their two worlds is the parents' job, not the child's.*

Everyone agrees that only bad parents would tell a young child: "I think you should do this, but your father thinks you should do that. So you decide." When parents disagree they are expected to confront each other about it. Whether they confront each other behind the scenes or in front of the child, with hostility or with dignity, is very important, but it is not the only important issue. What is equally important is that it is the parents' job to bridge their differences; even if they do their work badly no one would say that their child should attempt the job instead. Our society pins the success or failure of family conflict resolution squarely on the parents.

Making sense of two ways of life is an active experience for married couples. They have to work at it and some couples do it better than others. But even when couples are angry and avoiding each other—not actively bridging their differences or openly conflicting—the simple fact of the marriage holds them together and remains larger than the differences that divide them.

The unifying quality of being married is difficult to see, but it is a constant undercurrent in the life of a married couple. It is the background music between the fight scenes, the subtle strains that we don't hear until someone points them out to us. We see a married couple disagree. We hear about their conflicts. Sometimes we see them make up after a fight. We have to look more closely to realize that, in and around their periodic disagreements and reunions, they remain engaged in the lived process of simply being married—a process involving the countless minor compromises and charged negotiations summed up by bland expressions like "give and take." They go into the same bedroom at night and come out in the morning. They see to at least some of each other's needs as a matter of habit. Even if they are angry and avoiding each other, they still live in the same home and continue to share an identity as a married couple. Even when they don't particularly *feel* "married," they're still married. Despite their differences they are still a unit in the child's eyes—"parents"—and dealing with the conflicts between their worlds, however well or poorly they do it, is still their job.

Moreover, to focus on conflict and unhappiness to this extent is really to overstate the problem. Every married couple has conflicts but only some of them have very serious, ongoing conflicts that threaten their or their children's well-being. Divorce is an important option for these couples. For most married couples, however, the real need is to learn how to handle conflict better. In most marriages, the overriding achievement is the ever-unfolding, never-perfect, but nevertheless critical knitting together of two worlds into one marriage and one family life. Some married couples even find that as time passes, the rough edges between their ways of living begin to soften and their beliefs and values become more alike than different, although differences persist for all couples, and for some more than others.

Just as important, differences are not necessarily bad in a marriage. Married parents can offer their children quite different perspectives that ultimately benefit the child. Recently a friend told me about a meeting he and his wife had with their six-year-old's teacher. The teacher said their daughter was doing wonderfully in school. The only problem was that she sometimes pushed to the front of the line as everyone left the classroom to go the playground or cafeteria. When the parents talked afterward my friend's wife worried out loud, "Gee, I don't want her to hurt the other kids' feelings." My friend responded, "Gee, isn't it great how ambitious she is. That trait will take her far in the world."

Both parents were expressing good, but different, values. The mother was concerned about the child's relationships and ability to get along with others. The father was glad she had competitive instincts that would help her be self-reliant someday. By confronting their different values, alone and in front of their child, they are able to offer their daughter a nuanced and positive message: Do what it takes to get ahead, but be nice to people at the same time. Because her parents are together, their daughter knows these different values can be held together as well.

Naturally, when this child reaches adolescence and young adulthood and begins to separate from her parents, she will begin to develop her own, independent beliefs, values, and ways of living. But for now inventing a worldview is not her responsibility. Her parents confront each other, behind the scenes and in front of her, and give her something to work with. When she is ready, she will hold their worldview up to the light, compare it with what she sees around her, and begin accepting, rejecting, and blending parts of it with what she finds elsewhere.

Much of this process, while subtle, appears in intact families to be natural and therefore unremarkable. Of course married parents attempt to give their child one family and way of life. Of course most children, especially when they are young, see their parents as a unit with largely similar beliefs and expectations. This is the most basic stuff of family life, after all.

Except, for many children today, these basic features of family life cannot be taken for granted.

From Parents to Two Separate People

When couples divorce much of what our culture takes for granted about family life changes dramatically. Even the word *parents* takes on new layers of meaning. It still refers, at least for now, to the child's biological (or adoptive) parents. But after divorce, the unit dissolves—the parents are separated and become two people again. They move into different homes. The number of interactions between them typically drops from many times a day to perhaps several times a week to rarely, often only by telephone call or e-mail.

The divorce process further reinforces the parents' separateness. Litigation and conflict over possessions and children encourage them to define themselves in opposition to each other and to break all lingering ties, except those to the children.

In the ensuing years, some parents will continue to conflict openly with each other. However, experts recognize that doing so is harmful for children, and divorced parents today are strongly encouraged to avoid postdivorce conflict for the children's sake.

Some parents do manage to minimize conflict from the beginning. They avoid nasty disagreements over money and property. In the years after the divorce, their outward conflict might wane. They can pass the children back and forth without argument. A few even manage to achieve an amicable relationship. They both show up at important events in the child's life. They can stand in the front yard and chat when one drops the child off. These couples are seen as successful divorced parents who have achieved a "good divorce." They may smile when they greet each other. They may even remember each other warmly, as an old flame from long ago.

These parents are no longer conflicting. *But, at the same time, they are no longer trying to make sense of the differences between their two different worlds.*

It is at this point that the experts fall silent. There is a widespread assumption in our society that if parents manage to minimize conflict after the divorce, they will create something like an intact family for their children, because the children will still have a mom and a dad in their lives. This assumption is wrong. In fact, the postdivorce family, no matter what the level of conflict, is an entirely new kind of family that lacks many features of intact family life that might seem natural and unremarkable.

After a divorce the differences between divorced parents grow larger as they forge new identities. They have new homes and new challenges in their work and personal lives. They form new relationships. Their beliefs and values evolve. But, instead of rubbing the sharp edges of their worlds together on a daily basis, instead of sharing the same home and many of the same ties, their views develop on separate tracks in new settings. They are no longer the bumping cars of one train jostling down a single track, but two separate trains, diverged and steaming ahead.

At times these parents may conflict, but if they are seeking to minimize disputes they do so largely by staying out of each other's way. Observers may see an admirable absence of conflict, but from the child's point of view what these divorced parents have achieved is the creation of two separate worlds for their child to grow up in. It is certainly better for the child if there is little open conflict between the parents rather than a lot. A high degree of conflict reinforces the division between the two worlds and creates additional pain. But a mere absence of conflict between divorced parents can never begin to knit their worlds together in the way that being married does.

Travelers Between Two Worlds

Divorced parents stay out of each other's worlds, retreating to their own worlds. Where does the child stand? As children, we became travelers between their worlds. Sometimes we stood in one world, sometimes in the other, but in our own minds most often we were suspended uncomfortably somewhere in between. We were like the football I imagined myself to be as a child, hurtling between my two parents. When they divorced, our parents successfully separated their two identities. But we remained the bridge between them, seeking to make sense of two increasingly different ways of living as we forged identities of our own. In other words, *after a divorce the task that once belonged to the parents—to make sense of their different worlds—becomes the child's.* The grown-ups can no longer manage the challenge, so the child is asked to try.

Divorce is a problem for many reasons. It often causes the family incomes of women and their children to plummet. It often separates children from daily life with their fathers. It distracts children from doing well in school and increases their vulnerability to a host of social problems. But the central, daunting task that was suddenly assigned to us following our parents' divorce was this:

We, and we alone, had to try to make sense of our parents' increasingly different ways of living. The most important models for our own budding identities—our mother and our father—no longer had the job of rubbing the rough edges of their own worlds together in an attempt to hand us something reasonably whole. Like the parents in *To & Fro,* Mom may prefer the simple bohemian life of the country, while Dad wants to pursue his career dreams in the big city, but it is no longer their job to try to make their conflicting values and desires cohere. Instead, the rough edges of their worlds rub together in only one place—within the inner life of their child.

This theme emerged again and again in our national study of young adult children of divorce. Melissa, a twenty-three-year-old library assistant whose parents divorced when she was five, recalled: "It was just very hard to interact with my parents when I was growing up, because they were separate. They were two different people, two different places, two different ideas." After their divorce, Melissa's father started a new and eventually more affluent life on the West Coast. Her mother stayed on the East Coast, struggling with serious depression and often neglecting Melissa. Her very different parents could not do any of the work of bridging their differences and offering something whole to their child. That job was left to Melissa.

Many other children of divorce say the same thing. Jason, a thirty-two-year-old consultant whose parents divorced when he was fourteen, said: "My parents were so different. I mean, they were polar opposites. My mom had one way of thinking; my dad had another. But," he said, "it was never openly conflicting with each other. It was just different ways of being." It was up to Jason alone to make sense of his parents' vastly different ways of thinking and living as he tried to figure out who he was and what he believed.

Growing Up Watchful

We may have been quite young—only four or eight or twelve years old—when our parents split up. How did we take on the task of making sense of two very different worlds, something that our parents largely gave up on, something that *all* adults have a hard time doing?

We responded, in part, by becoming watchful. We observed our parents—their beliefs, their values, their ways of living—carefully. At times we invested all our energy in trying to *understand* each of our parents—what made them vulnerable, what made them mad, what they thought about the other parent, what they thought about us. To outsiders we may have appeared sensitive and observant, or rebellious and distant, but we were still watching.

Meanwhile, the child of married parents is on a very different journey. Before adolescence and young adulthood, before she begins separating from her parents and becoming an individual, she often moves through the world unselfconsciously knowing, or thinking she knows, her parents' beliefs. More important, most of the time she is not all that deeply concerned with what her parents think and feel. She is more concerned about *herself* and her own struggles and joys, her friends and siblings and school and games and fantasies. She is free to focus on these things, to stand in the center of her own world, because she knows at the deepest level that her parents are taking care of the big stuff. Together, they are protecting her, looking out for her, feeding her—in fact, it may often seem to her that they exist only to do these things for her and her siblings. Sometimes they may fight and the fighting may scare and upset her. But usually she feels confident they will get over it, and usually they do. Her attention, which has been temporarily diverted to her parents, returns to herself.

To outside observers, the children of divorced parents may look no different than the children of intact parents. We ran on the playground, went to school, argued with our siblings, played with blocks, drew pictures in our bedrooms. But we were also vigilant. When Mom came home we gauged her mood. When we stayed at Dad's we were often quiet and on good behavior. We paid close attention to the different rules at each parent's home and the conflicts in their expectations of us. We wondered if we looked or acted too much like our father and if that made our mother mad at us. We struggled to remember what we were not supposed to say, what secrets or information about one parent we should not share with the other. We adjusted ourselves to each of our parents, shaping our habits and beliefs to mimic theirs when we were around them. We often felt like a different person with each of our parents.

Our parents may no longer have been in conflict, but the conflict between their worlds was still alive. Yet instead of being in the open, visible to outsiders, the conflict between their worlds migrated and took root within us. When we sought our own identities—when we asked "Who am I?"—we were confronted with two wholly separate ways of living. Any answer we gleaned from one world could be undermined by looking at the other. Being too much like Dad could threaten the Mom-self inside us, and vice versa. These conflicts were not raised in conversation with or between our parents, or with anybody else, but internally. We were one in our bodies but we did not feel one inside. Even the "good divorce" left us struggling with divided selves.

Married parents do not live perfectly in front of their children. Far from it. Married parents can have major differences, and their children sometimes struggle with serious problems. But these are problems that our society is now willing to talk about. In the self-help section of the bookstore you will find entire shelves of books on alcoholic families, co-dependent families, incest, and child abuse. You will find books on mothers who love their daughters too much and mothers who are too distant, fathers who are workaholics and fathers who push their children too hard to succeed.

But you will find only a few books on divorced families, at least in proportion to the number of divorced families in this country, and most of them are upbeat guides on how to divorce rather than in-depth looks at the lives of children of divorce. Strangely, our culture seems only too happy to talk about dysfunctional intact families—to point fingers at all the ways married parents can mess up with their children—but it falls silent about divorce because no one wants to make divorced parents feel bad. Some people might even get the erroneous impression that the average divorced family is *better* for children than the average intact family, whose problems are so often bared to the world.

What are some of the consequences of a divided childhood, lived between two worlds?

Our study showed that children of divorce, even those who appear to be fine and successful later in life, are much more likely than their peers from intact families to share profound and moving stories of confusion, isolation, and suffering. Most people do not expect children to be deeply absorbed by their parents' needs and vulnerabilities, but children of divorce often say we were. Most people do not expect children to confront complex moral questions early in life, but as children of divorce we routinely did. Most do not expect children to feel like outsiders in their homes, but we often felt that way. Most do not expect children to keep secrets for their parents, but we often did. Likewise, most do not expect that children will approach God from a place of suffering and isolation, but that is how we often explain our spiritual journeys. Most do not expect children to feel like a different person with each of their parents, yet children of divorce are likely to say we did.

When our parents divorced we did not just suffer a bump, leaving us with a few bruises that quickly faded. Our childhoods were turned inside out in ways that have been largely secret and silent—until now.

3
Little Adults

When I was twenty-three, I ran into an aunt I hadn't seen in years at a family gathering. After we'd chatted about her sons, she gave me a warm smile and said, "Even when you were a little kid, you always seemed so mature. When you were five years old, you talked just like a grown-up."

All my life I had heard such compliments from adults. I was "mature," "resourceful," "trustworthy." I had learned to accept them with a shrug and then modestly change the subject. But this time something in my aunt's eyes made me pause.

"I always thought it was kind of sad," she added.

I froze. No one had ever said *that* to me before—ever. Suddenly, and for the first time, I saw my five-year-old self through her eyes. It *was* sad, I realized, for a small child to act so mature. Sure, some children naturally are more mature than others. But kids also need to be kids.

That moment has stuck with me. It was one of the few times that an observer departed from the usual line—"divorce is fine, your parents are great, it's terrific that you're so mature"—and recognized the complex reality of my life. My parents *were* great and I *was* mature—in some ways. But their divorce had caused me to grow up very fast.

Even my parents recognized this. With a mixture of sadness and awe, my mother often told me, "You raised yourself." She talked about leaving my dad when I was two years old and needing me to act older than my age, which apparently I did. Unlike many kids, I didn't throw tantrums or whine. I hung out with her and my new stepfather and their friends. I reveled in the attention from grown-ups. I was offended when I got sent to bed while the party was still going on. I found grown-ups more interesting to talk to than other kids.

By the time I was five years old I was flying alone to visit my dad. At the age of nine, when my mom and stepfather separated, I usually went where I wanted to go by myself. I wasn't the child whose mother shuttled her around town after school. I would walk or ride my bike miles away to a friend's house or the shopping center. If I couldn't get there myself, I didn't go. That same year I took care of my younger brother many afternoons—and, by the time I was eleven, some nights. Today, he and my mom agree that I helped to raise him.

My resourcefulness and independence were sources of pride. Sometimes this role was a burden, but I also accepted it as part of my identity. It didn't occur to me that there was another way of living. I felt I had only myself to rely on.

But if I was mature on the outside, inside I was still a child, often lonely, sometimes confused, and sometimes very scared. When I was home alone or taking care of my brother, I imagined strangers peeping in our windows or looking through the skylight of my attic bedroom. Unfortunately, my parents didn't have room for feelings such as these. My mother was too overwhelmed, and my father lived too far away even to know about them.

Children have to grow up too fast for all kinds of reasons: poverty, or a parent who dies or has a chronic illness. But divorce is different. Children know that it's the result of at least one parent's choice.

Kids, We Have Something to Tell You

The day a child learns his parents are divorcing marks a turning point in his young life. Some children who are old enough to remember date everything in their childhoods as "before the divorce" or "after." Yet that first moment of revelation is rarely as clear as outsiders imagine. Most of the time, the haphazard and confusing way that children learn that their parents are parting is a harbinger of the many baffling turns their lives will soon take.

Michael is a young guidance counselor based in a Chicago public high school. We met late one afternoon at a Vietnamese restaurant near his school. He rushed in late, looked quickly at the menu, and explained that a meeting about a troubled student had run long. It took him awhile to switch gears and start thinking about when he learned—at age five, twenty-four years earlier—that his parents were getting divorced.

He crossed his arms and leaned forward, balancing his elbows on the table. "My parents didn't fight in front of us," he said. "They would go in the bedroom and talk." He took a sip of his soda. "One day," he recalled, "when my brother and I were going to basketball practice—we had a little-kids' league—my mom said, 'You know, your father's left and he's not coming back.'" Michael paused. "We didn't say anything. She was like, 'Y'all don't have to go to practice if you don't want to.'" But Michael remembers being confused and insisting, "No, I want to go to practice."

Daniel, also twenty-nine years old, was seven when his parents divorced. No one even spelled it out for him. He remembers talking to his younger brothers one day and saying, "It's funny, we go to our mom's and then we go to our dad's, and we go back to our mom's and then our dad's." Only then did the meaning of it register.

Melissa was five years old when her parents split up. She remembers her dad losing his job and moving to the West Coast to look for work. The rest of the family was supposed to follow but never did. Eventually, she learned it was because her parents were divorcing.

Joanna doesn't remember being told her parents were divorcing either. One day she and her mother went to live at her grandmother's and her father did not come along.

Alex just remembers on several occasions being awakened, confused, by his mother, who would hand him his coat to put on over his pajamas, and say, "Get your coat on, we're going." One of those nights turned out to be his last in the home shared by his parents.

Samantha is not even sure when her parents divorced. She was somewhere between ages three and five, she thinks. She remembers a house, a pool, a swing set, then a blur. And then her parents were no longer together.

Some were told by a single, lonely parent, teary-eyed and tired— the abandoned one, the one forced to share the bad news with the kids. Sometimes they were asked not to tell their younger brothers or sisters yet, or sometimes they discovered that their older siblings had been told first. The divorce had begun isolating each of them already.

Ask a random person on the street, "How do kids learn that their parents are getting a divorce?" and they are likely to say something like this: "When parents decide to get a divorce, they gather the kids together, maybe in the living room or at the kitchen table, and break the news. They explain what's going to happen and where the kids are going to live." If this person is especially well informed, he or she might add, "They also reassure the kids it's not their fault, and they both tell them how much they love them."

Our culture has a script for divorcing parents. It's in books, on websites, in magazine articles found in therapists' offices. The instructions are always the same: Gather the children. Explain everything calmly, together. Tell them it's not their fault. Reassure them they are loved. Ask if they have any questions.

This is how to get the next phase of your lives off to a good start. This is the right way to divorce.

The problem, however, is that reality rarely follows a script.

Divorce is the ultimate breakup, and breakups are almost unfailingly messy, painful, and chaotic. When a marriage falls apart, often leaving one or both adults deeply wounded, the two adults are seldom equipped to function as a team.

The script also has a strangely ironic emphasis on togetherness. Both parents should tell the children *together*. The children should all *be* together and hear the news at the same time. The parents should be *with* the children and be extra attentive to them in the days after the discussion so that the children can express their feelings and ask questions that occur to them later. This is certainly good advice and, if parents must divorce, it is worth following as best they can.

But it quickly becomes clear that the divorce talk, if it occurs at all, is the last time that everyone will gather as one family. The children who remember it do so with sadness or anger, the togetherness an aching counterpoint to the sudden loss that overtook their lives and lasted for years.

Another problem with the prescribed script is that it assumes a fairly high level of verbal comprehension on the part of the children. Many children are quite young when their parents divorce, so as the divorce unfolds they may not remember what their parents said.

Ultimately, whether or not our parents turned out to be "good" at divorce is not the main issue. The splitting of one home into two opened a whole new chapter in our lives. Now *we* had the responsibility of bridging our parents' increasingly different worlds. The immediate loss of one parent and the sudden, unnamed burden that fell upon us loom larger in our memories than the words our parents hoped would be reassuring.

Children Pushed to the Edges

When a cell divides, it creates two new cells, each with its own nucleus. Likewise, when a divorce divides a nuclear family it creates two new families, each with *its* own nucleus. But divorce does something strange in the process of family cellular division. In intact families, the children are the nucleus and the parents protectively surround them. After a divorce, newly apparent adult vulnerabilities have a way of turning the family structure inside out. Each parent moves to the center of his or her own new world, and it's the *children* who are now on the outside, keeping a wary eye on them, even trying to protect them.

Children of divorce are quite frank about this rearrangement. I was surprised and disheartened to find in our national survey that almost two-thirds of people from intact families strongly agree that when they were growing up, "children were at the center of my family," but only one-third of people from divorced families do. Those of us who grew up in a "good divorce" are more likely to agree that children were at the center, but all of us are significantly less likely to feel this way than children whose parents had unhappy but low-conflict marriages or happy marriages. Divorce restructured our childhoods, making too many of us suddenly feel marginal.

Protecting Our Parents

When a teary-eyed mother or father tells a young child that his parents are planning to divorce, it is likely to be only the first of many times that he will see one or both of his parents feeling quite vulnerable. Just as a civil war exposes the weaknesses of a nation or the fissures during an earthquake expose the molten rock below, a divorce exposes adult vulnerabilities that had formerly been encased in a marriage. The adults are rocked by shock, grief, and anger. Absorbed as they are by their own feelings, they're often unable to protect their children from the same ones. Even more dangerously, some turn to their children for support—particularly those children who, after living along the fault line for a while, have become deceptively articulate, self-reliant, and mature.

As children, seeing our mother or father scared or hurt was frightening. They were, after all, our one line of defense against the scary world outside. They were supposed to be bigger than that world. Knowing that, parents usually try to avoid showing the raw depths of their feelings to their children. When parents divorce, however, they experience many blows at once. They might feel rejected and unloved, alone in a world of couples, wondering if they'll ever find someone to love again. They might struggle with depression. They might have had to divide up their possessions and move, and then faced sudden, urgent financial problems. They might have to think about getting a better job or finding a job for the first time in years. They worry about their children. They feel extremely vulnerable, and it is difficult to hide all this from the kids. Some children sense that their parents are falling apart and, in response, fall apart themselves. They are diagnosed with mental health problems such as attention deficit disorder, anxiety, or depression. They rebel or become violent or start drinking or doing drugs.

Others of us take a different path. We shift our gaze away from ourselves and onto our vulnerable parents. We try to guard our parents from things that might worry or hurt them. We grow up very fast. It takes a special kind of resiliency to respond to divorce this way, but it's not a test that adults should wish on any child. Those of us who could adapt in the face of such insecurity might grow up to become what "good divorce" proponents call "successful" young adults. We might look "fine" to everyone else, but talk to us about our inner lives and you will find, just beneath the surface, a potent mix of loss and confusion that haunts us to this day.

Allison is a young college professor with a baby girl. We met at a café in a busy urban neighborhood near the condo where she lives with her husband. She's a lovely thirty-two-year-old with a long, lean body and graceful movements. She is focused and friendly but a little cool, and she doesn't smile much. She seems to spend a lot of time thinking serious thoughts.

"Both my mother and my father grew up in the sixties," she said. "They were both liberal and sort of anything goes, whatever you want to do that makes you happy. . . . They both were open and accepting of whatever lifestyle anybody wanted, including their own." She fiddled with her bracelet and offered a rare, wry smile. "I guess the primary difference between them, which caused the demise of the relationship, was that my mother was not interested in being one of many women, while my father was on a quest to find as many women as possible." They divorced when their daughter was two years old.

Allison looked out the window for a moment and then turned back to me and shook her head sadly. She said, "I had a relationship with my mother where I was more like the parent and she was more like the child, because she was very young when I was born, and then my parents were no longer together. So I was always required to be more responsible than a normal child would have to be, and at a very young age." Taking care of her mother also meant protecting her from the judgments of her father and grandparents. "I would try to make sure that I never shared any details about what was going on in her personal life," she said.

"I just remember feeling pretty independent always. Sort of having to feel like an adult from a very young age." Allison did things "that children wouldn't normally do," such as flying by herself when she was three years old, or watching the clock at age five to be able to remind one parent when it was time to return to the other. "I've always been the responsible, organized, handle-it kind of person," she said. "It just completely defines who I am."

Yet this controlled approach to life has a downside. Although she is now in a loving marriage, Allison doesn't talk about her personal life very much and finds it difficult to get close to most people. Her greatest joy—the topic that made her break into wide smiles—is her baby girl. But before she and her husband had a baby, she was in therapy for "quite a while" to the tune of many thousands of dollars. "I wanted to try to make sure I was not screwed up before I had a kid," she explained.

Many of us from divorced families identify with Allison's experience of being a "little adult." The national survey revealed that of those of us whose parents had a "good divorce," half agree that "I always felt like an adult, even when I was a little kid," while more than two-thirds of people whose parents had a bad divorce say the same thing. Young people whose parents stayed married were far less likely to feel this way—and that applied not only to happy marriages but also to unhappy but low-conflict marriages.

In part, we felt like little adults because we so often felt overly responsible for taking care of our parents or siblings. More than half of young adults from divorced families, compared to just a third of people from intact families, say we felt the need to protect our mothers emotionally when we were growing up. Close to a third of us also say we felt the need to protect our fathers when we were young, an almost twofold difference compared to those from intact families. And close to a third of young adults from divorced families (well over twice as many as our peers from intact families) say we felt too responsible for taking care of our siblings when we were growing up.

Kyle's parents divorced when he was six years old. He grew up the youngest of four children living with his mother. We sat on a sofa in his living room one winter afternoon as the light grew faint outside. He ran his fingers through his hair and said, "Yeah, I felt like I had to protect my mother. You know, no news is good news. I wouldn't tell her about things that would upset her in any way. I mean, if it was below the radar screen and it was going to stay below the radar screen I wasn't going to bring it up. I definitely didn't want to add to the burden that she already had."

Katy said that protecting her mother took the form of being "on my best behavior" when she was visiting her father and step-mother. "I always felt like I represented my mother," she said. "I didn't want there to be a reason for anyone to look down upon her or say anything against her because of me." She cringed as she remembered that it also took the form of editing herself when she talked about events at her dad's home. "When it came to telling her stuff," she recalled, "with the sensitive things I was just careful on how I would word things. For example, if I had a story to tell, and all of a sudden I realized that this was an experience I had with my dad—let's just say it was about my stepmother's horse—I would say 'my friend's' horse. It would always be 'my friend.' I would do that on both sides."

Daniel, the oldest of three children, also protected his mom by keeping certain information from her. He explained matter-of-factly, "Like if I was upset or something I would never go to my mom and tell her, because I didn't want her to get further upset."

Some felt especially protective of one parent in the aftermath of the other parent's affair. Eric, a Web designer, and I sat at a picnic table in a park near his office building. He arrived with his Atlanta Braves baseball cap pulled low to shield him from the bright springtime sun. Reluctantly he told me about when his mother had an affair and divorced his father when Eric was eleven years old. He recalled, "When my mom was cheating on my dad, I felt like I had to protect my dad's feelings." But he recalled feeling protective of his mother as well: "I definitely would hold back my feelings toward my mom sometimes, because I didn't want to hurt her feelings. Meaning, you know, 'Mom, what are you doing?' " He slapped a palm against the side of his cap. "What's going through your head?"

Will, whose parents divorced when he was twelve, told me angrily that when his father had an affair, "I could see how much it was hurting my mom. And this is my dad, he's hurting my mom."

Perhaps not surprisingly, many young adults from divorced families say they continue to feel protective of their parents, even today. Kimberly spoke tenderly of her parents, especially her father. "He's been alone for years," she said softly. "He hasn't been as successful as my mom. . . . He hasn't dated in years. So he has these ideas that people are going to think he's not good enough or kind of a loser."

Sometimes our protective feelings even intensify as the years go by. Angela's parents divorced when she was four years old. She doesn't remember them badmouthing each other when she was a child, but now that she has grown up they are more willing to voice poor opinions about each other. This development has inspired a new protective instinct in Angela, more than twenty years after the divorce. "I think I feel more protective now," she said thoughtfully, tucking her fine hair behind her ear. "I'll say something to my father like, 'Oh, my mom forgot to pick me up at the airport,' and he'll say, 'She always was like that'." She grimaced. "And then I'll think, oh, I shouldn't complain about her to him because it's not fair, you know?"

Alicia did not recall feeling protective of her father as a child, but when her father's second marriage ended and he became suicidal, she was the only family member available to travel to where he was living and be responsible for him when he was released from the hospital. "I was twenty-two when I got the call that my stepmom was divorcing my dad. They said that I needed to go out there and be with him because he was falling apart. And he really fell apart. So I had to go."

Michael said that even now he protects his mother by reassuring her that she did a good job as a mother. "She always looks at herself and says, 'Maybe I did something wrong with your brother.' And I'm like, 'No, I mean, I turned out fine.'" He shrugged. "Not perfect, but I have a family and we're successful."

Not all young people from divorced families speak as sympathetically of their parents. Some offer a more hardened response. I sensed that these young people felt so unprotected by their parents that they decided, in anger, to offer little protection in return. Melissa scowled when I asked if she had felt the need to protect her parents as a child. "I figured if they needed protection they'd protect themselves," she said abruptly. "I protected my sister. She was older than me, but . . . she always seemed very, very fragile."

Ashley rolled her eyes and said that, even as a child, she felt as though "they're adults, they can deal with it."

Steve said that although he protected his mother when he was younger, their dynamic changed over time. "As things happened, especially when she got remarried . . . I started to feel like she's not watching out for me, I need to be taking care of myself."

In contrast, young adults who grew up with married parents are much less likely to say that they protected their parents. Many saw this as a simple yes-or-no question to which their answer was no. Some explained further: "I felt they were the main protectors. I could never think of any instances where I had to come to their defense." Or "My mom was such a strong individual and Dad's kind of a dad. They conveyed this idea that everything was going to be okay, no matter what. So I never really felt like I had to look out for them." Although not everyone from divorced families recalls protecting their parents, few of us felt so quietly confident that we would be taken care of.

Sometimes, when asked if they protected their parents, young people from intact families thought instead of how they protected themselves. When I asked one young man if he protected his parents, he replied easily, "Not really. If I protected them from anything it was just to save my butt." Another young woman thought a moment and said, "Well, I was arrested for underage drinking when I was in college and they still don't know about that." Still another said, "Yeah, if it was something about my sister or me . . . I might feel like I should keep something from them, but in the end I would tell them."

In a few cases, now that the parents were getting older, children from intact families were feeling the first stirrings of the need to protect them. But most still had relatively young parents, so these feelings were rare.

Being little adults doesn't just mean feeling protective of our parents; it often means feeling less protected *by them*. Over a third of us from divorced families, twice as many as our peers, disagreed with the statement "My parents protected me from their worries." As we'll see, being a little adult also means doing special things for your parents with little help from other adults.

Happy Birthday, Dear Mom

Each family has its own way of marking milestones such as birthdays. Some families have noisy, elaborate celebrations. Some let milestones pass without much notice at all. One insight into the different kinds of relationships children have with their parents is found by exploring how they celebrate their parents' birthdays.

Two main themes arise when people who grew up with married parents recall their parents' birthdays. Many say they were not a big deal. It was the children's birthdays that got the attention. These young people say things like "My parents' birthdays were never as big a deal as our birthdays" or "Theirs weren't big events. Ours were." One woman, the youngest of six children, said that although she and her siblings now make a big fuss over their parents' birthdays it was not that way when they were young: "Growing up, my parents' birthdays were just another day. . . . Now actually my parents' birthdays are more important. Ours are not so much."

At the same time, just as many people from intact families say that their parents' birthdays were lively events, with everybody in the family taking part. One woman remembered, "My sister and I would decorate for our parents' birthdays. And if it was my dad's birthday my mom would help, and if it was my mom's birthday my dad would get up on the ladder and hang things. . . . We'd do streamers and birthday banners and there was always a cake with candles. Then we would have dinner, and depending on what day of the week it was, sometimes family would come over. . . . Or if we were going to celebrate with everyone else then we'd do it again on the weekend."

Another woman remembered, "Oh, my parents' birthdays were always fun. Usually my mom would either cook some nice feast or we'd go to dinner. . . . Growing up, it was never really the gifts that mattered for my parents' birthdays. . . . It was definitely just like a nice meal. Just kind of appreciating the family. But birthdays were important."

The descriptions of children of divorce typically sound quite different. After all, we grew up in two worlds, each centered on a different parent, and unless they had remarried, one or both of our parents were often alone. In response, a surprising number of us tried to recognize and make a fuss over our parents' birthdays on our own, even though we were young and the challenge was sometimes daunting.

There were at least two hurdles to observing our parents' birthdays. The first was remembering the date. The second was having the money to buy a gift or the foresight to make a card or present. Often we made greater efforts for our mothers than our fathers. Children of divorce seem to worry about their mothers' birthdays a lot more than people in intact families do, while their fathers' birth-days often get much less attention than they would in an intact family.

Michael scratched his head, recalling, "I never celebrated my father's birthday." With his mom, though, "we just bought her a card. We didn't have a lot of money anyway. So it was just a card. And when I was little, I would usually make her something."

Rochelle said, "My sister and I would put our money together and buy stuff, especially for my mother. . . . And I would mostly call my father on his birthday."

Ashley recalled, "I really don't remember doing anything for them, you know, until I was older—like ten or eleven—and I had my own money and then I would do the cards and the gifts."

In contrast, people from intact families could usually rely on one parent to remind them that the other parent's birthday was coming up and they never mentioned being concerned about money to buy a present for their parent.

If children of divorce had stepparents or grandparents in the vicinity sometimes they could count on them to help. Alicia said, "I know we would make my parents cards and get them presents. A couple of times I do recall going with my stepmom to get some-thing for my dad. Like she would make a point of taking me shop-ping to get something for him." Kimberly recalled big occasions for each of her parents, orchestrated by grandparents and stepparents: "My dad's birthday we would celebrate at my grandma's house every year. . . . And my mom, same thing. We'd celebrate, my mom and stepfather, my sisters, every year. . . . Typically we'd have dinner and cake and presents. Like a big ordeal."

Most children of divorce, though, said they remembered their parents' birthdays on their own, without help from the other parent, stepparents, or grandparents. Stephen said that his parents' birth-days were "something I would keep track of," and he alone would remember to make or buy cards or presents for each of them.

Some divorced parents do demonstrate unusual cooperation in helping their kids to mark special occasions for one another.

Monique smiled and said, "I can remember my mom bringing cards home for my dad's birthday for us to sign. So it would be a card from the kids, or for Father's Day or something like that. When you're in fourth or fifth grade you don't always think about that stuff, but she always did."

After thinking about it for a moment, Daniel remembered, "My dad's birthday we usually celebrated at the beach. It was in the summer and we'd buy him a tie or something. My mom would give us money." He nodded, adding, "And I remember my dad would give us money for my mom's present. You know, 'Here, buy something for your mother.' And we'd wrap it up and make it a surprise."

For those children who didn't have help in remembering and marking their parents' birthdays, though, forgetting a birthday could cause a parent to express deep disappointment, and the responsibility of observing birthdays and special occasions could inspire lasting anxiety.

At first Eric, a child of divorce, sounded more like the young people from intact families when he said, "Our birthdays were always a big occasion, but theirs really weren't, for the most part. . . . I mean, sometimes I'd miss my mom's birthday altogether—not even a call." As he spoke his eyes drifted away to some kids playing touch football nearby.

"How did your mother react on those occasions?" I asked.

He looked back at me and said, as though it couldn't be more obvious, "She'd cry and say, 'You missed my birthday!'"

Samantha took a different approach. She remembers being careful to make a "big deal" about her mother's birthdays when she was growing up. Even today, she said, "whenever I have a friend or a family member with a birthday it's, you know, make sure I get a card out in the mail on time." She has noticed that her husband, who grew up in an intact family, is very different. "With his family it's kind of like what's the big deal? If he forgets by a few days that's okay too."

On its own, the topic of birthdays may not seem that important. But it can reveal a great deal about the children of divorce. Our need to recognize our parents', especially our mothers', birthdays, often reflects a larger need to protect our parents. Children do not have to worry much about their parents' birthdays. Little adults do.

Home Alone

If there is any single experience that unites children of divorce it is our feelings of loneliness as children. One of the most striking and far-reaching findings of the national survey is that just over a tenth of young people from intact families can identify with the experience "I was alone a lot as a child," whereas close to half of us from divorced families can. That's an extraordinary threefold difference.

When parents divorce, each of them is subject to enormous new pressures that make it difficult for them to be with their children as much as they once might have been. To support two households both parents must work, often for long hours, taking them away from their children. The financial strains of divorce can make it more difficult to find and pay for quality child care, especially after school. It is no coincidence that the term "latchkey children" was coined as the divorce rate began to rise and large numbers of financially stressed divorced parents began to leave their children home alone.

Other forces draw our parents away from us as well. Often they are intent on meeting someone new. To do that they have to get back into the dating world, and dating relationships are not usually welcoming of children, especially in the early stages.

When Michael's mother announced on the way to basketball practice that his father had left, it was only the first of many radical changes that would happen for Michael and his brother. His father at first moved into "a really dingy apartment" in the bad part of town and then eventually moved in with and married the woman with whom he had been having an affair. Michael had a doting mother, but she was lonely and eager to find a new husband. He explained, "One thing that changed after the divorce is sometimes my mom wouldn't come home right after work. She would go out with her friends and stuff." His mother also went out on most weekends, and Michael remembers these regular absences as "very lonely."

Melissa, whose father left to look for work on the West Coast when she was five years old and never came back, had a similar experience. During Melissa's high school years her mother was frequently absent—at work or on dates or spending the night with boyfriends. Melissa remembered forlornly that home was "just a house, and the house was always pretty empty, pretty lonely. It was just me and the cat."

Some of us felt lonely not only because we were often alone but also because we were isolated by intense and unacknowledged emotions. Will recalls feeling very lonely after his father left his mother for another woman, even though his mother was attentive and often home. He was overcome with anger at his father and with shame that such a thing had happened in his family. The depth of his emotions and his inability to share them with anyone else made him feel isolated: "I didn't talk to anybody about it because I didn't know who to talk to. It's just being young, like who do you trust? Who would I tell something personal like that?" He shook his head. "You've got all these emotions and you're running ragged."

Like all children, those of us from divorced families felt frightened at times and needed comfort. But we were significantly less likely to turn to our parents for comfort. When asked, "In thinking back on your childhood, when you needed comfort, what did you do?" over a quarter of those from intact families say they went to their mom, more than a third say they went to their parents as a unit, and a few went to their dad. The numbers are strikingly different for children of divorce. Almost a quarter of us say we went to our mom—not a great deal of difference—but fewer than a tenth say we went to our parents, and only a few went to our dads. In other words, over two-thirds of people from intact families say they went to one or both of their parents for comfort, compared to just one-third of children of divorce.

Where did the rest of us go for comfort, then, if not to our parents? More than a fifth went to our peers—either brothers and sisters or friends. Some went to our grandparents. An equal but small number of those from divorced and intact families cite prayer as a source of comfort. A few of us from divorced families say we dealt with it ourselves or did nothing. More than a quarter of children of divorce, then, remember seeking out our peers for comfort or dealing with the problem alone, instead of going to our parents.

Stephen, whose parents divorced when he was twelve years old, said, "The only one who knew about the divorce was my best friend who lived right up the street . . . and I can remember him saying, just once, 'If you need to talk about anything you can talk to me.'" He frowned. "But, you know, he's the only one, the only person that I can think of, that sort of went out of his way."

Kyle said that his older brother and sister reached out to him. "My brother, the second oldest, he kind of had some uncle qualities, because he was so much older." He smiled, remembering. "And my older sister, she was kind of a second mom as well. So she was kind of protecting."

A few others remembered unusual people, such as their friends' parents, reaching out to them. Jason vividly recalled, "Three of my four closest friends that I grew up with, in fifth grade all the way through college, had the same exact scenario where their parents got divorced. . . . And yeah, their families were very helpful in trying to explain things. Like the parental figures . . . in terms of taking my friend and me out to a ball game and saying, 'If you ever need a place to stay just come here.'" Although some of Jason's friends' divorced parents reached out to him, Jason recalled that he and his friends did not talk much with *each other* about their shared experience of divorce. Shaking his head, he said, "I can't remember one specific time that we ever really talked about that. I just think it was more of a taboo subject between us. . . . It was a subject of negativity, and we didn't want to have any type of negativity around us."

The divorce often seemed to be a "taboo subject" not only outside the family but within it. Monique, whose parents divorced when she was eight years old, said, "I remember my mom coming in one day and saying that the divorce was final and she was crying. . . . Outside of that moment I don't really recall talking about the divorce."

When Hope Seems Unrealistic

There are many myths about the experience of children of divorce. Most people assume that our parents sat us down and explained the divorce to us. Some think we grew up spoiled, guilt-tripping our parents into doing anything we wanted. And many people assume that all children of divorce entertain hopes of their parents getting back together. In fact, divorcing parents are commonly instructed to make clear to their children, in no uncertain terms, that they will *not* be getting back together. The idea is to squelch those fantasies at the outset, though experts warn that children may continue to hope for a reunion.

The reality is not nearly so simple. While some of us do say we hoped our parents would get back together, it is just as common for us to say we harbored no such hopes. Those who did not hope for a reunion often stress that the divorce seemed like a done deal. It was just part of our reality.

When asked if he ever hoped for his parents to reunite, Michael shook his head and said, "No. I don't know what it was, but I just knew it wasn't going to happen. So I never really spent a lot of time thinking they're going to get back together."

Anthony, who was five years old when his parents divorced, said, "I think it was pretty clear they weren't getting back together."

Samantha said bluntly, "At that point I just thought that's what happens and that's the way it is."

In my own case it never occurred to me to consider the possibility of my parents getting back together. After all, from my earliest memories they were apart. When I was growing up I never once cried about their divorce—that is, until I reached my twenties.

I was in my early twenties and dating a new guy who I was very excited about. I thought we might get married someday. I was lying on the rug in my bedroom, idly picturing our wedding day, when I wondered how I would handle the question of who would walk me down the aisle. It seemed strange to ask my father alone to do it and leave my mother out.

Maybe, I thought, they could both walk with me. I pictured myself in a wedding dress, walking down the aisle of a church with my father on one side of me and my mother on the other. In an instant I was shaking and sobbing on my bedroom floor. Never before had I pictured that unity, much less seen it in my life. I had no idea where the tears came from or what other hopes or heartaches might be inside me. I only knew that it had taken twenty years for me to cry even once about my parents' divorce.

Some children of divorce do recall hoping that their parents would get back together. But often they share these memories bashfully, as if they know it was silly to have hoped for such a thing. They often stress, too, how young they were when they hoped for a reunion, as though their youth helps excuse an otherwise irrational wish.

Melissa recalled that she had hoped for her parents to get back together "when I was very little—for a little bit. I just wanted to be normal. I wanted to have two parents." She faltered and tried to clarify, "I wanted to be able to say I had a mom and a dad who were together."

Kyle also remembers wishing his parents would reunite but knowing it wasn't to be. "I'm sure at some level I did hope for it," he said. "But I also kind of understood that this was a situation that they tried to rectify but it wasn't going to happen."

Others remembered that a remarriage brought an obvious and painful halt to such wishes. Joanna, now thirty-four years old, said, "I think I might have hoped for it when I was a kid . . . but my mom got remarried four years later. So I guess in that time frame I did hope they'd get back together."

Jason remembers the period around his mom's remarriage as being "the most rebellious time of my life. I think it's natural for children to want their parents to get back together," he said, "even if it's not going to happen."

Tammy's parents separated when she was eight years old, then got back together briefly when they realized a new baby—Tammy's little sister—was on the way. Soon thereafter they split up again, finally divorcing when Tammy was nine. She remembers getting "really depressed" when she was in high school, "when I realized my dad was getting remarried to someone else. Because then I knew they would not ever get back together."

Stephen also wished at times for a reunion. "Maybe the first year or so," he admitted, "I hoped that eventually they would get back together. I can remember watching the TV show *Growing Pains,* when the parents split up and then got back together soon after that. I remember asking Mom if that might happen. And she said no, it wasn't going to happen." Then he added, somewhat defensively, "I think even then I was realistic that that probably wasn't going to be the case."

The assumption that we yearn without exception for our parents to reunite may be based on an earlier generation of children of divorce. In the not-so-distant past, divorce was uncommon and children could still nurture "childish" hopes of parents reuniting. Our generation, on the other hand, saw divorce all around us. We *knew* that divorced parents never get back together (even though some do). In the face of this sad, sure knowledge, if your own parents come and tell you that they're getting a divorce, to hope they will change their minds is to show just how young and immature you really are.

Divorce does not transform all children into little adults. But it made it a lot more likely we would feel that way. Children of divorce feel displaced from the center of our families. We are twice as likely to agree strongly with the statement "I always felt like an adult, even when I was a little kid." We are more than three times as likely to say "I was alone a lot as a child." We have memories of trying to protect our parents—from other people's judgments and from our own sadness. As a consequence, we felt less able to turn to our parents for comfort and felt more unprotected ourselves. Even something as understandable as hoping our parents would get back together became, in the context of divorce, a silly, irrational, "childish" thing to wish for.

We little adults recall more burdens and anxieties than other children. In the national survey almost two-thirds of those from divorced families agree, "It was stressful in my family," while only a quarter of people from intact families say the same thing. This difference is enormous, of a magnitude rarely found in surveys of any kind. (Further, half of us from "good divorces" agree it was stressful in our families, compared to a third of those from unhappy but low-conflict marriages.) Even the most special holidays were more likely to be difficult for us. More than a third of us agree that "Christmas or Hanukkah was a stressful time in my family," which is more than twice as many as our peers from intact families.

We still looked like other children on the outside. We still played in the backyard and fought with our siblings over toys or clothes. But when we grew up we were less likely to feel that our childhood, as a whole, was carefree. Almost everyone we surveyed from intact families agrees, "My childhood was filled with playing," but just three-quarters of children of divorce say the same thing (and only 43 percent of us strongly agree that our childhood was filled with playing, compared to 70 percent of those from intact families).

The recognition that divorce can turn children into little adults should be enough to make our society question widespread divorce. But it is only the beginning. The impact of divorce did not diminish soon after our parents parted but continued to shape us well into adulthood.

4
Home

For most of my childhood my day-to-day home was with my mother, in North Carolina. Born in Greensboro, I lived there until I was four years old. Then, like many hippies at the time, my mother and stepfather wanted to get "back to the land," so we moved to a rural area, where they rented a four-room tenant farmer's house. A towering oak tree sheltered the wide front porch, and deep woods grew behind the house, leading to a river that ran brown after springtime rains. Briar roses wound over the tumbledown well house by our back door where skunks took up residence in the summers. We lived down a dirt road some distance from our neighbors, and in summer I often ran around in nothing but a pair of shorts, my fine brown hair flying behind me.

When we first moved in there was no bathroom, only an outhouse down by the woods. We took showers standing under a garden hose draped over the clothesline and I discovered how scary it is to be trapped on an outhouse seat while wasps hovered overhead. My mother and stepfather soon converted part of the long back porch into a bathroom with a view of the woods. They painted my bedroom bright yellow, built furniture for me, and covered my bedroom floor with a wall-to-wall carpet my mother sewed together from remnants. Every shade of green, gold, and orange appeared in its shaggy expanse. Then they tore out the kitchen ceiling—soot from the ages came tumbling down on their faces—and installed new, handmade cabinets and painted everything avocado

green, the "in" kitchen color of the time. An orange shag carpet
and a big, puffy plaid sofa in the living room completed the seventies look.

When I was six years old my brother was born in my mother and
stepfather's bedroom with the aid of a midwife. I was supposed to
be at the birth but he came early, while I was visiting my father and
grandparents in Florida. I returned on a warm March day to hold
my tiny, newborn baby brother for the first time. There is a picture
of that first time I held him, me sitting in the middle of my mother
and stepfather's bed with him in my lap. I'm smiling peacefully at
the camera, he's looking up at my face, and the whole scene is
bathed in a warm glow. I would come home from school in the
afternoons, grab an apple from the bowl on the kitchen counter,
and take my brother out into the yard. There I'd sit cross-legged
with him cradled in my lap and gaze down at his round cheeks and
little rosebud lips for hours.

It sounds idyllic and it was. I always missed my father, though. I
remember one night when I was about six years old, lying in my
bed and feeling suddenly overcome with sadness. I started crying
and my mom came in and asked what was the matter. "I miss
Daddy," I sniffled, not sure how she would handle it. She reassured
me and sat on the edge of my bed, stroking my hair, until I drifted
back to sleep. But it was unusual for me to express these feelings. From the time I was very young I learned to bottle up my
longing for my father until the instant I knew I would see him
again.

When I visited my dad I often traveled by airplane. We five-and-
ups were called "unaccompanied minors" and given a special button to pin on our shirts. I'd climb on a Piedmont Airlines plane at
the Winston-Salem airport, full of anticipation, and be taken under
the wing of a kind flight attendant. I always asked for a window seat
and would spend the forty-five-minute flight watching the tops of
the clouds go by. Shortly before we landed the flight attendant
would come by and tell me that once we were at the gate I should
wait until everyone else got off the plane so that I could be escorted

off. I'd nod solemnly, heart pounding as the plane began its descent, the anticipation of that always startling jolt on the ground mixing with the barely contained excitement that I was about to see Daddy.

I'd sit in my seat as we coasted into the gate, squirming, my heart bursting, until the airplane was finally empty and the flight attendant showed up again. As we walked together onto the jetway and rounded the corner I would see my dad at the entrance, beaming, and I'd start to run. From five feet away I would leap into his arms. One flight attendant joked to my dad, "Well, I guess I don't have to ask you for ID."

When I was seven years old my mom decided to go back to school to become a physician assistant. The first year of her program would be the toughest, so I went to live with my dad for third grade. It was the first time I'd ever spent a whole school year away from my mother and I was unprepared for how badly I would miss her, my stepfather, and my baby brother.

I loved my dad dearly but he was remarried too, busy working and going to law school at night, and he and my stepmother and stepsister had made a home of their own. My stepsister and I were only seven months apart—natural playmates, many would think, and we did play together a lot. But we jockeyed for security and fought a lot as well. I had claim to my father but she lived with him far more than I did. She had a bond with her mother, who I found intimidating. I remember once telling my stepsister that I lived there with her, her mother, and my dad.

"No," she retorted, "you're a visitor."

"No, I live here!" I insisted, frustrated.

Neither of us felt safe. I needed to believe I belonged there; she needed to believe I did not.

Throughout that year I longed for my mother and my home with a pain that rivals any I have felt since. My dad and stepmother's life was so different. They were more structured, living in a townhouse community with life taking place more indoors. They certainly tried to make me feel at home. They converted a dark paneled basement room for me, and my stepmother sewed a pretty pink bedspread and curtain for the tiny window near the ceiling. But it was worlds away from my sunny yellow bedroom in North Carolina.

When I felt sad I wrote letters to my mother, drawing pictures of life in the country and quoting corny John Denver songs. In case she missed my point I once let a tear drop on the page, then circled it and wrote "tear" beside it, with an arrow pointing. I'm a mother now and I can only imagine how much those letters broke her heart. But it wasn't my intention to hurt her. I just wanted her and our home so badly.

When the year was over I went back to North Carolina but things had changed. My mother and stepfather had moved to Winston-Salem, where she was attending school. I had a cute attic bedroom in our new house—again painted yellow—and I soon made a best friend who lived on the same block. But my mother and stepfather's marriage was starting to crumble. By the next spring he moved out and they eventually divorced. My mother was a full-time student, money was very tight, and my two-year-old brother and I were often alone despite my mother's efforts to find good day care and after-school programs.

I also came back from my father's feeling angry and distant from my mother. When she started dating again I seethed. Memories of life in the country quickly took on a hazy glow. Those memories burned all the brighter when my stepfather, a Vietnam vet who had long struggled with post-traumatic stress disorder and alcoholism, took his own life just a few years later at the age of thirty-seven. My mother and brother and I were left to mourn a man we had already lost through illness and divorce.

As a child, I could always take having a home for granted, in the sense that I always had a place to live, food on the table, a room of my own, a loving parent. But the early dislocations that I've described were only the beginning. They continued until I left home myself. I felt unsafe, not sure where I belonged, never certain that I could count on anything. Not until I married did I begin to feel secure. Only then did I feel as though there was somewhere, and someone to whom, I really belonged.

Increasingly, people think that joint physical custody—children spending quite a lot of time living with each of their parents—will solve many of the problems of divorce. The experts assure parents that having two homes is no big deal for children. But I wondered, do children of divorce really feel that way? I found that the reality is much more complicated.

For those of us from divorced homes, the splitting of a home did not simply add to what existed previously, creating two secure homes instead of one. Rather, growing up divided between two homes caused many of us to have a less secure sense of home. It often threatened our sense of emotional security and sometimes our physical security as well. It made us feel that things that were important to us—toys, treasured household items—could disappear at any moment. It made us feel less at home, especially in our fathers' homes. It also made it more likely that we would fear the loss of our homes entirely, because threats of being kicked out or kidnapped, while rare, were much more common in our lives than in the lives of those who grew up in intact families.

Safety

When children of divorce define what a "home" should be we often dwell on the idea of safety, probably because we are less likely to have felt that someone was watching out for us as children. In our national survey, most young adults from intact families strongly agree that when they were growing up, "I generally felt emotionally safe." But fewer than half of those from divorced families say the same thing. Young people who grew up in "bad divorces" are less likely to say they felt emotionally safe, but I was surprised to find that even those of us from "good divorces" felt significantly less safe than our peers from intact families with unhappy but low-conflict marriages.

The issue is not only emotional safety; almost one in five young adults who grew up in bad divorces say they did not feel *physically* safe, while practically no one from intact families says the same thing.

Michael was five years old when he learned, on his way to basketball practice, that his parents were divorcing. Before the divorce he and his brother had lived comfortably in a large house with his parents. After the divorce Michael's mother had to move through a series of ever-cheaper lodgings until they ended up in a sprawling apartment complex with a high crime rate where most of their neighbors were also women raising children alone. Michael was very conscious of not having a father at home to defend him if someone broke in. He felt uneasy in the afternoons when he and his brother were home alone for several hours before his mom got home from work, and he felt especially vulnerable at night.

I asked Michael if he felt safe as a child. "In the apartments, no, not at all," he said. "I was very worried. People would knock on the door late at night. One time," he remembered, "I woke up and there was somebody trying to get in one of the windows."

When our parents divorced we typically spent much of our time in a home without our father. New men may also have entered our home as our mother's boyfriends or, later, as stepfathers. For some children, having a new man in the house can be reassuring. After saying he didn't feel safe as a child, Michael then recalled, "When my mom got remarried I started to feel safe again, because there was a man in the house. And when you get scared at night, you just remind yourself that somebody was there and it'd be okay."

But others say that a new stepfather made them feel less safe. Samantha was pregnant with her first child when we met at the small apartment she shared with her husband. Sitting on an old wing chair with her feet propped up on the coffee table, she said that she "generally" felt safe growing up. Then she hesitated and added, "My stepdad was—I don't know how to say it—we weren't abused or anything like that. But there was something about him that just creeped me out."

Tragically, it is well documented that children are at significantly greater risk of abuse after their parents' divorce. More than seventy reputable studies document that an astonishing number—anywhere from one-third to one-half—of girls with divorced parents report having been molested or sexually abused as children, most often by their mothers' boyfriends or stepfathers. A separate review of forty-two studies found that "the majority of children who were sexually abused . . . appeared to come from single-parent or recon-stituted families." Two leading researchers in the field conclude, "Living with a stepparent has turned out to be the most powerful predictor of severe child abuse yet."

I did not set out to study child abuse for this book. I did not ask anyone I interviewed about it, but two of the thirty-five young adults from divorced families who I met with in person volun-teered heartrending stories. I began to wonder whether other stories had remained unspoken, stories that people were not comfortable offering to me, a stranger, in a two-to-three-hour interview. That was when I read more and learned about the astonishingly high risks of abuse that children of divorce face—risks that the culture remains largely unwilling to hear about or believe.

Crystal sounded a bit hesitant when we first spoke on the tele-phone. When we got together a few weeks later in a small meeting room at a public library around the corner from her apartment building, I learned why. She was a pretty young woman with ap-pealing, wide eyes. She was dressed casually in jeans and a sweat-shirt and sat straight with her hands calmly folded in her lap. Despite her calm demeanor, tears rolled down her face during much of the time we talked.

Researchers have found that children whose parents had a high-conflict marriage do better after a divorce. This may be true overall, but individual stories are not so simple. High-conflict marriages are often made up of one or two very troubled people. When the marriage dissolves there is no guarantee that a secure support sys-tem will suddenly appear for the child.

Crystal's parents, without a doubt, had a high-conflict marriage. Her earliest memories are of her father beating her mother, even when her mother was pregnant with Crystal's younger sister, who was later born with a collapsed lung. At times Crystal would try to stop her father, biting his leg as he pursued her mother, or distract-ing him when he was beating her younger sister so that he would come at her instead. For years Crystal hoped her parents would divorce and eventually, when she was thirteen years old, they did. It got better after the divorce, she said, but it was not easy.

After the divorce, Crystal was left alone with her sister and a brutalized, emotionally unstable mother. Soon a new boyfriend entered the picture. At first Crystal welcomed him. Her mother seemed happier when he was around and he was nicer than her father had been. But one night she woke to find him in her bed. "He crossed the line," she said to me, the tears starting even though she has told her story in therapy many times before. On two occasions the boyfriend sexually abused her, terrifying her. But what devastated Crystal even more was that when she told her mother about it, her mother did not stand up for her and only broke up with the boyfriend much later.

Caleb, too, continued to suffer even after his parents' high-conflict marriage ended. Today he is a successful actor and director working in Chicago theater. He came out as a teenager and he and his boyfriend are making plans to adopt their first child. He says he has hope now but as a child, he remembers, his overwhelming feeling was despair.

When Caleb was growing up his parents fought often, separating several times before his father moved to the other side of town for good soon after Caleb's younger brother was born. His mother struggled with bipolar disorder and attempted suicide several times. After the divorce she was often out or secluded in her bedroom. When she would try to make rules for Caleb and his brother, he recalled, "it was like trying to take direction from a bowlful of Jell-O."

Caleb summarized his parents' divorce by saying it "made some things better and a lot of things worse." His parents continued to fight over even the smallest things—such as the time their mother got mad when the boys got a haircut while visiting their father—although it was a relief that the fighting no longer happened in his home. But the divorce made things worse, Caleb said, "because of the isolation." After the divorce, he said, "there was no other adult around, no buffer between my mom and me."

Because Caleb's mother received no child support from his

father she was forced to rent out their second bedroom to students attending the nearby state college. Caleb remembered that students were often moving in and out, sometimes bringing suspicious friends with them. He suspects he was sexually abused as a child, although he's not ready to confront that part of his history. "I'm not looking for it," he admitted. "But there were a number of things that in looking back sort of add up." He reflected, "I don't really think that kids know a lot about sexual intercourse when they're six or seven, like how to do it. Probably you shouldn't know that. . . . But I remember really feeling that there's something weird about me that I know about this stuff and no one else does."

To deal with his fears, loneliness, and possible trauma, Caleb began drinking when he was seven years old, mixing hard liquor with sugar in big plastic cups he got from McDonald's. He continued trying to numb his pain with alcohol until he was twenty-one, when he entered recovery. At one point, when I asked him if he had ever thought about God as a child, he said he had asked only, "Why me? Why do you do this to me?"

Children are vulnerable after a divorce and—especially if there is a history of abuse, addiction, or mental illness in the family—they can be easy prey for abusers. As we've seen, children of divorce are left alone much more often than other children are. Many are too accessible to adults with bad intentions, especially to men who enter the home as a mother's boyfriend or new husband.

Of course, most of the partners that parents bring home are good people. Stepparents, especially, take on a tough and admirable challenge when marrying into a family with children. In time, many children of divorce come to love and trust their stepparents. Caleb, for example, eventually felt much closer to his new stepmother than he did to either of his parents. Michael was reassured by the new stability that his stepfather brought to his home life. Others speak respectfully of stepfathers and stepmothers who stuck around even when the going got tough, and they honor these stepparents with a special place at the wedding when they themselves get married.

But if our culture is going to confront the lives of children of divorce truthfully, it cannot ignore the fact that as a group, we were at much greater risk of abuse in our homes. The new generation of children of divorce is exposed to the same risks. For their sakes, our culture must be willing to believe the numerous studies and personal stories that document this tragedy.

It is also clear that a child's living situation can fall short of abuse and still leave a child feeling unsafe. Some of us from divorced families say that growing up we had a more generalized sense of feeling unsafe, a vague, persistent feeling of dread. When I asked Daniel if he felt safe as a child, he shifted uncomfortably in his seat. "No," he said, "I did not feel safe. I had problems sleeping. I would wake up feeling very alone or afraid. Like I had this fear of fires, of wars." He looked at me and tried to explain. "I always felt like I was watching out for something to go wrong. Not that I thought I was going to die or anything like that. But I always felt like things were lurking around the corners."

Will, whose father had an affair and left his mother, said he did not feel safe after his parents' divorce because "if your dad can hurt your mother, then anything can happen. Like what's going to happen next, around the corner?"

Steve said, "I think deep down I was always afraid of something happening to me. What that was, I'm not quite sure."

Compared to those of us from divorced families, young people from intact families are far less likely to cite safety as a concern when growing up. Children seem to find the presence of their fathers especially reassuring when they are worried about their safety. Not only did people from intact families usually recall feeling safe but some noted, in contrast to those from divorced families, that it was the presence of their family that made them feel safe despite threats outside the home.

Tabitha is a thirty-year-old software developer who lives in suburban Philadelphia. Her parents met years ago at Coney Island and are still married. She recalls that when she was growing up in a family with modest economic means in New York City during the 1970s "there was a lot of high-profile crime." "The first thing

I remember being afraid of was the Son of Sam," she said, "and I was in grammar school." But when asked if she felt safe growing up, Tabitha smiled easily and replied, "Absolutely!" "Even now," she said, "if I got out of here and I had a flat tire, I could call my father up in Brooklyn and say, 'Daddy, I have a flat tire. Can you come down and change it?' He'd be like, 'Okay, I'll be there in three hours.' Of course I wouldn't do that. But yeah, we always felt safe."

Joe grew up in Chicago, the son of a stay-at-home mother and a father who owned a thriving restaurant in Greek Town. His dad was at the restaurant until quite late almost every night. As a child Joe was the youngest kid on the block and he remembered that neighborhood bullies would taunt him sometimes. But even though his father was often not at home Joe still felt like he had a "defender." He recalls: "I felt like I had this great big dad, so I definitely didn't walk around scared too much. . . . He made calls to people if someone bothered us, so I always felt like I was protected growing up."

Similarly, Stacie remembered that she and her parents "lived out in the country, so there were these weird noises all the time." But because her family was always around, "it never crossed my mind that I wasn't safe."

Having married parents does not offer sure protection to children. Some children are victimized by their own parents, like Crystal, who was abused by her father as well as her mother's boyfriend. Tragedies within or outside the family can happen to any child, no matter what kind of family they live in. But on the whole, having both a father and mother who will look out for you, and not having unrelated adults passing often through the home, makes things safer.

Stuff

Another common topic when children of divorce talk about home is our "stuff." Many of us sound like nomads, talking about what happened to our stuff after our parents divorced, how much stuff we took with us to our fathers' houses, or how much of our stuff is left in our parents' homes today.

Monique and I sat on gliders one evening in the screened-in porch behind her house. I asked her how she defined "home." She said matter-of-factly, "Home is your place of residence where you live and you've got your stuff, and where you have dinner every night." Like her, Ashley said home is "where my stuff is." Rochelle said home is "filled with . . . the things that I like. And I can leave things there and know they're safe."

It is understandable why we focus on "stuff" when we think of home. In the economic downgrading that often happens after divorce some experienced the loss of a larger home filled with nicer stuff. Monique pushed her feet against the stone floor of the porch, shifting the glider back and forth, and with downcast eyes recalled with some embarrassment, "It sounds sort of shallow, but after the divorce we went from a really nice house to a sort of mediocre, not-so-nice house."

Others witness their stuff disappearing before their eyes in the sudden severing of a household. Jason was still amazed as he explained how he learned, at age fourteen, that his parents were divorcing. He stopped fiddling with a paper clip, twisting and bending it into endless shapes, and told me this story: "My dad and my sister and I drove several hours away to see our grandmother. . . . And I remember thinking, 'This is really strange that my mom isn't coming,' but I didn't ask any questions. When we got back home my dad told us they were divorcing. This was twenty minutes before my mom was coming to pick us up—like, that was the weekend my mom had moved all our stuff out of our house. And I got back and it was like, 'What? And where's all my stuff?' "

Crystal told me with a sad laugh about the day her father left her mother. She and her mother went for a walk and when they came home her father was gone—and had taken the trailer home with him. Trailer homes, of course, are designed for easy moving, but even children of divorce who live in houses on concrete foundations sometimes feel that if they look away for a moment their home — or their stuff — might not be there when they look back.

"Stuff" is also a concern because we usually had to carry it back and forth between our parents' houses. Some of us felt less at home at one parent's house because none of our stuff was there. Anthony is a young student getting his MBA at a northeastern university. He grew up living with his mother and brother and seeing his father routinely, since he lived in the same town. He recalled, "We packed our clothes and we'd take them to our dad's house. So there wasn't our little room and our space. . . . And when we left, there was nothing left of us. There was no connection to the house to make it a home. There was no home there."

Emily said of her father's house: "I didn't feel like I could leave stuff over there. And I'm sure he never said that I couldn't, but I always packed my bag and took all my stuff home."

Eric, whose father had custody, said that his mom's house was only "a second home." He drummed his knuckles on the picnic table where we sat, having a hard time sitting still. "I didn't have any of my belongings at my mom's," he said. "I'd sleep there on rare occasions, that was pretty much it."

When parents get divorced, one or both of them leave the family home. They divide up their possessions and may get rid of some things entirely. Some do not want to live amid physical reminders of the marriage. Others may need to sell pricier items and split the money. Some remarry, acquiring new things with their spouse and getting rid of the old. Sometimes even treasured things just get lost in the shuffle of multiple moves and marriages.

For all these reasons, when children of divorce return as adults to our parents' homes we are likely to see fewer physical reminders of our childhoods than our friends from intact families do. Ashley, now thirty-three and living on her own, said of her mother's home: "There's nothing there from my childhood. There's pictures . . . there's one mixing bowl I think my mom still has in the kitchen. That's about it, you know?" Old, otherwise unremarkable items remind us of our childhoods and signal belonging. For Ashley, the image of that one mixing bowl stood out as one of the few tangible reminders of her childhood, proof that her mother's home at one time had been hers.

Was Dad's House a Home?

Many of us did not feel our father's house was our home. Custody decisions may partly explain this feeling (among eighteen- to thirty-five-year-olds, almost three-quarters of us grew up living primarily with our mothers), but they are not the whole story.

Some children of divorce explain their father's house was not home because none of their stuff was there. Others say that their father's house was just not "homey." Kimberly told me her dad's home was a place "where he didn't want to be either." "It was a one-bedroom apartment," she explained. "He would always apologize that it was so small." And Kyle told me, "My mom always put a lot of effort into where she lived . . . and I didn't feel any of that at my dad's."

Others say that Dad's place was just not familiar enough to be their home. Samantha explained, "The place where my dad lived, it was usually a different apartment every time we went out there." She folded her hands over her pregnant stomach, remembering that when she and her sister went to visit her dad, "we had a good time, but we just kept thinking how we wanted to be at home, as much as he tried to make it home for us. We had our own rooms and everything; he'd have things planned for the whole time." She paused uncertainly. "But it was the unfamiliarity of the neighborhood and the surroundings, and he dated a lot."

When young adults from divorced families said that Dad's place did not feel like a home, I asked them what it felt like. At best, they described it as a vacation spot. Alicia said, "I guess it was like a vacation dad . . . and when I came home to my real house, I had homework and had to tell them if I got a bad grade and things like that." Kyle said his dad's house was "just a place to visit" and Ashley said it was "a little vacation area." Even Jason, who grew up living just blocks from his father and saw him several times a week, said that at his dad's he felt like "a guest at a hotel."

At worst, especially if there were people at their dad's house they either did not know or did not like, some felt like miserable outsiders. A bad divorce was especially likely to make them feel this way. One-fifth of those who grew up in a "good divorce" and almost half of those who grew up in a bad divorce say that at times they felt like outsiders in their homes.

Alicia said that her dad's house, with her dad, stepmother, and stepbrother all caught up in family dramas of their own, "felt like a complete unit that you were stepping in on." Alex said, "When my dad was living with that woman there were three kids over there and I hated going over there—it was always just this zoo." Will grimaced and said that his dad's house "was like visiting somebody in prison. It was their house," he said, "and I don't know how they felt, but I felt tension from the time I walked in the door to the time I left." Michael was tormented by his older brother and stepbrother at his dad's house, and his dad was often out at work or playing golf while his stepmother, not surprisingly, was overwhelmed and resentful. In general Michael did not speak heatedly about his childhood, but he said his dad's place "was hell. . . . It was awful, it really was, and I didn't feel like going there."

Shadow Homes

A vacation spot, a hotel, a prison, hell—the degree of tension varies, but the common theme is of being a visitor, an outsider, or an unwilling captive when staying with our fathers. Still, more than half of us who stayed in touch with both parents agree, "I felt like I had two homes." And that too is problematic. When people speak of home they always use the singular. They say, "There's no place like home," "You can't go home again," "Home is where the heart is." We, on the other hand, had two places that were, at least potentially, home.

It might seem at first that children of divorce are doubly blessed to have two homes. It is often nice to have two of something rather than one: two cars, two savings accounts, two graduate degrees. But home is different. Having two homes raised the possibility for us that while each place could be a home, each place could *stop* being a home as well.

Because we had two places that at least potentially could be home, the presence of the other home was always alive in our minds. It served as a point of comparison or a potential destination, a place to be desired or dreaded. Over time we came to see each parent's home as a shadow of the other. Our divorced parents each lived in, and were aware of, only their own homes, but we were connected to both places.

Having shadow homes undermined our sense of belonging in both homes. Some children of divorce even say the presence of the other home caused them to fear doing something wrong that would make them be sent there, even if their parents never said this would happen.

Angela is one example. Her parents had some disputes after the divorce, but for the most part they got along well. They lived far apart, one on the West Coast and one in the Midwest, but they spoke regularly on the telephone about Angela and her brother, and Angela felt close to both of them. Yet she noted, "I definitely felt like it was important to stay in everybody's good graces. . . . Nobody ever said, 'If you don't straighten up you're going to have to go live with your father' or 'with your mother.' Nobody implied that at all . . . but I do recall feeling, 'I've got to be really good.'" For Angela, though she had two loving parents with welcoming homes, the presence of another place to which she *could* be sent caused her to fear that a mistake on her part—being anything less than "really good"—would send her packing.

Some might say that Angela was simply a hypersensitive child. Why would she think that her mother would send her to live with her father if her mother never said so? Yet when I talked with other children of divorce I saw that Angela had a point. The presence of two homes can influence divorced parents' behavior, causing some of them to behave differently than married parents.

In any family, whether intact or divorced, adolescent children argue with their parents. These conflicts are a normal part of the separation process but sometimes they become so heated or frequent that they throw the whole family into turmoil. Yet in the typical intact family these conflicts would have to become extremely severe, and all other options would have to be exhausted, before parents would consider forcing their children out of the house.

In divorced families the dynamic can be different. When one parent, for instance the mother, has difficulty controlling a rebellious teenage son, it seems reasonable to consider sending the son to live with his father. After all, his father is not some stranger and his home is an equally appropriate place for the child to live. Thus in a divorced family it can be more likely that tension between a parent and child will cause the child to be sent somewhere else to live.

I'm not saying that married parents are more saintly or patient than divorced parents. They can feel just as fed up with their teenagers and are probably just as likely to daydream about having a teen-free home. But married parents who are having troubles with their children usually have few other options. Besides sending their kid to military school or maybe Grandma's house, no one else is likely to volunteer to raise their child. Only in the most severe circumstances—if their child is an addict, stealing from them, or physically threatening them—might they begin to consider kicking him or her out. Otherwise they have to stick it out. The children, in turn, know their parents have few options. They may feel at times that they hate their parents, but most of them know that, come hell or high water, this is their home.

Of course, being kicked out of the house and being sent to live with your other parent are two different things. A teenager who has been kicked out of the house must fend for himself and may end up on the street. A teenager who has been sent to live at his dad's house still has a roof over his head. But the feeling of being rejected or forced from a home is present in both experiences, if in different degrees, and it is this fear of rejection that is more likely to be felt by a typical child of divorce. A child of divorce is also more likely to fear this loss of home at much lower levels of conflict, or even, as with Angela, when there is little apparent conflict at all. A child of divorce knows that her parent has an option that married parents do not have, even if the divorced parent never says so or never even thinks so. *A child of divorce sees the shadow home that the parents do not see.*

Angela's parents did not send her packing, but the parents of other children of divorce did, or threatened to. Though the numbers are small overall, children of divorce are more than three times as likely to say they were kicked out of the house while growing up. Kimberly was one of these children. She fought frequently with her mother when she was a teenager, seeking her mother's attention and reassurance. She remembered, "My mom would say things like, 'Go live with your dad, I don't want you here.'" Kimberly loved her dad but still felt painfully rejected by her mother on these occasions. She told me that one day her mother finally said, "Get out, just get out. I don't want you here. You cannot live here anymore." Kimberly went to live with her father, but she remembers this as the day when her mother "kicked her out of the house."

Kidnapping

One measure of the impact of divorce on our society is the way it has changed the language. Divorce has ushered in new terms to describe events that were formerly rare or nonexistent, and it has given old terms new meanings. *Custody* and *visitation*, words that sound as if they should apply to a prison population rather than to children, are now used routinely inside and outside the courts when talking about children's lives. Perhaps most strangely, when one parent takes their child against the other parent's will or against a court order, it is called kidnapping.

Kidnapping is a frightening term. It makes us think of a child screaming as a stranger snatches him away from all that is known and familiar. The thought of such a thing terrifies a child and is a parent's worst nightmare. But today the word *kidnapping* is more commonly used to describe a different kind of tragedy. When two parents are so alienated, or when one parent is so threatening, that the courts have decided when and how these parents can see their children, and when one parent violates this order and takes the child away from the home the courts have decided is best for him, it is called kidnapping.

Kidnapping in the sense of abduction by a parent rather than by a stranger is for the most part unique to children of divorced or single parents. I should not have been surprised that kidnapping came up as often as it did in my conversations with young adults from divorced families, but I was. In contrast, no one from intact families ever brought it up.

In the national survey, I was taken aback to find that 7 percent of children of divorce but virtually no one from intact families (0.3 percent) agreed that "at times one of my parents suggested my other parent may try to kidnap me or my sibling." Further, about half of those who said a parent suggested they might be kidnapped actually *were* kidnapped by one of their parents.

As a child I too encountered the threat of kidnapping. After my mother and stepfather split up when I was nine years old, my stepfather moved first to a small apartment in another part of town, then to the coast of North Carolina. My younger brother and I went to visit him the first summer he lived there, bunking together on the fold-out sofa in his efficiency apartment. I stayed for a week, then went on to visit my own father. My brother stayed longer and went back a few more summers as well. He says those summer visits with his dad when he was three, four, and five years old "are like a dream" now. I think it was frightening for him to be away from our mom and me but he loved his father. Those short weeks spread over a few summers ended up being all the time he had left with him.

As time went by I saw my stepfather less and less. One day when I was thirteen years old my mother came to talk to me. She had just learned that my stepfather had quit his job, moved out of his apartment, and seemingly disappeared. She confided in me that because of several threatening phone calls she was worried my stepfather might come to town and try to kidnap my brother. "Please," she asked, "when you're outside playing with your brother, keep an eye out for Rob's white van."

I gulped and said nothing. Now I understand that there was a real risk that Rob in his confused mental state might have followed through on his threats. But at the time I had no idea what to believe. I adored my stepfather. He was my in-the-home father from the time I was three years old until he moved out when I was nine, and I couldn't believe he would do such a thing. On the other hand, my mother seemed genuinely afraid and that made me afraid too. For months afterward I kept my eye out for a white van as my brother and I played in the backyard or rode our bikes in the street. I was confused about what I would do if I saw one. I missed my stepfather and if I had seen him my heart would have leaped with excitement. Yet I was also supposed to keep him from kidnapping my brother.

No white van ever appeared. Instead just a few months later we learned of my stepfather's suicide. Kidnapping fears gave way to waves of grief. For years, though, if I was walking down a street and saw a white van I would feel a mixture of foreboding and excitement, a desperate desire to see Rob again coupled with a nagging sense of fear.

I discovered that I shared this ambiguous and confusing experience with other children of divorce. Several recalled that their mothers were quite anxious that their fathers might try to kidnap them. Katy and I met one evening in a faculty office at a law library near her home in Atlanta. She arrived a few minutes late and plonked her cell phone down on the heavy mahogany desk, telling me apologetically that she was expecting an important call. As a resident psychiatrist at a drug treatment program in the city, she was often consulted after hours when a new patient was admitted.

We pulled two chairs together in front of the desk as Katy filled me in on the details of her early childhood. She told me that she grew up spending most of the year with her mother and maternal grandparents, visiting her father, who lived several states away, for one month each summer. As we talked she recalled, "Kidnapping was a big thing when I was growing up. My mom and grandparents were fearful that my dad would kidnap me. So they never wanted to really tick him off, because they wanted to see me again after the month."

Like her, Peter recalled his mother worrying about his father kidnapping his two younger siblings. On outings with his father, Peter felt responsible for keeping an eye on his father and his younger brother and sister to make sure his father would not run off with them.

Sometimes the mother's worries may have been legitimate; in other cases the mother may have been overanxious or even manipulative. Whatever the case, the mother's suggestion that the father might kidnap the child, whether it was justified or not, fostered a high degree of mistrust in these children of their fathers and, surely, of the world in general. After all, if your own father can kidnap you, what else can happen?

Kidnapping actually comes up a lot in discussions about children of divorce. For example, Constance Ahrons, author of *The Good Divorce,* describes her own divorce: "For two miserable years my husband and I battled constantly over custody, visitation, and child support. There were private detectives, a kidnapping, several lawyers, and two years of legal fees that took me ten years to pay off." Not only were her own children kidnapped but Ahrons reveals that a portion of the couples in her study had "ongoing escalations that went as far as kidnapping."

The fact that, as children of divorce, we were often home alone also made us fear more traditional kinds of kidnapping. Caleb told me that when he was growing up he was often by himself after school, taking care of his younger brother. One afternoon while watching television he saw a public service announcement warning of the dangers of leaving children home alone. In the ad, a boy is in his house by himself when a stranger breaks in. The boy is seen running through the house and up the stairs while the stranger, whose face is never shown, chases him. Caleb was terrified.

———

We have seen that for children of divorce, even something as elemental as home cannot be taken for granted. Even if we were lucky enough to maintain contact with both parents, divorce divided one home into two and in the process made each one feel less secure. But home, it turned out, was only one of many ideas we would feel compelled to reexamine.

5

Early Moral Forgers

As a child I was passionately devoted to my parents, perhaps because I longed for each of them so much when we were separated. Yet the worlds they embodied were so different.

My mom is a petite woman, only five feet three inches tall, but she is all muscle. Because she was a breech birth her grandmother used to say she was "born feet first and kept running." She grew up on a farm, driving tractors, hauling fertilizer, and balancing on beams high up in the rafters of tobacco barns as others handed her long sticks sewn with heavy tobacco leaves to hang and cure. Eager to leave the world of farming behind, she went to college and professional school and completed a doctoral program. She has always moved fast through the world and that intense physical quality makes her stand out even in her fifties. Today her silver-gray hair is a sparkling mane. She still runs, still hauls fifty-pound bags of fertilizer and mulch to tend her garden, and still impresses mechanics by knowing more about her car than they do.

My mom's passion for life made her larger than life. One of my favorite larger-than-life memories of her was the time she piled into a van with some good friends and drove out to the West Coast for a couple of weeks. I was seven years old and in school, which meant that I had to stay home with my stepfather, but my six-month-old brother was still nursing, so she took him along. I was excited about my mother's adventure and wished I could have gone too. But the rest of her family was scandalized. One of my older aunts, appalled, told everybody who would listen that my mom was hitchhiking down the West Coast with my brother on her back.

My mom came home with chopsticks from San Francisco, a new taste for hoisin sauce, and a wealth of stories. She didn't do any hitchhiking, but I remember vividly her tale of seeing the Grand Canyon for the first time. On a sweltering day under a brilliant blue sky she and her friends hiked a long, winding trail down to the bottom of the canyon and then slowly climbed back out again, with my brother on my mom's back the entire time. I loved that story because it embodied what is best about my mother: her stamina and determination, her deep need for the wide-open spaces of the outdoors, the flash of excitement in her eyes when she's cooking for friends or having a party. And at the same time she's a mother, nursing my brother on a rock in the Grand Canyon, changing his diaper who knows where, showing him how the sun sparkles on the crystal water, and pulling a floppy hat over his head to keep him from getting sunburned.

Life with my mom was free and unstructured. We had meals and I had bedtime, but she expected me to follow my natural instincts through much of the day. And I did. I was a big reader. I played outside. I found secret hiding places. Some evenings I would sprawl on the grass watching the sun set before heading home again.

But the lack of structure had a downside too. Once she and my stepfather moved away from the country and life got tougher, I was often on my own. I came to be a child who needed — and had — a lot of freedom but struggled with the loneliness and fear that came along with it.

My father's world sparkled too, but in a different way. He grew up in Pilot Mountain, a small town in North Carolina known on the *Andy Griffith Show* as "Mount Pilot." His was a world of Boy Scouts, summer camps, sports, and impressive academic achievements. His grandfather was a tobacco auctioneer, a banker, and a state legislator who built one of the nicest houses in town, on Main Street. When he died, my dad's parents moved into that house to raise their children. I think my dad had his share of disappointments, but he's never been one to talk much about them, and his childhood has always sounded idyllic to me. Like my mom, he was highly ambitious, always looking ahead. He seems to have known from his earliest years that he wanted to work someday in Washington, D.C.

When my parents split up my dad finished a master's program and headed to Washington. As a young man in the seventies he sported a thick mustache and floppy light brown hair. The summer I was five years old he rented an apartment with several other guys in an old brownstone on Capitol Hill. When I visited him I was fascinated by the noise and activity of the city. My dad and I would walk to the gritty urban park near his brownstone while teenagers playing funk music pounded by in their cars. Each morning he dropped me off at a day-care center where I was one of the few white kids. When I tried to fit in by imitating the other kids' playful jive walk, the teachers cracked up.

After work my dad would pick me up and take me to softball games on the Mall, where he played with other young staffers working on Capitol Hill. I loved watching my dad at bat. His jaw would tighten, his eyes would fix on the ball flying toward him, time would stop for just a second, and then in a flash he'd swing— biceps bulging, cutoff shorts twisting—and kick up dust around the batter's box as he tore into a run.

In my dad's world there was a lot more structure, and that worked well when I was young. I liked the dinners he made: fish sticks or pork chops, cottage cheese, applesauce, or, on nights when he wanted to kick back, bacon and eggs. But as I began to get older, and especially after he married my first stepmother, it was tougher adjusting to the structure of their home.

At my mom's, as long as I wasn't caring for my brother, I came and went as I pleased, leaving a note if I was going far. At my dad's in the Washington suburbs I hung around the house more. I didn't know anybody outside his family, so there wasn't really anywhere to go. At my mom's I had a bedtime but that just meant I had to go to my room, where I usually read before tucking myself in, and bath times were pretty much up to me. At my dad's, bath time always followed dinner, and at bedtime my dad would tuck me in. I liked his company in the evening—I would have liked to have my mom tuck me in too. But I also felt constricted by life indoors, on a schedule, in a neighborhood I didn't know.

While my parents were good people with good values, their values were *different,* and I alone had to reconcile those differences. My mom valued freedom, new experiences, personal growth. My dad valued moderation, safety, predictability. My mom wanted to challenge social norms. My dad preferred a traditional life that balanced work with pastimes such as baseball. At my mom's I was a hippie kid and independent—which led to speaking up in class debates on behalf of the underdog. At my dad's I wasn't sure what I was. It's not that I couldn't talk freely—I loved, and still love, debating social issues with him. But I was always uncomfortable in his world and felt I stuck out.

My parents' worlds would collide forcefully in ways that were largely invisible to them. For instance, language was an issue. At my mom's, we talked about things being "screwed up." But when I used "screwed up" at my dad's, he corrected me firmly. "*Messed* up," he said, intending only the best but leaving me feeling silly and ashamed. One example has stuck in my mind for years. During the year I lived with my father, when I was in third grade, I went home at Christmas to visit my mom. I had missed her so much—and I'd especially missed her food, which is weird because I usually complained about all that tofu and tamari cooked in a cast-iron skillet, the tabouli that none of the kids in my rural elementary school could make heads or tails of, and the homemade whole-grain bread and granola that I'd love to have someone make for me *now*. But then I was a kid and wanted Fritos. It didn't take many lunch periods to figure out that no six-year-old would trade his Fritos for my tabouli.

When I went home that Christmas, though, I loved it all. So when it came time to go back to my father's, my mom filled a cardboard box with all her specialties, including crunchy whole-grain crackers. I think it gave my mom a lot of pleasure to send a bit of her life along with me, but it seemed to be a source of annoyance to my dad, who probably thought, "Does she think we don't know how to feed an eight-year-old?" A week or so later I was passing by the kitchen when I saw my stepmother crunching on one of those crackers. *My* crackers, from *my* mother. I was furious. When she left the kitchen, I stole the box and hid it in my room, knowing I could get in trouble because at my dad's house, unlike at my mom's, I wasn't supposed to take food to my room.

I don't think I ever dug those crackers out again. Probably they sat behind the books on my shelf, moldering, until my dad and stepmom found them months after I was gone. But how that silly box of crackers has stayed with me, one of many seemingly harmless examples of the clash in my parents' values that left me feeling torn between their worlds.

No matter how agreeable or disagreeable our parents' divorces, all of us had experiences like this. And the dividing line that ran through our childhoods meant that we lived out, on a daily basis, the conflict between our parents' often widely differing values, beliefs, and ways of living. If we were to survive, we had to become early moral forgers. To figure out who *we* were, we had to wrestle early and often with the sometimes subtle and sometimes blatant contradictions between our parents' different ways of life.

Forge has several meanings. A blacksmith forges iron in the intense heat of a roaring fire. A bushwhacker forges through a thick forest, cutting a new path in the dense underbrush. As children of divorce, we had to do both. We had to forge our own values and beliefs in the intense heat of our inner lives. We cut our own path through the forest of contradictions between our parents' ways of living. The children of married parents were able to watch their mothers and fathers confront each other about their many differences. But we worked alone. And like the bushwhacker struggling through the frontier, the work we did went largely unnoticed. The moral drama kindled by our parents' divorce has burned quietly inside us for years—for all our lives.

The Morally Vigilant Child

Daniel is a soft-spoken twenty-nine-year-old medical resident with dark hair, gray eyes, and a solid build. We met one morning in an empty classroom on a sprawling, private university campus. He apologized as he sat down, explaining that he'd had very little sleep and might not be too coherent. With a big, proud smile he told me he had delivered his first baby the night before.

As we began to talk I noticed that he met my eyes only when he wanted to make a strong point. Otherwise he gazed thoughtfully out the window, watching students walking back and forth between classes, as he recalled the years that had passed since his parents' divorce.

Daniel's parents were immigrants from Germany and divorced when he was seven years old. He grew up the oldest of three boys who lived primarily with their mom but often stayed with their dad, who lived nearby. When Daniel's parents got together on rare occasions after the divorce, he worried that they might fight—even though they rarely did. Still, he often felt "conflicted"—he used the word several times.

Daniel's parents' marriage ended when his father moved out to live with another woman. His father remained loving, yet he was an intimidating figure—his home more formal, his expectations of his boys higher. Daniel's mother was devastated. She never dated seriously again, devoting herself instead to her three sons. For Daniel, his father's fateful decision opened up a whole new realm of complex moral issues. He learned in Hebrew school that infidelity was wrong. But he loved his father and did not think he was a bad person. He loved his mother too but felt burdened by her needs. Her refusal to pursue her own life made Daniel, the eldest son, feel as if he had to care for her emotionally, especially as he got older. As a teenager he sometimes chose not to go out at night because he knew that his mother would be alone. He learned to avoid going to her when he felt sad or scared because she would become overwhelmed with guilt, calling herself a bad mother, and he would find himself instead comforting *her.*

Daniel tried to figure out how each of his parents was right and how each was wrong. "I would wrestle with it all the time," he says. "I would go back and forth, not for five minutes but for an hour. I remember being up at night thinking about these kinds of things."

Daniel's preoccupation with the moral intricacies of the aftermath of divorce began to shape the kind of child he was. He became the boy who tried to rein in other boys' childish behavior. "I remember my brothers wanting to go into this moving truck," he says. "Someone was moving and the workers were somewhere else. And I said, 'No, no, don't go! It's not right!'" He took a sip of the water I had set out earlier and reflected, "I look back on that now and think, at the time that was normal kid stuff. Why didn't I just go and take a look and get yelled at? But I was very concerned with not being a bad kid. . . . I think that was a huge part of my identity formation." Struggling with his dad's infidelity and his mom's emotional dependence was the opening foray in Daniel's early and lasting confrontation with complex moral questions.

A fierce moral drama unfolds in the wake of our parents' divorce, revolving around a core of common questions. Some are questions with which *all* children must eventually grapple: "What do my parents think and believe? What do I believe? What is the right thing to do?" Yet divorce requires us to face these questions much earlier in life, and *alone*.

Other moral questions are ones that uniquely and powerfully confront children of divorce: "Which parent do I choose? Which of my parents is right and which is wrong? Where do I belong?"

What Do My Parents Think and Believe?

Almost from birth, children begin absorbing their parents' values by listening to their parents' words and—even more so—observing their parents' actions. It's a kind of background noise that children hear without even realizing it. And they rarely have to think about those values—which ones they will share and which they will reject—until they're well into adolescence or adulthood, perhaps not even until they have children of their own.

Children of divorce, in contrast, begin consciously reflecting on their parents' values almost immediately after the divorce, even if it happens when they're very young.

People from intact families often observe that their parents' values seemed pretty similar when they were growing up. They say things such as "I don't think my dad's values ever differed a lot from my mother's" or "I really can't think of a specific instance where they would ever be different" or "They both feel the same way; they're a totally united front." Others note differences in their parents' values but typically describe these differences as complementary rather than conflicting. They say their dad values hard work while their mom values nurturing, or their mom is compassionate while their dad prefers to be a straight shooter.

Young adults from intact families do recall conflicts between their parents' values, but it's relatively rare. Several people in the study said that their mother was religious, while their father was not. Others said that later in life they realized that while their mother was scrupulously honest, their father was capable of breaking traffic laws or otherwise bending the rules. Still others noted that one parent was less generous and kind than the other. People from intact families were sometimes aware that their father or mother had been unfaithful, although others may never have been told about such serious problems if they existed.

Young adults from intact families might not have known everything about their parents' values. They probably did not believe that their parents were faultless. But on the whole they saw those values as either unified or complementary.

By contrast, young adults from divorced families rarely perceived their parents' values as unified or complementary. They were much more likely to portray those values as in conflict or even as opposites. Kyle told me that his mom was open and accepting of all people, while his dad was class-conscious and given to stereotyping. Daniel said his immigrant father's most important goal was to make his family blend in as Americans, while his mother despised that idea. He also said that his father wanted his sons to excel at sports, while his mother was overprotective, fearing that the boys would get hurt. I heard that one parent valued hard work while the other parent had no work ethic and even that one parent valued commitment while the other did not.

This sense that our parents' values were in stark conflict influenced our feelings about them. It can be said that in life there are a few core beliefs we all need to have in order to feel good about ourselves and the world. One is that our mothers and fathers are good people. In our national survey, virtually all young adults from intact families strongly agreed with the statement "My mother is a good person." Most children of divorce thought so too—but they were less likely to agree strongly. This weakened sense of a parent's goodness is even more pronounced with fathers. Almost everyone from intact families strongly agrees that their father is a good person, but just over two-thirds of children of divorce feel the same way.

The differences are even greater when it comes to respect and forgiveness. Almost one-fifth of today's young adult children of divorce agree with the statement "I love my mother but I don't respect her." That's a threefold difference compared to their peers from intact families. One-quarter agree with the statement "I love my father but I don't respect him"—an almost fourfold difference.

Even more strikingly, more than a third of young adults from divorced families agree, "There are things my mother has done that I find hard to forgive," and over half agree, "There are things my father has done that I find hard to forgive." These are threefold differences. And if this study had included the many children of divorce who lose touch with their fathers altogether, the numbers would certainly be even higher.

Of course, there are plenty of children of divorce who admire one or both of their parents deeply. In particular, divorced mothers who focused on their kids and worked hard earned a lot of respect in their children's eyes. Samantha said, "The concept of family is really important to my mom and she did whatever she could to give my sister and me that. And she's got a very strong work ethic. When she was raising the two of us she was working second shift, going to school, all kinds of things. Even now she's still working crazy hours. But now she's worked her way up and she's got a really great job."

Anthony said, "Every morning my mom would wake us up, and she would cook, like, bacon and eggs, and they'd be ready when we got up. She took care of us and she sacrificed a lot for us. I know she went a long time without ever having a new dress. She sacrificed for us instead."

It made a similar impression when children saw their father sacrificing for them. Eric said, "For probably seven years, from the point my parents got divorced until the time he got remarried, everything my father did was for me and my brother."

What Is the Right Thing to Do?

To please their parents and to avoid getting in trouble, children want to know what is the right thing to do. Household rules are one way parents convey their sense of right and wrong. Yet even in this practical area, it is much less common for children of divorce to say we received consistent guidance from our parents.

In the national survey, fewer than half of us who stayed in touch with both parents agree that our parents' household rules were the same, while most of the people from intact families do.

The quality of the divorce makes little difference when it comes to that consistency. Just 58 percent of us whose parents had a "good divorce" agree that our parents' household rules were the same, compared to 32 percent of people from bad divorces. In comparison, 81 percent of children from unhappy but low-conflict marriages say their parents' rules were the same—as do 94 percent of children from happy marriages.

Some people from intact families recalled that household rules were set mutually ("Whatever one said, the other would stand for it"). Others said that one of their parents, often the mother, set the rules and the other parent backed him or her up. "Dad enjoyed fun things with the children but Mom basically set the rules" is a typical explanation. Or "Dad would be in the background and he would sort of be the second wall, so if we broke through what my mom told us to do then my dad was always there." Some did not know who set the rules but figured their parents talked about it behind the scenes.

By contrast, young people from divorced families often found that few if any of the rules at one home were in place at the other. There might be a firm structure at Mom's house but none at Dad's, or vice versa. Daniel remembered his mom's house as "sort of chaotic, and she would basically do everything," whereas his dad would have "little jobs for us." In a few cases, there seemed to be no rules at either house.

Some of the children of divorce recalled that whatever rules existed before the divorce fell away when their parents separated. Melissa is a recent college graduate with light blond hair and an eager, friendly personality. She had a plateful of freshly baked brownies ready when I arrived at her apartment. Before the divorce, she said, there had been homework and bedtime rules, and her mom was "fun . . . very much a parent and the authority figure, but also, like, cuddly." After the divorce, both the rules and the cuddles disappeared as Melissa's mother struggled to remake her life. Thereafter, the rules at her mom's and dad's houses were minimal, arbitrary, and different. Melissa wiped a brownie crumb off her chin and gestured with one hand. "So you'd go with one and they'd be like, 'Ah, stay out till ten! You can walk to the playground!'" Then, gesturing with the other hand, she continued, "And then the other one's like, 'You can't go anywhere! You have a bike but you have to ride it in the yard!'"

Similarly, Sara recalled that after her parents separated when she was ten years old they no longer shared regular meals at her mother's home. Like Sara, 32 percent of children of divorce say their family was not in the habit of sharing a daily meal after the divorce, while just 8 percent of those from intact families say the same thing. It was only many years later, when she was in high school, that Sara's mother managed to plan family meals again, but at that point Sara was angry and resentful. She remembers challenging her mom, "Why are you coming around now instead of eight years ago? Where were you this entire time?"

Some recalled that there were very few rules *before* their parents divorced. Jason broke into a wide grin as he said, "My parents were definitely baby boomers and yeah, it was great growing up in that household in terms of rules—there really weren't any." But after the divorce when he was fourteen years old there were new, strict rules as his mom tried, mostly unsuccessfully, to rein in Jason's rebellious behavior. Like him, several people noted that if there were any rules in their divorced families it was in response to troublemaking on the part of the kids. The "good kids," on the other hand, were not constrained by rules but also received less attention.

Several others pointed out that the divorce effectively ended their dad's role as a rule setter or enforcer. Will said his father was a strict disciplinarian before the divorce, but after the divorce "Dad's not around . . . I felt like 'I can do whatever I want, Mom's not going to stop me.'" He reflected, "It felt great, but looking back now, it's not a good thing." Anthony too said that his formerly strict father never disciplined him or his brother again after the divorce, even though they saw him often.

Many said that they spent too little time with their dad for rules to be required. Stacie recalled, "The relationship that we had didn't really call for rules. We were there for two nights every other week, and if I was there during the week it was for a couple of hours." No matter how often the children of divorce saw their noncustodial fathers—from weekly to only once a year—they frequently made this observation.

In some cases there were very dramatic differences in rules at each parent's home, even to the point of having the freedom to drink, smoke, or view pornography at one home—practices that were unthinkable at the other. In these cases it was always the noncustodial parent who provided the party atmosphere, although it was not always the father. Eric, who lived primarily with his father, recalled that in high school "we could have drinks at my mom's, we could get drunk if we wanted to," while his father would have been livid if he knew this. Sara recalled that in high school her mom was very strict about drinking but that her dad would buy beer for her and her sister when they visited him.

Other respondents also recalled parents who attempted to bond with them by appealing to their impulsive desires. Anthony's mother was devoutly religious and provided a highly structured home, but when he and his brother went to their dad's "we had freedom, too much freedom. . . . We knew we could do whatever we wanted." Anthony and his brother could curse and drink beer at Dad's house, and a formative experience in his life was when his father showed him a pornographic video in high school. At the time, he said, "it was exciting." Now it is one of many examples of why he does not respect his father.

Yet it was the more subtle differences between the rules or practices in our parents' homes that were the most confusing. After all, it didn't take Anthony long to realize that his dad was wrong for showing him a porn video, and Eric knew his mother shouldn't be serving him unlimited quantities of alcohol in high school. But it can be bewildering to children of divorce when neither parent is doing anything wrong but their rules and habits are simply *different*.

Katy offers one example. She spent most of the year living with her mother, stepfather, and grandparents. During the summers and school holidays she lived with her father, who remarried twice after her parents' divorce. Katy's parents had many differences. Her mother was religious and her father was not. Katy was the center of attention at her mother's house but felt more peripheral at her father's house, though she knew her father loved her. But some of the most confusing situations for Katy occurred when she confronted her parents' competing values in everyday situations.

Katy's mother was a penny-pincher and at her home, Katy remembered, they would "conserve every little scrap of paper." At her father's house money flowed more freely. "That was a little hard for me," Katy said, "because the leftovers on the table would get

thrown out at my father's house. And I was very used to the way my
mother did things." She remembered, "One time at my father's
house I ate everything on my plate and then ate more so that it
wouldn't get thrown out." In fact, Katy ate so much that night that
she ended up with a bad stomachache. She did not say anything
about her father and stepmother's practice of throwing out leftovers because it "would be rude," but she also had difficulty tolerat-
ing it. Her mother valued thrift and her father valued abundance.
Katy was caught silently in the middle, stuffed and uncomfortable.

Everyone has ended up at times in uncomfortable social situations, not wanting to offend someone. But for children of divorce
the differences between our two homes were between not just any
two people but our *parents*, the earliest and most important role
models we had. These crossed signals about right and wrong went
to the heart of our identities. Katy's confrontation with the leftovers was only one of many times she felt caught between two competing value systems in a way that was largely invisible to her
parents. After their divorce, her parents no longer had to decide
together what to do with the leftovers, nor did they have to discuss
or argue about the deeper values their decision might reflect. Yet
the need to sort out their different values did not disappear.
Instead it fell to Katy.

Every household is made up of these kinds of distinctive rules
and customs. In some households, for example, no one rushes to
answer the telephone when it rings. If the parents are eating dinner or otherwise busy, they let it go. In other households, answer-
ing the phone is a priority. Parents answer the phone no matter
what time of the day or night it might be. In the first case the parents value privacy and family time over being instantly available to
others. In the second case parents value being available whenever
anyone might need them, regardless of what else is going on. When
parents are married they have to find some way of merging contrasting values such as these, and some may never firmly sort it out.
But no matter how they handle it, the disagreement about whether
to answer the phone is their responsibility, not their child's.

When parents divorce they create separate households, and in the best divorces the child remains a part of both households. The parents no longer have to sort out issues such as how they will answer the phone—each can do it his or her own way—but now the child lives in both homes, confronting on a daily basis the parents' different ways of living. At her mom's house the child may often answer the phone and call out to her mother when it's for her. Then one day at her dad's house she is standing in the kitchen when the phone rings. She's about to answer it when she remembers that the last time she did so her dad was annoyed by the interruption. The phone continues to ring and she stares at it guiltily, wondering if it might be an important call, trying to figure out the right thing to do.

It's true that all children have to adapt to different rules all the time, whether it's at home, at school, or at a relative's house. But the key point is that in order to adapt, those of us from divorced families had to study our parents' different ways of living with a vigilance that children in intact families typically do not have to muster. In that one place in the world in which any of us should be able to let down our guard—our home—children of divorce have to keep their magnifying glasses up and their thinking caps on. For children of divorce, even benign, everyday decisions—"Should I answer the phone? What should I do with the leftovers?"—become fraught with tension and moral drama.

Who Do I Choose?

Perhaps the most significant moral decision many children of divorce have to make—one that is utterly foreign to children of married parents—is the choice between our parents. Fortunately, many people recognize that it is agonizing for children of divorce to have to choose between their parents. Divorcing parents are typically urged to make the decision themselves about where the child will live and how visitation will be arranged.

Unfortunately, despite our society's awareness of this potential burden, the choice between our parents—either soon after the divorce or years later—is almost unavoidable due to the structure of divorce. In the national survey, one-third of young adults from divorced families say they were asked to choose which parent to live with at some point in the years after the divorce, but even that fairly high number tells only part of the story. In other cases the choice between our parents was alive in our minds even if our parents did not raise it. Of the two-thirds of children of divorce who were *not* asked to choose which parent they would live with, one-third say they wanted to have that choice but apparently did not.

Even when custody arrangements were fixed and we neither were asked to choose nor wanted to choose which parent to live with, as we got older we were routinely confronted with new choices between our parents as we began to make our own decisions about where we would spend our time. The need to choose between our parents was an issue that stayed alive for many of us throughout our childhoods and well beyond.

Although most divorcing parents know they should not ask their children to choose between them, it still happens. Parents feel extremely vulnerable during a divorce. A parent who has been abandoned is dealing with deep feelings of rejection and may fear losing the love and loyalty of his or her children as well. Kyle was six years old when his parents divorced. He remembered sitting on the front stoop with his father when his father asked if he wanted to live with his mom or his dad. Kyle reflected, "I was a little kid, and he was upset at the time, but . . . it's a tough thing to ask a six-year-old. I think he was just obviously pretty torn up. I mean, my mother started the divorce proceedings." Because Kyle's father had been struggling with alcoholism for years, it was clear to Kyle where he would live when his parents divorced. He felt pressed to say something, so he told his dad he wanted to live with his mom, but he has regretted having to answer that question ever since.

Daniel's mother too was quite vulnerable after the divorce, and this led her at times to put her sons in difficult positions. Daniel remembered that his mother would ask them to choose between her and their father. "The question I remember was, you know, 'Who do you love more?'" He took a swig of water and said, "And we would never answer who do we love more, so I think she tried to phrase it, 'Well, who would you rather live with?'" He remembered, "I was old enough at the time to say, 'I don't know.' But I remember my brothers would say, 'Well, maybe Dad. Well, no, maybe Mom.' Like they were really thinking about it. But for me, I sort of knew what was going on."

Daniel says that if he and his brothers bring up that memory today, "my mom swears that she never asked us that. She gets very sensitive, very defensive if I even mention the fact that she had asked us that. But I remember clearly being very bothered by that question [because] I couldn't possibly choose. And in my mind I had to force myself to go through each one of them and sort of [decide] what's good here, what's bad there, what's good here, what's bad there. And even thinking about that would make me feel guilty."

When children are asked to choose between their parents, they try to evaluate the moral status of each of their parents. What is good and bad at each of their homes? How are they right and how are they wrong? Who should the child choose?

Children feel terribly caught if they are asked which parent they want to live with. But older children especially can feel very resentful if they are *not* allowed to make the decision about where they will live. Jason's parents divorced when he was fourteen years old. In the wake of the divorce Jason and his mother fought bitterly. Even today Jason complains, "We didn't have a choice. That is one of the questions I asked my mom when they split up. I was like, 'Why are we living with you?' And she said, 'That's the way we've decided.'" Jason remembers retorting, "Who the hell are you to make a decision on my behalf? I know you're my parent, but what if I don't want to live here?"

Although custody decisions are first made at the time of the divorce, the issue of where the child will live can remain an open question for years. When I came to the door of Angela's home in the suburbs her little boy answered the door, with Angela not far behind him. She got him settled with a video in the next room and invited me to join her at the dining room table.

Her parents divorced when she was four years old. At the time they decided that she and her brother would live with their mother on the West Coast during the school year and with their father in the Midwest every summer. But years later, when she was in seventh grade, Angela was confronted with the choice between her parents. "Apparently my mother had made some kind of deal with my father when they divorced," she said. "That when she was doing some part of her schooling we would go live with him for a few years. And then it got to be that time and she reneged." Angela went on softly, lowering her voice so that her son wouldn't overhear, "So my father talked to a lawyer and I guess the lawyer told him that a custody fight would not work in his favor unless it was the kids' decision."

In response, Angela's father set up a meeting between his children and the lawyer, thinking perhaps that it would be easier for the children to reveal their feelings to a neutral party. But when Angela sat across the desk from the lawyer she felt "like I was at risk of betraying everybody. Like if I said that I was unhappy with my mother or that I wanted to live with my father, then I would be betraying my mother. But if I said I didn't want to live with my father that would be betraying my father. So I felt very anxious. And I really wished that it wasn't my problem."

Angela's experience reminded me of my own. Like her, the issue of where I would live resurfaced many years after my parents' divorce. They split up in the early seventies, when it was rare for fathers to get custody. My father has told me that at the time he talked to a lawyer about the possibility of suing for custody, but the lawyer explained that he would have a chance of winning only if he was able to prove that my mother was unfit. My dad thought my mom did a good job raising me and he didn't want to trump up charges about her, so he backed off and went along with the plan for me to live with her most of the year.

Some years later, though, the question came up again. The year that I spent living with my father and stepmother—the year in which I was happy to be with him but desperately longed for my mother and my home—came about because of a choice that was given to me. I was seven years old when my mother decided to go back to school. She knew the first year of her program would be very challenging, all the more so because my brother was still just a baby. I was playing with paper dolls on the front porch one afternoon when she sat down on the steps next to me. What did I think about living with my father for a year? She'd be really busy and maybe it would be more fun for me. "Think about it," she said, "and let me know what you want to do." I was intrigued by the idea of living with my dad, but as soon as she walked away I forgot about the question.

A few days passed and my mom brought the idea up again. So, she asked, had I thought about whether I might like to live with my dad for a year? Truthfully, I hadn't thought about the question even once since she last brought it up. But when she raised it I again felt intrigued by the thought of living with my dad—after all, I often missed him. At the same time, I could not imagine a whole year without my mom, having never lived without her for such a long time before. I had no idea how to make this kind of decision, so without thinking it through for more than two minutes, with a seven-year-old's logic I said out loud, "Well, I've always lived with you. So I guess I should live with Daddy for a year." It was like sharing on the playground. My mom had had the chance to have me for a while, so now it was my dad's turn.

The decision was made and the wheels were set in motion. Months later we packed my things, I said goodbye to my mother, stepfather, and baby brother, and I went to live with my father. And though I was happy to see him, it would prove to be one of the hardest years of my childhood, when I missed my mother and my home with a searing intensity I could never have imagined. The fact that it had been my decision made the year all the more difficult. I thought my sadness was my own fault—this was, after all, my choice—and it was up to me to deal with it alone.

As we got older, the choices between our parents could take surprising forms. For example, Katy had always found her dad a bit intimidating after her parents' divorce when she was three years old, but she loved him and never doubted his love for her. So she was thrown off guard when she was about ten years old and her mother asked if she would like for her stepfather to adopt her, which would require Katy's father to forsake his parental rights. Because Katy was close to her stepfather and because her mother and father had clashed for years over child support payments, it might have seemed natural to Katy's mother to suggest that Katy's stepfather become her father now. But Katy remembered, "Even though I really considered my stepfather to be part of my family . . . I still felt it was important that I considered my biological father to be my father as well. I had a good relationship with him, and I didn't want to give that up." After much soul-searching Katy told her mother no, but the profound importance of the decision presented to her at ten years old stayed with her.

Years later, when Katy's mother and father were embroiled in suits and countersuits over her college tuition costs, her father's anger at her mother boiled over onto Katy as well. Katy and her father had a nasty argument. She recalled, "He said something to the effect of 'If you walked out of my life right now it wouldn't even matter to me.' . . . He has a bad temper at times and he really let it rip."

Katy was deeply hurt. She remembered thinking, "I was the only one who stuck with him all those years." She told me that she wanted to ask him, "Why would you ever think that I would go anywhere?" "I had that choice," she said, "which I don't even know if he knew about." In Katy's mind she had a secret trust with her father, one they never discussed and which he likely never even knew about—that in spite of her mother's wishes she had chosen him. That secret trust made his callous remark years later burn all the more.

As children of divorce, we also had to make many smaller but equally loaded choices between our parents. When we were young children we were usually told what our schedule would be. Mom and Dad arranged where we would live and visit, who would pick us up and drop us off, and more. But as we got older it increasingly became our own decision about when to stay and when to go. These days parents who are trying to construct a "good divorce" for their children might even live within a short distance of each other. They say one of the benefits of living close by is that the children "can go back and forth as they please." They believe they are creating a structure similar to an intact family in which the child has equal and easy access to both parents.

The problem, though, is that locating divorced parents' households very near one another—even buying a duplex in which Mom lives upstairs and Dad lives downstairs—does little to change the burden that falls to children when their parents divorce. If anything, locating the parents' homes close enough that a young child can walk from one to the other can increase the child's burden. Suddenly it is no longer the parents' job to determine when the child will travel back and forth between their two worlds. Now even a child who is not old enough to drive can come and go "as he pleases." Now it becomes the child's choice, not the parents' decision, to decide which parent to spend time with and for how long.

Jason was one such child. After his parents divorced when he was fourteen years old they moved into separate apartments a short distance from each other. Many afternoons Jason would drop by his father's apartment after school and sports practice to hang out for a while, have dinner with his dad, and watch some television. He remembered, though, that while lying on the sofa in the evenings watching television he always tried to avoid falling asleep. Outwardly he may have looked relaxed, but inside he stayed alert and vigilant, fearing he would inadvertently drift off and end up sleeping at his father's place. Instead, at some point in the evening he would rouse himself and get up to go back to his mom's. Even as he did so, he always felt guilty about leaving his dad. Jason sensed that his dad wanted him to stay longer and it felt like there was no good way of deciding when to leave. He had to make an arbitrary choice and that just made him feel worse.

Some might be surprised that Jason felt his comings and goings would affect his parents so much. But, years later, Jason talked about those evenings with his dad. His dad said to him, "Yeah, it was always hard for me to see you go." Parents are only human and of course they feel sad when their children leave them. And children can sense their parents' sadness, even if the parents try to shield them from it.

By contrast, in an intact family the children do not have to think about being with their parents. They may spend more time with one parent than the other, but they do not have to plan it or pay attention to their parents' feelings about it.

Of course, most divorces do not involve parents living so near one another that their young children can walk between their houses. Parents typically move farther apart and sometimes live very long distances from each other. But if we were not required to choose how much time we would spend with each parent when we were still living at home, we soon had to make the choice once we left home.

Many children of divorce tell stories about the dilemmas they faced when they first went away to college or moved away from home. Angela's father was hurt that she no longer spent long summers with him when she went off to college, because she now had limited amounts of time to split between her mother's home, her father's home, and other opportunities, such as jobs or travel. Katy remembers doing her "East Coast tour," cycling between her mother's and father's homes, which were several states apart, on short breaks from her Ivy League university.

Stephen says that even now it is stressful visiting his father and mother, who still live near one another. When he goes home, instead of relaxing in one place he's "the one trying to juggle everyone." Stephen feels guilty if he spends too much time with one parent, but he also feels resentful if his parents don't recognize what he's trying to do and help him out. One time recently, he said, "it had been awhile since I'd been home. And the only time that weekend that I could see my dad was on Sunday, and I remember he played golf that day. I remember being really annoyed with that, like I'm always the one making time to see everyone else."

The choices become still more complicated when children of divorce marry and have children of our own. Our family obligations are multiplied with the addition of in-laws and sometimes our spouse may have divorced parents too. When grandchildren come along all the grandparents want to see their grandchild, but the ever-constricting amount of time and the expense of travel makes the choice about which parent to spend time with even tougher. For children of divorce, the choice between our parents lives on as long as we and our parents do.

What Do I Believe?

Given the contradictions between our parents' beliefs and values, as well as the fact that we were so often alone, children of divorce are more likely to develop our own values independently of our parents. Many people know that children of divorce end up being more independent, but Professor Glenn and I were surprised at how different they looked from their peers from intact families. For instance, young adults from divorced families are much more likely to say they do not share similar moral values with their fathers and mothers. A small number, about 6 percent, of people from intact families feel this way, but 24 percent of people from divorced families say they do not share similar moral values with their fathers, and 17 percent say the same thing about their mothers.

Similarly, almost a quarter of young adults from divorced families disagree with the assertion "My father taught me clearly the difference between right and wrong," and more than a tenth say the same thing about their mothers, while a tiny number of people from intact families say the same thing—just 3 and 1 percent, respectively.

When asked where they got their sense of right and wrong,

many children of divorce will name mothers (and, rarely, fathers) as important sources, but they often name other sources as well. Katy said her values come from her mother and her faith. "If I need to make a decision about something," she said, "I think more what would my mother do? Because she's very religious and I'm very religious." Joanna said her values come "from the church and my mom." Louisa said her values come from "number one, my mom; number two, my friends; and number three, the church."

While today's young adult children of divorce are *less* religious overall than our peers from intact families, a surprising number of us feel that we are *more* religious than our parents. Almost one-third of us agree with the statement "I think I am more religious now than my mother ever was," which is a twofold difference compared to young adults from intact families. About half of us, compared to fewer than a third of those from intact families, agree, "I think I am more religious now than my father ever was."

Other children of divorce say that rather than looking to their parents or a faith tradition they looked inside themselves as they tried to figure out right from wrong. Melissa said her response to her parents' conflicting guidance when she was a child was to "make up my own rules." She glanced down at her chubby cat, curled contentedly in her lap, and scratched his neck as she told me, "I developed a strong sense of what I thought was correct when I was young. I didn't really have any guidance. I didn't really know what to do, so I thought, 'Well, if this feels right I'll do that.' " This approach worked for Melissa and kept her out of some dangerous situations—one of her personal rules, for instance, was to avoid sexual activity as a teenager—but it is clearly a risky strategy for many children and teenagers.

Even among those children of divorce who complete college and are successful, some are blunt in talking about their struggles to do the right thing. Eric was about to become a new father with his girlfriend and he said that his life until recently involved "going out every weekend drinking. And definitely getting into drugs as well, but not hard core." Now, he said, "I've pretty much altogether stopped, just trying to save money, and we're moving into a new house. . . . Now I'm back with my head on straight." When I asked Eric where his sense of right and wrong came from, he tugged on his cap and looked away. "I think my sense of right and wrong is very, you know, cloudy—which is bad." He went on, "My loyalty to women was probably not as good as it could have been for many years." Eric was trying to do the right thing these days as best as he understood it. But he seemed hesitant and ambivalent about his values even today.

Where Do I Belong?

The question "Where do I belong?" would seem to be relatively easy for a child to answer, especially a young child. But growing up in two worlds plants the question of belonging deep in the moral and spiritual lives of children of divorce. We traveled between two worlds and in a sense we belonged in both. But these were not just any two worlds. Each world revolved around a parent who had rejected or been rejected by the other parent. These two worlds were not just different but fundamentally at odds with each other, making even simple questions feel loaded with moral importance.

The question of belonging was the deep undercurrent running beneath many of the questions that confronted us. In each moral quandary we searched for belonging and feared exclusion. We puzzled over our parents' conflicting values and beliefs and tried to determine whether we shared them. We scrutinized our parents' different household rules—not just to avoid getting in trouble but also to try to fit in. We asked ourselves, "If I choose one parent, will I be rejected by the other?"

Perhaps nothing signals belonging more than physically resembling someone else. Yet, paradoxically, we often found that resembling one of our parents marked us as an outsider, as someone who does *not* belong, rather than as an insider.

In an intact family, resembling a parent signals belonging. Parent and child can enjoy sharing a single, powerful family identity that extends even to the shape of their nose or the texture of their hair. Looking or acting alike is the ultimate way of feeling like you're insiders in the same group. All kinds of organizations, whether gangs or clubs or professions, try to some extent to mimic the bonds that families share by having their members sport the same jackets or uniforms or tattoos.

In a divorced family resembling a parent can mean something very different. In our families, looking like our father or mother could just as often mark us as outsiders—as members of that other, rival club.

When I talked with all kinds of young adults it became clear that in many families, whether married or divorced, it is apparently not uncommon for mothers to cry out in exasperation, "You're acting just like your father!" Yet while young people from intact families recall their mothers uttering these words, the comparison never had much sting—even when their mother's frustration was clear—because these young people knew without question that their father was a full member of the family. They loved their fathers and almost all of them felt confident that their mothers loved their fathers too. How bad could it be, then, to be compared to him?

By contrast, when a divorced mother compares her child to her ex-husband, the child experiences tension and fear. As children we perceived each of our parents as being at the extreme end of a continuum. No one could be more different from our mother than our father, and vice versa. To be compared to one parent by the other sounded terribly threatening. Even a mild comparison, not meant to upset us, still carried a powerful undertone: "You resemble the outsider. You do not fully belong in my world." No doubt it is the rare divorced parent who actually feels that the child does not belong in his or her world. But because our parents lived in two separate worlds that were opposed in our minds, these hints of potential exclusion are what *we* looked for, heard, and felt.

I noticed that for young people from intact families the question of resembling a parent is usually lighthearted. Some will say that they look like both of their parents and will even point out which features come from which parent—"I have my mom's eyes, my dad's nose, her complexion," and so forth. Often they smile, as though they are recalling entertaining family discussions during which children and parents speculated about who looked like whom. Others will say that their looks or personality more closely resemble one parent, either the father or the mother. But those from intact families almost never thought about such resemblances as a problem.

Some from intact families did remember feeling threatened by such a comparison, but the threat did not go deep. One woman recalled that when she was a child her father sometimes said she acted like her mother. She remembered, "I guess initially I thought, 'What does that mean?' And then I'd think, 'Well, yeah, I am just like my mom, so deal with it, you know?'"

Similarly, another woman said, "When I was being irresponsible my mom would be like, 'Stop acting like your dad.'" She grinned and shrugged. "But I always thought my dad was great. I didn't think my parents could do any wrong. So I was all right with it."

More often, young people from intact families remembered one parent favorably comparing them to the other parent. One man recalled his mother looking at his school picture and saying proudly that he looked like his father. Several women said they resembled their mother in looks or personality and this was a source of pride for their father. One remembered fondly, "My dad would say my mom is so sweet, and he would often say he was so glad his daughters took more after my mom than him."

Genetically, of course, children of divorce and children from intact families are no different. But young adults from divorced families do not recall lighthearted family discussions in which their nose was identified as their father's or their smile as their mother's. Instead, many of us remember feeling anxious and deeply threatened about possibly resembling one or both of our parents.

Anthony, whose parents divorced when he was five years old, grew up living with his mom and younger brother but saw his father, who lived about fifteen minutes away, often. Anthony had many good memories about his mother and talked at length about how much she sacrificed for him and his brother. But thinking about being compared to a parent brought back a painful memory: "I'll tell you something that used to bother me," he said uncomfortably. "My mother would call me Mr. J —— [the same last name as his father's] when I would do something to make her mad at me. Meaning 'You're acting like your dad,' and I knew that she didn't like him and she thought he was not a good person."

Kyle felt the same way. As a child, he thought his bad temper came from his father because that was what his mother always said: "She'd say, 'You're just like your father.' That would hurt me. I would feel like it was a put-down."

In other cases a divorced mother might exclaim in a fit of frustration that the child was acting like his father but backpedal when challenged to explain what this meant. Daniel said that when his mother accused him of acting like his father he felt "very angry, because it wasn't with a smile that she said that, it was with a scowl, and it was just very negative." He folded his hands together, gripping his knuckles tightly. "I would just feel my blood boiling at that point. And I would say, 'Well, what's wrong with that?' That would come up a lot. Every time we did something she didn't like she would say, 'Oh, that's just like your father.' We were definitely primed. We knew that being like our father was bad, so anytime she said that I felt she was telling me I was bad."

He relaxed his hands and looked at me, frowning. "I remember having it out with her several times, saying, 'You're implying that I'm bad.' Then she would say, 'No, I didn't imply that at all.' It was very confusing, very mixed messages."

Being compared to the other parent did not always sting. For example, Eric grew up living with his father and brother and visited his mom often. Because he lived with his father he saw how his father sacrificed to care for his sons every day. At times Eric's mother would say with frustration that Eric had a bad temper like his father, but this tended to annoy Eric more than anger him, because he was confident that his dad was not a bad person.

In still other cases, even when the mother did not compare the child to the father, the child nevertheless wondered and worried. One woman said that acting like her father "probably was an issue for my mom but she never would say it." Another said she looks like her dad and "I sometimes thought it was an issue with my mom. I'm like, 'Oh, she thinks I'm way too much like him, and I look like him.'" Another recalled, "I think sometimes my mom resented me because I look just like my father."

Growing up, I had the same fears. From the time I was extremely little I recall people saying that I looked just like my father. I heard it so often that I accepted it as fact, though as a girl I sometimes wished people would also compare me to my mother, who I thought was beautiful. My mother would also compare me to my father and, unlike other people's comments, this was something I never got used to. She would say that I gestured with my hands the way my father did, or that I had his goofy sense of humor. Usually she pointed out these similarities with a curious fascination, interested to see how genetics led me to be so much like the father I didn't see on a daily basis. But when she made these comparisons I would freeze inside, searching her face for signs of disapproval. Suddenly I was aware of the potential for exclusion, for identification with someone who, I thought, couldn't be more different from her.

As children, being compared to our fathers was the more typical experience for us. We tended to spend a lot more time with our mothers and it may be that mothers in general more often make these comparisons. But children of divorce can also fear resembling their mothers. Katy leaned back in her chair and remembered, "Because of my dark hair I look just like my mother. When I was with my father's relatives, I always felt like I was the odd person out." She gestured toward her face. "I was genetically obviously derived from somebody else too, you know? Like 'Gosh, where is she from?'" I understood what Katy was saying up to this point, but her conclusion surprised me. "So if I was in a car with my dad," she said, "I always had this fear that people would think I was his mistress." Not only did Katy feel that looking like her mother marked her as an outsider within her father's family and community, but as a budding adolescent her status as an "outside" female raised uncomfortable sexual overtones, even around her own father.

When the children from intact families were compared by one parent to another it could be a point of pride or a source of frustration. Yet even when the parent making the observation was obviously frustrated, the children of intact families had the internal resources to bounce back, like the young woman who told her dad, "Yeah, I am just like my mom, so deal with it." The children of married parents know that even if a parent is angry or annoyed, both the parents and the child, for better or worse, belong in the same family.

Those of us from divorced families lacked this unquestioned sense of shared family identity. Even if our parent intended to make an innocent or complimentary comparison, their words were not uttered in a vacuum. We were already intimately familiar with a history of serious conflict between our parents' worlds, and it was this conflict we tapped into when being compared to a parent. In even the smallest exchanges we scrutinized our parents' words and deeds, looking for signs of inclusion or exclusion, rejection or security, in a lasting quest to understand where we truly belonged.

Polar Opposites

The tough moral questions that arose from the clash between our parents' different worlds seemed all the more urgent because those worlds quite often seemed completely polarized. The majority of us—two-thirds—agree that after the divorce, "my parents seemed like polar opposites of each other." By contrast, only one-third of people from intact families say the same thing about their parents, and 43 percent of them strongly disagree that their parents seemed like polar opposites.

Of course, some children of divorce may have viewed our parents as polar opposites even if our parents had not divorced, just as some of the children of intact families do. Simply put, some parents may divorce because they fight so much that they seem like polar opposites of each other. But we found that the children's perception that their parents were polar opposites does not have much to do with the amount of conflict they remember. In the national survey, only a fifth of young adults from divorced families say their parents conflicted a lot after the divorce, yet two-thirds say their parents seemed like polar opposites. Clearly, something about the divorce itself made our parents much more likely to seem to us like polar opposites. Looking at marriage and divorce from the child's point of view helps explain why.

All parents, whether married or divorced, are different, just as any two people are different. But parents who are married share many experiences that draw them closer together. They live in the same home, spend time with each other's families, share many of the same friends, and their economic fortunes rise and fall together. Children arise from their union, typically sharing biological ties with each of them, and the parents raise those children together. In their work lives, their personal lives, and in the world at large, they are treated by others as a couple, the fact of the marriage like a banner over their heads announcing that what connects them is larger than what divides them. They will always have differences, but by being married and living as a married couple their two worlds increasingly overlap as the years go by.

In contrast, for children of divorce there was little that brought our parents' worlds together once they parted. They no longer shared a home or spent time with each other's families and friends, nor did they appear before the world as a couple. Their financial lives were still intertwined through their mutual responsibilities to us, but their fortunes could and often did rise or fall quite independently of each other. The only links between their two worlds were their ties to us. Otherwise each was free to form new ties, to take new risks, to try new things. With no structure remaining to knit them together, their differences grew larger over the years, and their worlds seemed increasingly polarized. When they gave up trying to make sense of their two worlds, that decision caused us to see them as polar opposites.

Just as important, our normal cognitive development disposed us to see our divorced parents as polar opposites. Children's early thinking begins with contrast and opposition; we think in terms of big and little, near and far, light and dark. Similarly, we also think in terms of good and bad, right and wrong. When confronted with two powerful forces that were separate and set in opposition to one another—our divorced parents—it was natural for us to view Mom and Dad as another polarity, like big and little or light and dark. But this polarity went to the heart of our inner lives.

The children's book *To & Fro, Fast & Slow,* described in Chapter 2, quite astonishingly uses the organizing theme of a child traveling between her divorced parents to teach young children about opposites. The whole book is organized around the split that brings about the child's experience of growing up in two starkly contrasting worlds. Of course, the book portrays the child happily bouncing from home to home, welcoming the rich variety of experiences that she finds in each place. Yet although children certainly enjoy a visit to the animal farm in the country followed up with a jaunt to the science museum in the city, growing up in two starkly contrasting worlds is far more difficult than that.

As children of divorce, each time we confronted a new and complex moral question—"Where do I belong? What do my parents think and believe? What is the right thing to do?"—we looked not just to any two worlds for clues, but to two worlds that seemed as different as night and day. The chasm between the two worlds made reconciling even their smallest differences seem much more daunting, perhaps even impossible. Outside of the picture books, those of us who grew up in divorced families did not bounce unselfconsciously between our parents' worlds so much as get mentally stuck in between them.

There is still another reason why our parents' divorce made them seem like polar opposites to us. Divorce, like marriage, can be seen as an institution. Our parents were related to one another not through a structure that emphasized their unity—marriage—but rather through one that emphasized their difference and opposition: divorce. Unlike the banner of marriage announcing their unity to the world, the banner of divorce announced to everyone, including us, that the differences between them were larger than anything they might share in common. Even if *they* did not feel starkly opposed to one another the structure of divorce nevertheless made them seem that way to us.

I recently talked with a fellow Gen X-er named Stephanie Hanley, a fiber artist and doula who lives on the East Coast. She identified strongly with my idea that divorced parents seem like polar opposites to their kids. She said her parents especially seemed that way when it came to their religious beliefs. Her parents had gone to church together before their divorce. Afterward her mother stopped going, but Stephanie's father and stepmother joined a strict Baptist congregation where the girls had to wear skirts, not pants, to church on Sundays. Stephanie and her younger sisters stayed with their father every other weekend and struggled to adapt to living in their parents' different worlds. Sometimes, though, these two worlds collided in moments that Stephanie found bewildering. She remembered, "It was weird to be at Wal-Mart with my mom and run into my friends from church, and I'd be wearing pants."

When Stephanie left home for college she became a fiber arts major. Her senior art project, years ago, was a large, freestanding woven sculpture that explored themes of light and dark. One side of the sculpture was water, with jellyfish floating in it, a reference to a childhood memory with her father. The other side of the sculpture was a forest with leaves, which represented her mother's profession. The two sides of the sculpture were looped at the ends but not woven together. Stephanie remembers looking at her art, at what she now realizes was a depiction of the polar parents who shaped her sense of self, and thinking, "Is this sculpture a symbol of me or the wall I have to get around?"

Only one-quarter of young adults from divorced families, but three-quarters of our peers from intact families, strongly agree,

"When my parents had conflicts, I always knew they would get over it"—yet another enormous difference (and for this question, like most, the children of divorce were asked to comment about *after* the divorce, not before). Just a minority of us remember our parents actually conflicting a lot after the divorce, but their divorce itself made it seem to many of us that their worlds existed in a permanent state of conflict. In contrast, the majority of people from intact families were very confident that when conflict arose between their parents they would "get over it."

Many people I interviewed for this book are still clear in my mind, even as months and years pass since the time I met them. Daniel is one of them. He struck me as a deeply thoughtful and sincere person. He wanted to talk seriously about the big questions in life. At a young age he had started a family and was already making important gains in his profession. He tried hard to do the right thing. He seemed conscientious and extremely independent.

Some may say that if divorce requires children to become independent thinkers capable of complex moral discernment, that's a good thing. But the problem is that requiring children to confront confusing moral questions, early and alone, is an uncertain strategy for raising healthy, secure young people. Children may figure out what is right, but they may also struggle and end up doing what is wrong. The need to develop a value system with less clear guidance from parents may help to explain (as one of many reasons) why, as a group, children of divorce have higher rates of substance abuse, teen pregnancy, depression, juvenile delinquency, and suicide. Some children are able to cast a wide net and find the answers they need. Some are not. They feel overwhelmed by the burden of growing up too soon and flail desperately.

Even those who make it are distinctively shaped by this history of growing up in two worlds. Daniel and the other children of divorce I interviewed spent their childhoods studying their parents and their worlds rather than living freely immersed in their own world. They still managed to have fun, like most children do, but they wear a mantle of seriousness and vigilance even today that sets them apart from their peers. Childhood is about gradually maturing to become an adult who is able to think independently about complex moral issues. But children are not meant to take on this task alone.

Some of the questions raised in this chapter are ones that children from intact families face too. In an intact family, however, the married parents take the lead on confronting these moral questions. It's their job to sort out their conflicting beliefs and experiences and come up with consistent guidance about right and wrong. If they fail, it's clear where the failure lies. Children of married parents must reflect on moral questions but more often they can do it on their own timeline, when they are ready, and they are more likely to have the presence and aid of their parents when they do so.

Certainly, children of married parents can also be hit with arduous experiences early on. Someone in the family may get ill or die, a parent may lose a job, or other tragedies may befall them. And in every childhood smaller but deeply felt losses are likely to strike — pets die, families move, friendships are lost. Yet when these tragedies do happen, most parents try their best to be there for their kids, to comfort them and help them with the loss.

Still more important, the most glaring losses felt in intact families are quite often beyond the parents' control. Most parents try their best not to get sick or go bankrupt. But divorce is a massive blow to a child that the parents — at least one of them — have control over. Sometimes it must happen, but often it does not have to.

In a "good divorce" the big moral questions can be especially confusing. Often we are told that the divorce is nobody's fault, that the marriage just has to come to an end. Parents tell the children that they simply don't love each other anymore. Or, even more confusing, they tell the children that they still love each other but simply can't live together anymore. In a "good divorce" both parents are typically presented as "good" to the child. Neither Mommy nor Daddy is blamed for the failure of the marriage. Yet as children we nevertheless struggled with a series of often unanswerable questions: "If my parents do not agree on what is right, which of them is right and which is wrong? Where do I belong? What should I do?"

When I wrestled with these questions as a child I did not know that the first responsibility for dealing with them should lie with my parents. Instead I struggled alone and the lack of acknowledgment for my task only isolated me all the more. No one said that my parents may have handed me an overwhelming task—on the contrary, everyone around me affirmed that my parents were good people having what's now called a "good divorce"—so as a child I was left to assume that if I couldn't handle the burden it was because there was something wrong with *me*.

There is perhaps greater moral clarity for children of divorce when one parent is called "bad" and the other "good," but that is not easy either. For instance, when a father is blamed for having an affair and wrecking the marriage, and when a mother is seen as good and blameless, it may be easier for the child to figure out which model to follow, but a great deal is lost along the way. The child loses the ability to respect one of his parents and absorbs a lesson that one way to deal with a troubled marriage is to leave your spouse and take up with someone else. In addition, when one parent is blamed for the failure of the marriage and for all the problems that crop up afterward, it may lead to an overly rigid way of judging the world. The "good" parent is never all good, but that parent's mistakes are overlooked. The "bad" parent is rarely all bad, but that parent's good qualities are dismissed.

In the end, no matter what kind of divorce our parents had, we were set at once on a different course, required to forge our own values and beliefs in the raw heat of our inner lives. But growing up in two worlds did even more than foist complex moral questions upon us. The dividing line between our worlds was drawn and reinforced by a wall of secrecy and contested truths. This wall contributed to a troubling secret within us, a feeling of being divided inside. In the deafening silence of the "good divorce," when we felt confused or overwhelmed we felt we had only ourselves to blame.

6
Secrets

As a child I got more practice keeping secrets than I wanted. And usually the secrets were not my own.

Once, when I was ten years old, my father and I were sitting at the kitchen table in the house he shared with my stepmother, surrounded by the blue-and-white patterned wallpaper that looked for all the world like wedding china. I was chattering about something that had happened recently at home with my mom when he interrupted.

"Is Paul living with you and your mother?" he asked.

I froze. My dad's eyes were kind but he also had a very direct, don't-lie-to-me look. If he was asking me the question, it was because he didn't know the answer. And if he didn't know, it was probably because my mom didn't want him to know. But it was hard to hide the fact that my mom's boyfriend was indeed living in our house; if nothing else, his name popped up in too many stories.

I don't remember what I said. Probably I turned red and looked pained and my father, taking pity, backed off. But I remember it as another instance when my two worlds collided, when aimless chatter led to a dangerous breach in security, when one parent's secret was almost revealed to the other—all because of me.

Families routinely make decisions about what kinds of information to share with the outside world. But when a family breaks in two, those decisions suddenly multiply for a child. Children travel from one parent's world to the other's, learning a thousand private details about each of them. At the same time, they soon discover that each parent wants to keep some of these details from the other parent.

Some parents explicitly ask their child to keep secrets. Experts discourage this practice and many divorced parents manage to avoid it. But what parents and experts alike do not realize is that secrets are almost inevitable when children must travel between two homes.

Divorced parents are like any other couple that has broken up. They feel sensitive to news of their ex-spouse, especially if it involves a new romance or money. As children we quickly learned a lesson—the information that might have provoked these feelings of anger or hurt should not have been shared.

Of course, not all divorced parents remain concerned about what their ex is up to, nor do they particularly care what the ex knows or doesn't know about their lives. But this attitude sends a troubling message to children as well. Parents who show little interest in our other parent's world might seem as if they have little interest in *our* lives when we're in that world. It can feel as if each half of our childhood is a secret from one of our parents.

Therapists and other professionals typically view secrets as a serious problem. Secrets, they say, stunt healthy communication, which harms the well-being of children and families. Yet for an entire generation of children of divorce secrets are epidemic, an almost inevitable part of growing up in a divorced family.

What Don't I Tell Mom? What Don't I Say to Dad?

"I was not supposed to tell my father anything about the finances," Katy recalled. "That was a no-no topic, because it could tip the boat just a little bit. Somebody might get an idea not to pay child support." She paused and anxiously twisted the thin silver band on her finger. "Even now when I'm talking about it I'm thinking"—her voice fell to a whisper—" 'Oh, that's family business.' "

Alicia recalled that when it came to her parents, "you didn't talk about money, how much somebody made, how much you were spending."

Melissa leaned back in the kitchen chair and said, "Especially when we were little and we'd go visit my dad, my mom was always like, 'You can tell him this and you can't tell him that and you can't tell him that.'" She grimaced and said that when she and her sister came back from their father's, "we were like little spies. My mom would give us the whole Gestapo debriefing. 'So what did they do? What did they wear? Where did they take you? What did they say? What did they say about me?'"

Indeed, 27 percent of today's young adult children of divorce agree, "At times one of my parents would ask me to keep important secrets from the other parent," compared to only 10 percent of children from intact families. Yet even these data reflect only those children of divorce who were explicitly *asked* to keep secrets. It does not count those who, for whatever reason, felt the need to keep secrets. I found that these more subtle yet still divisive experiences of secret-keeping were common in our lives.

Infidelity is a secret numerous children of divorce say they had to keep, and certainly one of the most painful. While infidelity is a serious problem in many marriages, not all marriages that suffer from it end in divorce. Yet when the veil of a marriage is lifted and the parents' actions are revealed, children of divorce are more likely to learn about an unfaithful parent's behavior. A number of them told me they were aware of a parent's infidelities before the marriage ended, in some cases even before the other parent knew.

Eric grew suddenly heated when I asked about this: "When my parents got divorced my mom was definitely cheating on my dad, and I knew about it and didn't say anything." His jaw tensed. "It was a shitty feeling. I hated my mom for a while."

Jason also recalled knowing, at one level, that his mother's infidelity had ended the marriage but not wanting to admit it to himself. He looked me in the eye and said, "You don't want to think that your mom's an adulterer."

Some children of divorce said they learned especially early about a parent's infidelity. Will, whose father cheated on his mother, recalled, "When you're in seventh, eighth grade and you know what your dad's doing, it causes a lot of pain." I sensed that Will had known about the affair before his mom did, and asked if that was true. "Yeah," he replied, "when I was ten or eleven he'd take me to baseball games and she was always there, the girlfriend. It was like, 'Now I'm going home, what don't I tell Mom? What don't I say to Dad?' You're in the middle and you're too young for that stuff. It just sends your life into a complete tailspin."

Infidelity is far from the only secret to which children of divorce are more likely to be exposed. There is, for one thing, the divorce itself. Some children of divorce recall being told about the impending divorce before their siblings, or even before their other parent.

Stephen was twelve years old when his mother dropped multiple hints that she was planning to divorce his father, information he felt compelled to keep from his younger sisters. He kept the secret through the Thanksgiving and Christmas holidays until his parents finally sat down with the three children, after New Year's, and told them the news.

My own parents largely avoided asking me to keep secrets, for which I am grateful. But as their personal lives unfolded in the years after the divorce there were ample opportunities for me to learn about important new developments before I was meant to. One of these revelations occurred during the autumn when I was nine, after I had returned to live with my mother, stepfather, and brother. Looking back now, I can see the tensions that were brewing that year, but I was caught completely off guard when my stepfather and I were sitting on the front steps and he said, "I think your mom and I might be getting a divorce."

I don't know why he told me, and it only occurs to me now that he was upset about it and hoping to talk. Maybe he was even hoping for reassurance that I loved him. If so, my reaction must have been sorely disappointing. I simply could not comprehend that he would leave. He'd been central to my life since I was three years old. Trying to picture life without him made my brain shut down. So I just nodded, probably looking as if I was taking it in stride. We never talked about it again.

Several months later when I was up in my attic room I heard the back door close with a soft click. The sound was nothing out of the ordinary but something about it set me on edge. I crept down the stairs and found my mother sitting in the Kennedy rocker they had bought when my brother was born. Her face looked empty.

"What happened?" I asked, dreading the answer.

"Rob has left," she said. "He's gone."

The floor seemed to slide out from under me. My stomach twisted and my face was suddenly burning hot. I flung myself onto my mother's lap, sobbing uncontrollably. She held me tightly and slowly rocked. Every time in the past when I had solemnly nodded, taking things in stride, every time I had looked in control when really all I felt was numb fear—all that suppressed emotion came flooding out of me. It terrified me that Rob had disappeared into the night. I was afraid for my mother to let go of me.

"Where did he go?" I wailed.

"I don't know," she said.

"Why aren't you crying?" I demanded.

"Because I've cried so much already," she said. "I don't have any tears left."

I had learned about this secret months before but it was too enormous to grasp, so I had swallowed it. Only when the door finally swung shut did the reality of their divorce hit me full force.

Strangely, that night was the only time I ever cried about it. Though I often missed my stepfather, it wasn't until a few years later, when he died, that I cried again about losing him. After that I cried many times, for many years to come, and always alone. When I was crying for him I think that I was also crying for the life we'd all had together: my mother and stepfather, in love and hopeful, building a home together in the country, joyfully welcoming my baby brother. Piece by piece the foundation of that life had slid out from under me, leaving me feeling so alone, able to look grown-up only by ignoring the feelings that surged forth as each of my parents' lives kept hurtling along.

The years wound on and the big pieces of news kept coming. One afternoon when I was thirteen my mother came to me to say that she had talked on the telephone with my father and learned that he and my stepmother were planning to divorce. My father was going to tell me when he came down to visit later that month, but she wanted to go ahead and share the news. I'm not sure why she told me his secret. I think maybe she thought I would be happy. For years I had complained about my stepmother, and though my stepsister and I had a lot of good times together, our regular fights had made me miserable.

But it's hard to celebrate divorce, no matter what the circumstances. I felt nothing, just numbness once again. Weeks later my father came to visit. As we were driving on the highway to my grandparents' he cleared his throat.

"Um," he said, glancing over at me, "I have some news."

He looked back at the road as I sat there feeling completely guilty, knowing what he was about to say.

"Katherine and I are splitting up," he said. "We're getting a divorce."

I nodded as if this were new information. I didn't want to tell my father that my mother had already told me because I knew he would be angry. About the news itself, I didn't know what I felt. Sure, the years of their marriage had been tough on me. But my stepmother and stepsister had been a known quantity since I was five years old. I looked back at the road in front of us. Now, once again, the future—in one half of my life or the other—was completely unknown.

I felt not just loss but anger. One confusing thing about the divorce of a parent and a stepparent to whom one doesn't feel close is the sudden switch in messages. I experienced that kind of divorce once when I was thirteen, and then again in my early twenties, when my mother and second stepfather—who had married when I was thirteen—got divorced.

When your parent remarries it can take a while to gel with the new spouse—years, often. And a piece of information that the grown-ups usually don't share with the child is that maybe the stepparent shares some of the blame. As a child I was told to get along with my stepparents, to cool it, to get with the program. Too often it felt as if I had put my feelings on the line with stepparents who often hurt my feelings in return.

Then all at once the parent and stepparent decide they can't do it anymore. For whatever reason the relationship is over, and the child no longer has to struggle to get along with that stepparent. This was my experience—not once but several times. Far from rejoicing, however, I was left angry and mystified. "What was it all for?" I asked myself. Despite those years of pain and whatever semblance of family unity we cobbled together, when the grown-ups decided to call it quits I was supposed to go gamely along once again.

Of course, secrets also involve activities far more mundane than parents' plans to divorce or their affairs. The simplest, most everyday events can become fodder for secrets, leading some children of divorce to suggest that *everything* was a secret. Kimberly said briskly that she kept secrets "all the time. If I would say to my dad that Mom screamed at us and didn't talk to my sister for nine months, he would be upset and say that's not right. So I just wouldn't tell him, and the same with Mom. If Dad was mad at me, if he threw something across the room, I would never tell her that because she wouldn't know how to react to it." She set her empty teacup back on the saucer and concluded, "I knew the difference very young, that this is my life here and that is my life there."

Allison arched an eyebrow as she recalled, "I basically had compartmentalized parts of my life. Each person had their own set of truths, and I tried not to share the information between them unless it was absolutely necessary or they found out on their own."

Joanna said, with barely muted sadness, "My whole life's a secret to my dad."

Other children of divorce remember being put on guard by one of their parents. Daniel remembered his mother giving him ambiguous warnings about his father that he later learned were baseless but which nevertheless made him clam up around his father. He recalled, "When they were separating my mom said, 'Be careful with your father,' and she'd stop right there. I'd go, 'What do you mean? What?' And she said, 'Well, I'm concerned he might be trying to brainwash you, tell you things that aren't true about me.'" He looked out the window for a moment. "I can honestly tell you that I never really trusted my dad for a long time, because I assumed that my mom was right. I consider myself an honest person, but every time my dad would ask me a question that was a little more sensitive, I was very evasive."

Others recall keeping secrets about their parents' new postdivorce relationships. Often they knew about their parents' new partners when they met them while visiting. Stephen said, "I remember when my dad first started dating my stepmom. He brought me over to meet her and I got along really well with her, but I never said anything to my mom. A couple weeks later my mom found out and she was upset that I hadn't said anything." He rolled his eyes. "I felt like, 'This is another thing that I'm being put in the middle of.'"

Still others said that there was an eerie silence about one world when they were in the other. Alicia sounded puzzled as she said, "There were no secrets, but I don't know how well my parents communicated as far as letting each other know about their personal lives. That was pretty much nonexistent. They would say, 'My business is my business and your business is yours. The only common thread we share is the kids.'"

The concept of being asked to, or feeling the need to, keep secrets was foreign to most young people from intact families. Of course, very troubled intact families harbor damaging secrets as well. One young man from an intact family had a father who was an alcoholic. He said frankly, "Yeah, growing up and my dad's drinking, you wouldn't want to tell Mom that something happened or that he had a beer, because she would just flip out."

Others who grew up in intact families said there might have

been a few secrets, but they were typically mild—and, curiously, they often seem to involve what the mother spent while shopping. "It would be some stupid minor thing," said one woman. "'Don't tell your father I bought this pair of shoes.' Otherwise, they're together a lot, and neither of them traveled for work, so I don't think there were secrets."

Another woman said lightly, "Yeah, shopping. My mom and I would go shopping and she'd say, 'Don't tell your dad about this,' or 'Don't tell your dad you need money, just call me.' Nothing major."

The other young people from intact families said that there was no information they kept secret or guarded for one parent about the other. They said things like "No, they didn't make stuff public," or "They kind of had their own thing going." Some, though, would break into broad grins as they admitted that *they'd* had plenty of secrets of their own when they were growing up. Interestingly, no one from divorced families ever used this question to launch into a discussion of their own secret lives as children or teenagers, nor did this question ever make them smile.

Secret Worlds

Although as children of divorce we were exposed to a lot of secrets, we were not necessarily more knowledgeable about our parents than children in intact families. Far from it. Few outsiders realize that whenever we were involved in the life of one family we were missing life in the other family. We may only have found out about certain events the next time we visited that family, if at all. Not only was each half of our life too often a secret from our parents but our parents' lives and their worlds in general could also be secret from us.

Angela's mother and father each moved several times when she was growing up. They always chose to move while she was away visiting her other parent. Angela recalled how disorienting it was to return to a whole new life at the first parent's home—a new house, neighborhood, school, and more. "It was very scary to come to this new house that I'd never seen before but was already set up," she said softly. "You'd feel like a guest for a little while . . . and I didn't know where anything was and I didn't know how to get to school."

Sounding a more cynical note, Katy laughed and said that as a teenager her standing joke was that each time she visited her father there would be "a new car, a new house, or a new wife."

Another child of divorce remembered that as a teenager he had been shocked and hurt to learn, only months afterward, that his father, with whom he felt close, had been admitted and treated at the hospital for serious heart problems.

In an intact family, a child would know that his family is moving or that Dad is in the hospital or that his parents have bought a new car, simply because he would be there to see it and be a part of it. In a divided family, life continues rolling along at each place even though the child can only be in one place at a time. While we may at times have been exposed to more information than children from intact families — especially sensitive or secret information that was potentially explosive — at other times we knew far less.

These secret family experiences shaped our long-term relationships with our parents in lasting ways. Shared experiences become the memories that families recall when they gather in the years to come. An intact family sitting around the dinner table might recall stories of how Johnny was afraid of the basement when they first moved into their new house, how Janie picked the color when the family purchased their first new car, or, more seriously, how scary it was that time Dad was in the hospital.

As with all children of divorce, my memories, like my childhood, are split in two. I share some memories with my mother and others with my father. Children of divorce typically say that at least one and often both of their parents were not aware of large parts of their lives growing up with the other parent. Ashley told me, "I don't think my dad knows how much we were alone when we were at my mom's. Like after my grandmother died when I was twelve, how much my mother wasn't home and how much we had to more or less fend for ourselves."

Samantha's forehead knitted as she said, "I know that my dad doesn't know what it was like with my stepfather. He doesn't know everything that went on there." Then she shrugged. "And my mom was like, 'They're just going out there to visit at their father's. They're going to go camping and do whatever and come back.'"

Allison told me, "I don't think they knew much. They just assumed I was doing whatever kids do. My life at each place was not a topic of discussion."

Alicia said, "When I came back from a weekend at my dad's, my mom might ask, 'Oh, what'd you do? Did you have a good time?' I'd say, 'Oh, we had pizza or da-da-da-da-da.' I don't think they knew about what the other one was doing. And once they got remarried they were pretty much into their own lives."

Some said there are annoying misunderstandings that one parent continues to harbor about their life with the other parent. Daniel said, "I think they have a good idea of what our lives were like, but my mom has this idea that every time we were with my dad it was a grand old time, and it wasn't."

Joanna recalled with frustration, "My dad thinks that we grew up being brainwashed. But my mom always said, 'I don't care what you think, I don't want to hear you talking bad about your father.' That's why I get really upset when he says stuff like that."

Many also noted that now that they are grown up, their parents are often surprised or curious to hear what happened years ago at the other parent's house. Rochelle said with a grin, "My mother doesn't know about my life with my dad. I think some of the things that I tell her have shocked her."

Chameleons

Children only have so much ability to keep facts straight, so keeping secrets is especially tough. How, then, did we adapt to the demand to keep our two worlds divided, to remember the information that could and could not be shared with each parent? Some of us adapted by becoming a different person with each parent.

Professor Glenn and I were astonished to find that children of divorce are more than twice as likely to agree that "I felt like a different person with each of my parents." Almost half feel this way. In this case, as in others, a "good divorce" is better than a bad divorce, but it's still more than twice as likely as a happy marriage to make children feel like a different person with each of their parents, and it is even slightly worse than an unhappy but low-conflict marriage.

Jen Robinson, a young Gen X poet, writes tellingly about the lasting effects of feeling like different people with each of her parents. "[The divorce] wasn't supposed to affect me; my parents were having a 'good' divorce—still on speaking terms with each other, each still wanting to actively parent. . . . Everything was just fine. Of course, that wasn't quite true."

One effect of her parents' divorce, Robinson writes, is that when she left home for college, "I made friends easily, but always in distinct groups that seldom interacted. When they did, I felt internally pressured to please both groups and at the same time to negotiate the interaction between them. . . . Occasionally such situations would become unbearable, and I'd end up making one set of friends both mystified and angry by ignoring them altogether. I realized at some point that I needed to reintegrate myself, to let myself be the whole of who I was with everyone who knew me."

Robinson's story of how in order to heal she had to confront the divisions in herself, seeking to "be the whole" of who she was with everyone around her, is familiar to many of us. As they try to explain how they adapted to each parent's world, some children of divorce describe themselves as being a "chameleon" or an "actor." Allison's eyes widened as she told me, "Children of divorce are the biggest chameleons on the planet. You are forced by your circumstances to be everything to all people. My husband says to me, 'You're an Academy Award–winning actress, because you can be whatever you need to be in the circumstance.' I see that also in my friend who is a child of divorce. You put us in a circumstance and we can mirror the behavior of a person that we're with and make them think we're similar, because we did that as children. We knew how to play the game."

Kimberly described a similar phenomenon: "I knew very young how my parents were. To me it was just obvious—like 'This is how Mom is, this is how Dad is. This is how you learn to deal with them.'" She stopped and thought, "Now, I don't know how I figured that out. I just think it was through experience, through doing it. We lived with my mom and we stayed with my dad the whole month of July. So you actually had a substantial amount of time to live with that person and understand their personality—what makes them tick, what makes them laugh, what pisses them off. You think all the time."

Daniel too felt the need to blend into each of his parents' worlds, but he also worried that too great a resemblance to one parent could upset his ability to fit in to the other parent's world. He told me, "At different times I thought, 'Oh, I'm just like my dad,' and at other times I thought, 'Oh, I'm just like my mom.' And that would worry me. But in general I can't say I'm more like one than the other."

I asked him, "Do you think that balance is something you've tried to achieve?"

He nodded and replied, "Yeah, I'm very conscious of it, and I've worked at it. I have an alarm going off if I'm being too much like my mom or if I'm being too much like my dad."

Like the others, Rochelle sounded like a chameleon when she said of her two families, "I think I move in and out of both sides fairly fluently."

Jason agreed enthusiastically with the "chameleon" characterization: "Absolutely! That's a fantastic analysis. Because I think that a lot of divorced kids suppress their feelings. . . . They wear different hats in different situations. They're not very consistent with their actions."

Chameleons change their skin color to adapt to each new environment, but for children of divorce the changes go much deeper, to the heart of our inner lives. Stephen's story is a remarkable example.

Now twenty-seven years old and a camp director, Stephen was twelve years old when his parents divorced. When he first came through the door for our meeting, I noticed his good looks—strong shoulders, curly hair, dark eyes. He looked so self-assured. But as we introduced ourselves, his handshake seemed overly quick and eager. When we sat down, he radiated tension. He seemed to be holding his breath while we talked, and he had a habit of starting most of his sentences several times before finding his words and finishing them.

Stephen first found out about his parents' impending divorce when his mother dropped so many hints that he was able to figure it out on his own. Until that time, Stephen had no inkling that there were problems in his parents' marriage: "There was nothing at the time that I thought was out of the ordinary." He later learned that it was his mother's unhappiness that brought about the divorce, though he was never told much more than that.

When his parents divorced, Stephen and his sisters were spared many of the major changes that often happen to children in the aftermath. His father moved into a nearby apartment, and he and his sisters stayed in the same house with their mother. He saw his father for much of every weekend but there was also flexibility if he wanted to do something with his friends instead. His mother never moved, and Stephen was able to continue going to the same school and live near his best friends and his grandparents. Each of his parents remarried within a couple of years but these unions brought no other children into Stephen's families. Except for some early friction with his stepfather, Stephen got along well with his new stepparents. Neither of his parents divorced again, and today he considers all four of them—his parents and stepparents—to be his parents. If there was ever a child growing up in a "good divorce," Stephen was that child.

Nevertheless, although his family life was reordered in ways that would appear to minimize the losses, the parting of Stephen's parents produced two new worlds for him—worlds built around division and secrets. The first major secret was the one that Stephen's mother had shared with him and that Stephen had kept from his sisters and father—the fact that his mother was planning to divorce his father. The next major secret was revealed the night his parents sat down and told their three children about the divorce. For many months Stephen's father had often been "working late." But now his parents said that on those nights his father in fact had been searching for a new place to live and setting up his new life. By the time the other children were told, his father had a new home to go to that very night. Stephen was shocked by the news and by the sudden discovery that "the only family situation that I'd known was radically changing."

From that point, the division between his two worlds grew. Very soon Stephen began to feel subtle pressure to identify with his mother's point of view. His mother did not want Stephen and his sisters to badmouth their father, but it was clear that she *did* want them to believe that she was right when it came to the divorce and conflicts over money with their father. Stephen, however, felt the need to defend his father, which led to many arguments with his mother through his early teenage years. At the same time, he also felt the need to protect his mother. When his father started dating the woman he later married, Stephen decided not to tell his mother, fearing the news would hurt her feelings. Several weeks later his mother found out from a friend at the supermarket and was angry that Stephen had not told her. In those instances and many more Stephen felt caught between his parents and their conflicting needs.

What I found most striking in talking with Stephen was that he responded, seemingly unconsciously, to many of my questions by talking sometimes about his "rational" side and other times about his "emotional" side. First he would say something that appeared to reflect his true feelings. Then he would apologetically say that this feeling was not "rational" but rather "emotional," and he would reframe his response to reflect what he believed the "rational" response should be.

When he first talked about his teenage conflicts with his mother he said forthrightly, "Maybe *angry*'s the right word. I think at the time I blamed my mother for the fact that my parents aren't together.

I think I still do." Then he continued speaking slowly and carefully. "And, you know, it's not a rational thing. At the time, I was aware enough to see that it was for the best, but I think I blamed her because she was the one who initiated the divorce. If she hadn't put the wheels in motion my parents would probably have been together for a while. Maybe would still be together." As Stephen continued to speak, his own feelings as a child began to peek through again: "So that might have been part of my resentment towards her—that I was happy in the previous situation. We had a normal family, at least that is the way I saw it, and now we don't."

Then he shifted in his chair and switched back to a defense of his mother: "Part of me felt that she was right and a big part of me didn't want to admit it to myself or to her especially."

I waited a moment, then asked, "Did any part of you think she was wrong for leaving your dad?"

He paused and thought. "Yeah, I guess more the emotional side of me . . . and I think that's where blaming her comes in. Where the rational side of me could look at it and say, 'Yeah, this is best for her. And probably best for the family too.' But another side of me, more than anything else, wanted the family to still be together and was angry with her." Later Stephen shook his head and said that as a result of the divorce, "I follow the extremes. In certain aspects of my life I'm very rational, and in certain aspects of my life I'm very irrational."

Now completely intrigued, I asked, "What does *rational* mean for you?"

He explained, "That I can look at a situation objectively and I can make sense out of it. . . . To be emotional means that if a situation upsets me, I . . . make it out to be a lot worse than it really is. I have a more extreme reaction than I would if I were looking at it rationally."

When I thought about it later, it seemed as though Stephen's attempts to look at issues "rationally" were his somewhat desperate, though by now habitual, attempts to make sense of the two contradictory worlds he was handed after the divorce, even if trying to reconcile those two worlds meant ignoring his own feelings.

Even today his authentic, deeper feelings still well up. Yet Stephen has apparently been told, or has come to believe, that these deeper feelings are overreactions or extreme—not valid responses to an upsetting situation and certainly not rational.

This inner division continued to show up throughout our discussion. When I asked Stephen how he felt when his two parents were in the same room together after the divorce, he replied, "Rationally, looking at the positive side of it, I think I'm pretty lucky, compared to most kids who come from a divorce situation, that my parents can do that."

After he had talked for a while about his positive feelings, I asked, "Do you feel anything else?"

He replied, "Well, I remember being under a lot of stress when we all went out to dinner together after my college graduation." When his parents are together, Stephen said, "I feel like I have to make sure that everyone is okay. To keep everyone happy." Still later in the interview, when I asked him how he got along with his stepparents, he said, "I get along really well with both of them. Again, I think that's the rational side coming out. That, okay, yes, my parents aren't together, but they're much happier now."

Perhaps it is true that Stephen's parents are happier than they would have been if they had stayed together. But that is their truth. As he told me about his life Stephen seemed to find it difficult or impossible to acknowledge *his* truth and let it stand—that his parents' divorce had devastated him, that he blamed his mother, that he longed for them to still be together. Instead, he talked about himself as if he were two Stephens, the rational Stephen who desperately tries to make sense of his two worlds by accepting his parents'—especially his mother's—explanation of events, and the emotional Stephen who defends his father and cries out at the direction his family life took. When I talked with other young adults from divorced families they often noted that they felt like different people inside, but Stephen vividly described, in explicit and often painful detail, his inner conflict as he tried to come to grips with his parents' two very different worlds.

What Is True?

The struggle with secrets gives rise to a central moral dilemma for children of divorce. In one way or another, as children and as young adults, we were confronted by the question "What is true?"

Our national survey revealed, astonishingly, that more than half of young adults from divorced families, compared to just a fifth of people from intact families, agree, "What my mother said was true and what my father said was true were often two different things."

One reason why truth becomes a central problem is that after a divorce some parents feel tempted to reveal the "truth" to their children. When parents are married they tend not to point out all of their spouse's mistakes or failings; they more often cover up for each other and try to protect the child from learning about each other's less desirable traits. After a divorce, however, the parents no longer feel such a strong need to portray themselves as a cohesive unit, and each parent may have an interest in revealing the short-comings of the other to help explain why the divorce occurred, or to shore up their own positions in ongoing conflicts with the other parent.

Tammy said that when her parents divorced, "I started to learn things, different things, that had been going on that I was not privy to," including details from her mother about her father's affairs.

Rochelle said, "My mother never tried to shelter us from things. She always raised us to be kind of independent thinkers and try to tell us the truth," including the truth about their father.

Melissa recalled that when her parents were married, "my father was an alcoholic and was drinking very heavily." Before their divorce, she said, "I think my mom tried to put us off in a little secluded room so we didn't see any of the ugly stuff, so that we could be perfect little children. . . . But once the family fell apart and she had to try to do everything herself, she couldn't keep up the facade. So all of a sudden you see the fact that there was no money in the savings account, no money to pay the electric bill."

In a family struggling with alcoholism, infidelity, or other serious problems, the truth will at some point have to be faced, whether the parents stay together or not. But when a divorce occurs it is also the case that lots of information, often quite troubling, is likely to be spilled all at once on the child. The child goes from an admittedly troubled life in which her mother is nevertheless trying to shield her from family problems to hearing, say, that her father has left, he is an alcoholic, and there is no money to pay the electric bill.

It is very important for families to face up to their problems, and families struggling with very serious problems need help; the parents might indeed need to divorce. But this does not mean that the sudden revelations that follow the divorce are easy for the children to handle. Often too the "truth" in question is not so clear.

Some young people say that after the divorce one of their parents told them information about their other parent that they came to distrust in later years. Steve said when he was in eighth grade his father contacted his mother requesting visitation rights that would let him take the children out of state. He remembered, "My mom was really scared that he would try to kidnap us—she filled our minds with that. And it always made me a little anxious when he would come to visit. I was always wondering, 'Is he going to try and take us?'" Years later Steve was shocked to learn that his father had wanted the new rights simply in order to be able to take the kids across the state line to his brother's house when he came across the country to visit, rather than having to get an expensive hotel room each time. This flexibility would have allowed him to visit more often. But, Steve said angrily, "I didn't know that at the time. All I was told by my mother and stepfather was that 'He wants to be able to take you to his house, and if you go there he's never going to let you leave.' And so I believed it, you know? It's my mom. She's not going to lie to me. Or so I thought."

Others recall their parents clearly misleading them. "My dad used to take us out and buy us stuff," said Sara, "I think because he wanted to make us love him." Years later she learned to her dismay that "he would act like he was buying us things, but he would just take it out of my mom's alimony."

In other instances, children feel as though they must defend the truth about a parent in the face of accusations made by the other parent or relatives. Daniel remembered anxiously his parents accusing each other after the divorce: "They would say things that would really hit my buttons. I just wanted to say, 'No, that's not true. My mom never did that.' Or 'No, that's not true. Dad never said that.'" But rather than say anything, Daniel remembers, he would "just sort of sweat inside" and keep quiet.

Alex said that during visits with his father, his aunts would bad-mouth Alex's mother, blaming her for the problems in his father's life. "They would say that certain problems were my mom's fault, or that my mom is evil. . . . Maybe not those words, but that was always the implication. I just let it go in one ear and out the other, even at that age. I knew that I lived with my mom every other day of the week and that this wasn't the case."

The problem of truth is a recurring theme in portrayals of children of divorce. On a recent special episode about children of divorce on the *Oprah Winfrey Show,* a seven-year-old boy sat between his two divorced parents, who clearly loved and were worried about him and his brother. He looked up at Oprah with wide eyes and said, "My dad, he tells truths. My mom tells truths. So I don't really know. I trusted my dad but he lied, and like I trusted my mom, but she lied, so I can't trust either."

Even researchers who are strongly accepting of widespread divorce have recognized the phenomenon of divorced parents holding different truths. In *The Good Divorce,* Constance Ahrons writes of the divorced couples on which she based her study:

> As I expected, differences in the two halves of an ex-couple's [sic] story emerged; in fact, once their names were deleted, we often couldn't tell who had been married to whom. Partners differed on such essential details as when they first separated, who had decided to divorce, what were the reasons, how involved fathers were with their children, the amount and regularity in payment of child support, and the actual time each parent spent with the children.

Clearly, if divorced couples often do not agree on even simple facts, such as when the separation first occurred or how much child support the father is paying, there are likely to be many other points, for years to come, on which they differ as well.

Still another researcher found that even when couples have largely the same understanding of their marital troubles while they are married, their stories begin to diverge sharply after their divorce. The contentious nature of divorce encourages both of them to begin revising their stories, portraying their ex-spouse more negatively and themselves more favorably. For the child who lives alternately with both, two different truths emerge, and the child alone must decide which truth to accept or reject.

Most divorced parents do not intentionally burden their children with secrets. Quite the opposite. Although they are more than twice as likely as married parents to ask their children to keep secrets, the majority try to follow the expert wisdom and avoid handing their children such burdens. Yet by listening to children of divorce it becomes clear that when a family splits there are new structural conditions that override the parents' good intentions, making secrets almost inevitable.

As children of divorce, we tried to adapt to our parents' different worlds. We confronted their different truths and felt it was up to us to make sense of the contradictions. Some of us felt so burdened that we lost the ability to trust our parents. Truth became a murky thing, something malleable, something that could even be taken advantage of.

Nevertheless, growing up in two worlds gave us at least some advantages. If we pulled through, perhaps we gained skills that have served us well in adulthood—an ability to wear different hats in different situations, to evaluate contradictory pieces of information, to act as a diplomat shuttling between conflicted lands.

But even for us "successful" children of divorce, much was lost: a sense of being the same, authentic person no matter who we were with. We lost the rich memories that come from sharing life with all

the members of one family. Perhaps most important, and sadly, we
lost the unselfconscious assurance—a feeling that is the right of
any child—that we didn't have to study our parents and their
needs. When we should have been caught up with harmless childhood fantasies, we learned instead, as one child of divorce put it,
"how to play the game."

7

Child-Sized Old Souls

O ne of the major findings of our study was a strong connection between children of divorce and belief in God. This surprised me. As I reflected on it, though, I realized that the connection mirrored a similar journey in my own life.

When I came of age and left home, spiritual questions were much on my mind. My parents had been involved in different faith communities at different times. My father had attended a Baptist church, which I went to when I was visiting. My mother was part of a groovy United Church of Christ congregation that I liked a lot. They had a large stained-glass tree-of-life design in the sanctuary, contemporary hymns written in homemade songbooks, and a kind, thick-bearded pastor who made needlepoint name tags for all the congregants. At my dad's church the pastor seemed to notice me and the other kids only as he greeted parishioners when we filed out the door, but at my mom's church the pastor (and all the other adults) paid a lot of attention to the children. They talked to us at coffee hour, included us in discussion groups on social issues, and had potluck suppers at which we were welcome.

When my mom met the man who would become my second stepfather he had no interest in church, so they stopped going. The church was a couple of miles from our house so for a while I continued alone, walking back and forth each Sunday. But I felt adrift there without my mom and when I was about twelve I quit too.

It thus came as a great surprise to everyone who knew me when, three years later, I started going to a large Pentecostal church near our new house. At first I went reluctantly with my boyfriend, feeling like I was being dragged along but also curious about the source of his sudden interest in faith. He soon left for college, but I kept going alone. It has taken me years to figure out why.

For many people, the Pentecostal theology is rich and life-affirming, and I respect them for it. But I came to find it soul-destroying. The only message I heard was that I was a sinner. Perhaps that's why I kept going. I had reached a critical point in my adolescence when I was just beginning to come to grips with my deeply divided identity and feeling unworthy of love. Denial of the self seemed like the right choice, maybe my only choice. The message of salvation that I heard, meanwhile, seemed to be intended for someone else—maybe the guy sitting in the pew in front of me.

The whole experience was profoundly isolating. I never became friends with other members. I was never invited to be part of a small group, nor did I even know such groups existed. I never met with a pastor. On one level, that congregation failed me. But it's also true that it never occurred to me to seek anyone out. I sat there by myself, a sponge soaking up the message that I was unworthy, that the things I enjoyed—going to movies, reading novels, making out with my boyfriend—were terrible sins. I could try to ask this fearsome, faraway God to come into my heart but it was likely I'd never be good enough for him.

When I went to that church I stopped writing in my journal and stopped reading anything except the Bible and my schoolwork. My friends largely gave up on me, mystified by the grim, utterly joyless person I'd become. My boyfriend and I were still dating but he was at college hours away and we didn't see each other much. My mother fretted about what was happening to me and forbade me to go to that church, but I went anyway, and she didn't know what else to do. She tried to talk to my father about it but he—far away and seeing little of it—replied that if their biggest problem was their teenage daughter's constant church attendance he didn't see the problem.

My new stepfather, meanwhile, was disgusted with the path I'd taken. He ridiculed my Christian music: a few rounds of Amy Grant's "El Shaddai" drifting from under my bedroom door would turn him purple with rage. My mother later said that if I'd gotten into drugs she would have had some idea how to help me but she had no idea what to do with a daughter who'd suddenly become a fundamentalist Christian—and a very unhappy one at that.

I'd stumbled onto an appealing and effective way of rebelling against my mother and her new husband but I don't think that this was the main reason I stuck with it. I think it was for the same reason that some young women on the cusp of adulthood get caught up in anorexia or bulimia—an attempt to control their bodies and numb their feelings. I struggled with body image problems as well, but mostly I was absorbed with the utter unworthiness of my soul.

It was an awful time in my life but fairly short, less than two years. One advantage, certainly the only one, was that since I had little to do besides read the Bible and do homework my grades improved dramatically. I had been in honors classes for years and scraped by in some subjects but had also routinely gotten C's and D's on my report cards since I was ten years old, mainly because I almost never did my homework, studied for tests, or turned in projects on time. With college on the horizon, my turnaround happened not a moment too soon. Based on a couple of years of excellent grades and my status as a faculty kid—my mom was on the medical school faculty of a good university—I was able to leave high school a year early and enroll as a freshman just before my seventeenth birthday.

When I started college I left the church, broke up with my boyfriend, and walked around thoroughly scared for the first few months, feeling that I would be almost literally struck by lightning for turning my back on God. Eventually I settled in, found a new boyfriend and new friends among the few alternative types at that school, and started down the bumpy road of young adulthood, hungry for almost any idea or experience so long as it had nothing to do with God.

Several years later, the same week I got married, I began classes at the University of Chicago Divinity School. The old friends who knew my history were shocked. The newer friends were just confused. They'd never heard me express any interest in religion. All they knew was that I'd just gotten married and enrolled in a ministry program. To them I had fallen off the deep end.

Like a lot of people, they didn't understand what divinity school is about. I went there to study meaning. I wanted to read and learn and talk about the big ideas—love, suffering, hope, maybe even God. My time there was an emotional roller-coaster ride and an intellectual bonanza. For three years I studied ethics and theology and early Jewish and Christian history. I passed a tough year of Greek with flying colors. I interned as a student pastor at a diverse downtown Chicago congregation, struggling to interpret biblical texts and preach sermons every word of which I could believe.

I spent one endless summer working as a chaplain at a big urban medical center. Every day and many long nights on call I witnessed suffering and death and families' grief, and then every morning I met with a small group of other student chaplains as we tried to find the sense in it all. I sought out the solitude of the on-call room and cried many times: For the gentle old woman on a ventilator in the ICU, dying in mute agony while her family never visited. For the fourteen-year-old girl who had a late miscarriage and asked to see her baby one more time, swaddled in a blanket—brought up from the morgue by another chaplain and me. And I cried the hardest the night after I had to tell a seven-year-old boy whose parents were divorced and who himself had cancer that his young father, clearly the light of his life, had just died in the ER. I cried for him, and for my brother, and for myself.

"Where is God in all this?" I asked, and still do. I've struggled with anger at God for many years. In one sense anger at God is not a bad thing. Many of the great prophets and theologians spent most of their lives shaking their fist at God. But anger has also kept me distant from God. Too often I've embraced a false sense of control, moving through the day checking items off a list so that I could avoid having to feel.

Though I'm still uncertain about where I stand in relation to God and the church, gradually I've come to believe that some meaning can be found in suffering—that love somehow survives, that an insistent life force keeps surging forth. Babies are born every day—an incredible miracle right before our eyes that counters that loss and somehow outlives it. It might not be enough, but it's about all I've figured out so far. And the best spiritual practice I've found is to write about it.

Lonely Spiritual Journeys

Through interviews for this book I came to realize I was not alone, that the spiritual journeys of children of divorce are often winding, lonely, and surprising. Growing up, we deal early and alone with profound losses and confront big questions of meaning. We search for explanations in a culture that too often denies our loss, dismissing our questions as cute or precocious or ignoring us altogether. We are child-sized old souls. When we come of age and leave home, we are less likely overall to be religious. We long for spirituality as much as our peers from intact families do, but loss, suffering, lack of trust in and anger at our parents, and even anger at God are more defining qualities of our spiritual journeys.

As children of divorce, we know loneliness. Compared to those from intact families, three times as many of us agree, "I was alone a lot as a child." As adults 22 percent of us say, "I don't feel that anyone really understands me," compared to 14 percent of our peers. Twenty-three percent of us—almost twice as many as our peers from intact families—agree, "I feel like I can depend on my friends more than my family."

Of those whose parents had a "good divorce," more than half agree, "I have experienced many losses in my life," and close to two-thirds of those from bad divorces say the same thing. By contrast, 42 percent of those who grew up with parents in unhappy but low-conflict marriages and just over a third of those who grew up with parents in happy marriages say the same thing.

For some of us, our suffering has caused turmoil in our relationship with God. One-fifth of us agree, "When I think about bad things that have happened in my life I find it hard to believe in a God who cares," a difference one and a half times greater than our peers. Yet suffering is not always a roadblock in our spiritual journeys. Three-quarters of us, compared to two-thirds of our peers from intact families, agree, "My spirituality has been strengthened by adversity in my life."

For many of us, loss and the search for belonging provoke us to seek the meaning and comfort that can be found in practicing a faith. Yet unlike people from intact families, it was not uncommon for us to seek out a faith on our own, showing up at church without our parents even when we were young. But for others of us, religion as we have encountered it ignores or, even worse, painfully evokes the losses that resulted from our parents' divorce. When we grow up we are more likely to confront spiritual questions alone, without being a full part of a faith community and without having the model of our parents to look to.

Yearning and Fearing, Searching but Repelled

Many young adults from divorced families I met were, like me, struggling with questions about their belief in God. Angela is a deeply thoughtful young woman who seemed to me stuck in a spiritual middle ground, deeply interested in a life of faith but somewhat cynical, and wary of any beliefs that smack of hypocrisy.

After we had talked for some time I asked Angela whether she believed in God. She stared at the floor. "I don't believe in God," she finally said slowly, "but I do believe in some sort of connectedness between people and nature. Not in a cosmic sort of way, but just that human beings share so much in common. Our lives are so short. At the end we break down to nothingness again, and if we don't look after each other while we're here then there won't be any goodness for us." She looked up at me. "That this is our chance, you know? And the only chance that you have to improve the world is to try and be good to other people."

Angela went on to say that she had not always been so certain that she did not believe in God. Her parents divorced when she was four. Her father was Jewish and her mother was raised Catholic but converted to Judaism when they married. After their divorce Angela's mother did not practice Judaism anymore but Angela found an example of committed faith in her Lutheran stepmother.

"I admire people with faith very much," she said. "My stepmother is a woman who believes in God so sincerely. I admire her for having so much faith and for always trying to do the right thing — and say the right thing and feel the right thing — because of the obligation that she believes she has to God." Angela went on: "When I was twelve or thirteen, I decided that's what I wanted. I wanted to have that kind of faith and have that kind of sense of belonging because that's the other thing that I see with religious people. They join a church or a synagogue, and they have this built-in group of friends and supporters and people who care about them. So I prayed and I went to church and put a lot of effort into it. . . . I really tried to find faith in the Christian faith."

Angela was attracted to her stepmother's faith, but she was also troubled by it. As the daughter of a Jew and a former Catholic, she felt that the church held out so much promise but too often fell painfully short of the vision laid out in the Bible. "I was always disturbed by the historical problems of the church," she recalled. The summer she was twelve years old she remembers saying to the pastor, "How do you respond to questions about the Crusades? That was terrible. People died." She paused and shook her head. "He was like, 'Oh, you know what? You don't have to worry about that.'" His response offered little solace, nor did it take seriously the genuine problems she was encountering in her pursuit of a life of faith.

When the summer ended, Angela went back to her mother's home on the West Coast. She recalled, "I said, 'I want to be a Christian and I believe in God now,' and she said, 'Oh, that's nice.' Then she said, 'You know, your grandparents are Jewish.' And I said, 'Yes.' And she said, 'And now you think they're going to hell.'" Angela took a sip of her coffee and said, "I think she was just teasing me for being completely wrapped up in things the way twelve-year-olds are. I think that she saw it as just a phase."

But for Angela it wasn't a phase. Her quest to discover and live the right kind of life, her search for belonging, her struggle with the deep paradoxes of faith as we live it out—these were serious questions that would not go away. Early adolescence is a tumultuous time in which many young people solidify or break away from their ties to faith traditions. Children of divorce are no different. Yet young Angela, already attuned to paradox and suffering, was dismissed by the grown-ups in whom she confided. Angela remembers, "After a while I realized I just didn't have it. When it came right down to it, I didn't believe that there was a God. . . . I decided that you have to have something else to base your life philosophy on."

Even though Angela told me she doesn't believe in God, she continues to be attracted to a life of faith because of her loneliness as a child and the sense of belonging that might be found there. "It's nice to have a group where you can know people and they will care about you," she says wistfully. "At my stepmother's church they still announce if somebody's in the hospital and then everybody prays for them, and they would go visit them. And it's nice that these people would be willing to care for you even if they don't know you very well. Just because you belong." But her adolescent cynicism, born of dashed hopes, still leads her to keep her distance: "The flip side is what about the people who don't belong? Like shouldn't you care about them too? And isn't it a little fake to care for people just because they're sitting in the same room with you for two hours on a Sunday? And so I go back and forth. Sometimes I find the idea so comforting, and then other times I find it a little hollow."

When God Imitates Life

Others experience tensions even greater than Angela's. These young people have experienced so much loss, they're unable to find meaning in a faith that does not recognize it. For them, the faith itself evokes the losses they felt in their families so many years ago.

Melissa's parents divorced when she was five years old. Her father left for the West Coast to find a job and never moved back, though she continued to see him occasionally. Melissa considers herself only slightly religious today, though she does believe "there's something out there—I usually call it God." Yet her lack of interest arose in part from the way in which religious faith painfully revived her sense of loss.

"When I was really little, my mom was fairly active in the Episcopalian church," Melissa recalled. "They always teach you prayers. . . . So when stuff was happening that I didn't understand, I'd be like, 'Maybe I should pray.'" She remembered, "I'd sit down and go, 'Okay, now how do I pray?' You'd usually start it as a letter. 'Dear God, how are you? I'm fine. Today was warm. I was hoping that you could help me.'" She paused and laughed. "But then you kind of wonder about it because they never answer. So that made me wonder, 'Well, I wrote to him. I didn't get a letter back. *That sounds like Dad!*'"

By the time she was a teenager, Melissa said, "I pulled away from organized religion. They promise so much, and when you're little and especially when your parents are divorced, you want something that's consistent." As a child of divorce, she said, she felt "very bouncy." "You bounce back and forth between this parent and that parent and this role and that role, and you're never quite sure what's going to be happening, so when in religion they say that God's always there and he's always constant—you know I'm going to embrace that." She thought a moment and said slowly, "It's hard, though, because it's not that type of consistency, that type of stability that you're looking for. It's not somebody you can just walk up to and be like, 'This is God, I am holding God.' . . . It's so much built on faith and at that point in my life I'm like, 'Faith?'" She looked at me, eyes wide. "Faith in what? What am I going to believe in? I believed that my parents were going to be there. . . . Now what do I believe in?"

The problem, Melissa eventually realized, was that a relationship with God "wasn't like a substance. I couldn't touch it. And I wanted to touch it, feel it, taste it, bite it, break it. It had to be real. I didn't want to deal with what-ifs or promises or dreams. I was like, 'If I can't walk up and hug it, I'm not even going to think about it.'" Melissa's young hopes swelled when she contemplated the thought of an ever-present God, but for her the possibility of loss was already inherent in the hope. A God she could not touch was too much like a father she rarely saw. As a teenager she pulled back to prevent the possibility of losing again.

Over and over again I found this connection between a child's experience of her parents and her feelings about God.

Unlike Melissa, Will grew up in the church and continued being a part of his Catholic community well into his early twenties. Will's childhood had been derailed by his father's affair with another woman, which Will knew about before his mother did. He was close to his mother after the divorce but could not share his anger with her since she was nursing her own wounds. Instead Will bottled up his feelings until they erupted years later in his relationships with girlfriends.

"I think with my parents getting divorced, I had a lot of anger inside me," he told me. "And I didn't know how to express it. I felt like everything was against me." He remembered that when he was in church, a young man barely out of his teens, "I was mad. Like, 'God, you know, I come in here, I pray, I pray to you all the time and there's no change. I just don't understand.' I'm a very angry person and this isn't good." He observed, "I guess that's why I stopped going to church."

Around that time Will went to a therapist and for the first time was able to express his feelings about his wayward father and the divorce. "It kind of slowed everything down and brought me back to reality. Brought me some kind of closure so I could move on. I don't have all this anger. And in my relationships with other people, I have more trust." As time passed, "the feelings became something I could control . . . put that over here now, instead of trying to drag it with you." He sat back in his chair and concluded, "But yeah, I believe in God now and stuff like that. I just don't go to church too much."

Will's relationship with God today is distant and wary, much like that with his father. He doesn't want to reject either of them completely, but neither does he trust them.

Waiting for a Sign

Ashley was thirty-three years old when we met, a single information technology consultant who lived in her own condo near the suburban community where she had grown up. Ashley had an appealing sense of humor, both sharp and self-deprecating, but when the conversation turned to serious issues she often lapsed into tried-and-true responses, as though it was futile to dwell too deeply on it all. "Life is short," she said many times. "Love my mother, don't like her," she concluded almost every time the subject of her mother came up.

Ashley's parents divorced when she was five years old. The youngest of four, she and her siblings grew up living with their mother, who worked long hours, including many Saturdays, as an administrator at a Fortune 500 company and kept up a busy social life in the evenings. Ashley's grandmother lived with the family, and it was she who made dinner every night "at six sharp," did the laundry, and brought home treats for the kids. She filled the gap in the family's life. She died when Ashley was twelve, and the void she left was large, especially for Ashley. Ashley and her siblings were left on their own—the older ones going their own way and often getting into serious trouble.

After her grandmother's death Ashley found little companionship or understanding in her family, and her spiritual life has been much the same. She grew up in African American Baptist churches and was taught a punitive image of God. From Sunday school teachers and sermons at the several churches she attended, she learned that God is a judge whom we must fear and there is little we can do to live up to God's expectations. As a child, she said, "I didn't think about what God looked like or what he or she was like, but I thought a lot about what God thought of me. Am I a good person, am I doing the right thing? I guess I had this fear of God. If I do this and I know it's wrong, am I going to go to hell or be judged poorly?"

When Ashley was very young her grandmother would take her and her siblings to church while their mother stayed home. But by the time Ashley was school age she and her brothers and sister got on the bus and went to church on their own. Eventually her older siblings stopped going. "I would go by myself," Ashley recalls. But when she was fourteen years old she too gave it up.

She remembered that she was not the only child at church without her parents. "There were a couple other kids who, you know, the parents would slow the car down and let them out." She also recalled that "the kids who were there with their parents were in pews that were close to the front."

I found Ashley's recollection of where those children sat in church incredibly poignant. Perhaps it was not always the case that the children who came with their parents sat in the front, but Ashley's memory of things reflects her sense of being set apart. Like Angela, like me, she was another child-sized old soul sitting inexplicably alone in the back of the church.

Ashley told me she went to church alone every week as a child because she was looking for "consistency, something familiar." When I asked if she prayed as a child she responded uncertainly, "Not a whole lot. I've always thought that you're not in control of your own destiny. I've thought that for a long, long time." Even today, she said, "my friends always get pissed off because I don't plan anything. They ask me, 'Want to do this and this?' I can only deal with today, I tell them, and they look at me like I'm crazy. They're nice ideas and if they actually pan out that's wonderful. But if they don't, oh, well. So I don't remember praying or asking for too many things." In fact, Ashley dealt with loss by trying not to need or want much of anything at all.

But Ashley does have needs and wants. For instance, she wants to get married and have children. "When or if I get married," she said, looking down at her hands in her lap, "I'd like to be married in a church by someone who knows me." She looked up at me. "But I don't think that's going to happen. And then when and if I have children I would like to have a religious background. I think it's very important, but right now I'm just kind of drifting."

It's not that Ashley isn't making a conscious effort to find a faith community. "For the past five years," she said, "I've been, literally, pick a religion. At least once a month I go to a different church with my friends. Nothing's grabbed me yet. I sit there and I'm just going, 'Are you guys for real?' I guess it's just not speaking to me and where I'm at right now in my life. I don't know what sign I'm waiting for or what exact sentence is going to click and go, 'Hey, this is the place for me to worship.'"

I asked Ashley if she was looking for a place where she would feel known or understood.

She responded heatedly: "People don't understand other people. They just kind of go, 'Mm-hmm.'" She nodded with a look of mock concern. "And they think they're listening and they feel they understand. No, they don't."

What Ashley wants, she said, "is inner peace." "That's it. Quiet my mind and just be at peace with myself and at least know that I'm a good person and giving back to society and contributing to something." But then she shrugged. "If I knew what I was looking for maybe I would find it."

It was clear that Ashley had thought a lot about her spiritual life. Even her plan to visit churches once a month was carefully thought out. At one point when I mistakenly asked, "So what do you think brings you back to church every week?" she corrected, "Once a month." Yet even as Ashley seeks a place where she can find peace, can feel a part of something, can feel that people are really listening to her and not just, as she said, mouthing the words "I feel your pain," she maintains a careful distance. Going every week hurts too much when her unvoiced hopes go unfulfilled once again. So Ashley goes once a month and keeps on looking.

In God We Might (or Might Not) Trust

At first blush Allison seemed different from the others. Her parents were not religious and they divorced when she was two years old. Allison's only model of religion was her maternal grandparents, but she experienced their strict fundamentalist beliefs as unloving and harsh and she made no effort to find faith on her own. Yet in her twenties, when she met her future husband, she converted to his faith—Catholicism—and married in the Roman Catholic Church. Today she attends church regularly with her husband, prays with him and her young daughter, and hopes to give her daughter the strong faith she did not have as a child. How did Allison's conversion come about?

In fact, her conversion remains a cautious one, still deeply influenced by the loss of trust that has afflicted her since early childhood. "My husband and I go to mass every Sunday together," Allison said. But "in terms of a deep sense of spirituality I don't really feel that. I'm kind of hoping that as I get older I'll be better at defining that and feeling that way." She told me, "I can look at my husband and see he is both deeply religious and deeply spiritual," and she wants those same deep feelings for herself and her daughter. "But out of the two of us," she concedes, "I have to say I'm going through the motions more than he is."

Allison has thought a lot about why her husband's faith is stronger than hers. She explains, "My husband grew up with a very happy, sheltered, loving childhood. So I feel like he has more of a base for it, because he can trust in certain things." In contrast, Allison reflects, "I'm kind of a neophyte. I mean, I have just found trust with him in the last few years." She thinks her story is not uncommon.

Allison told me that she sees "huge problems" with being a child of divorce and trying to believe in God. What so many young adults from divorced families told me so movingly was reflected in Allison's words. "Fundamentally," she said, "if the most important relationship in your life, which of course is the one with your parents, is irretrievably broken at a young age, and one of the defining components of your life is that that core relationship was not there, you have to have fundamental trust issues. So I think that it's easier for my husband to trust in something because he's always had something to trust in. It's a much harder leap of faith for me to say, 'Okay, I can completely trust in a superior being. I can completely trust in God' when, you know, I never had a base to build that on."

The notion that God is like a parent is common in many religions. Christianity, especially, is steeped in language comparing God to a father. I asked Allison if she thinks that God is like a parent.

She thought a moment and replied, "Maybe that's part of the problem. Because if I view it like that, then that would be a negative relationship for me . . . I don't have good models of parents, so I wouldn't associate happy feelings with that feeling."

When God Becomes a Father

Others do find spiritual healing and joy in the church. At a young age Michael embraced the church. Yet like so many children of divorce, he came to God and the church alone, without the company of his parents. "I wasn't raised in a religious home," Michael recalls. "My mom was Catholic and my stepfather is too, but not practicing. They would go to church on Christmas and Easter and that was about the extent of it." When he was fourteen years old, though, Michael's best friend invited him to go to church. "It was a Baptist church and they had a separate youth worship service and it was really, really neat. The more I went, the more it became somewhere that I felt safe and like I belonged." After a while, he told me, "I gave my life to Christ and started going to church regularly."

Michael sat back and smiled as he recalled, "I remember being very excited when I got my first Bible. I can remember the smell of it. And I just would spend hours in my room reading it and thinking this is the most exciting stuff in the world, you know, that God cares for me, that all this is possible for me. There had been this

huge void in my life," he told me. "But once I accepted Christ, from
that point on, I really looked at life differently." As a child, he said,
"I had always believed in God, but now it was like God could be
with you. . . . God wasn't out there anymore. God was walking with
you and living in you." Michael's newfound faith changed every
part of his life, including at school. "I had been doing mediocre in
school at that point. But it just really gave meaning to life for me, to
excel in life. I got more involved in school and my grades got really
good."

When Michael was in high school, he started going to a different
church with the girlfriend who would later become his wife. "It was
a Presbyterian church. And I started to learn then that you could
question your faith. It didn't have to be that this is what you believe
and that's it. Doubt had a place. That was really important. So I
joined their youth choir and sang with them. The church became
my home away from home."

Michael's growing relationship with God helped fill a huge void
created by his tense relationship with his father, who had left his
mother for another woman. At his father's house the children of
his first and second marriages vied with each other and Michael's
older brother would often turn on him, teasing him mercilessly.
Meanwhile, Michael's father was often out at work or playing golf.
"God really became my father," Michael said. "He was that father
who never leaves and is always there. Who you can always talk to
and who will listen to you." Children of divorce are almost twice as
likely to agree, "I think of God as the loving father or parent I never
had in real life," with 38 percent feeling this way compared to 22
percent of those from intact families. If we had included in our
study the many children of divorce who lose all contact with their
fathers this number might well be higher.

The Struggle to Reconcile Faith and Family

Yet struggles persist even for those wholly committed to their faith.
Katy's parents divorced when she was three years old. Her mother
moved back home with her parents and raised her daughter in the

Catholic faith, eventually meeting and marrying another man who Katy came to think of as a second father.

Katy grew up embracing the rituals of Catholicism and today finds deep comfort, joy, and challenge in her ever-growing faith. Now married and pursuing a busy career as a resident psychiatrist, she turns regularly to God and the Catholic Church to find meaning and to help confront difficult questions in her life. She told me that she thinks of God as a force that "has a plan. Not necessarily like a master plan . . . It's more like he's on my side. He cares for me and loves me, and he has a purpose for me."

As a child Katy was taught that Jesus was her friend, "this good person who loved you. It was a very loving relationship, a very forgiving relationship." As she traveled from her mother's home to her father's home, and back again, "I developed the sense that God was always with me. Especially if I was going from place to place I could always know that God was in both places. And everywhere in between."

This child of divorce took comfort in knowing that God was with her as she traveled between her parents' different worlds.

At her mother's home Katy practiced her faith in the company of her family, but when she visited her father going to church was a solo endeavor. She regularly sought and found a Catholic mass on her own, even when she was quite young. On the major holidays her father and stepmother might come with her, but typically Katy attended alone, enlisting her father to drive her there.

Even though as a child Katy felt strong in her Catholic faith, at times when sitting in church she confronted serious conflicts between her need to accept the beliefs of her faith and her equally important need to see her parents as good people. She talked about the New Testament passages on divorce, in which Jesus says that a man who divorces his wife, except on the grounds of unfaithfulness, causes her to commit adultery. Katy remembered, "That passage caught my attention repeatedly because it reaffirms the fact that divorce was not good. I couldn't twist it around and say 'Well, it's okay,' or 'This was acceptable.' No."

Katy was even more troubled by one of the Ten Commandments.

"'Thou shalt not commit adultery.' Because I came slowly to the conclusion that my dad had done this. That was a definite calamity. And they're not suggestions, they're commandments." There was a catch in Katy's voice as she remembered, "There was always that little discrepancy in me. Not whether I forgive my father, but *will my father be forgiven?*"

Another troubling conflict arose when Katy learned that her parents had obtained an annulment—in which the Catholic Church says that the marriage was not valid in the first place—in addition to a divorce. "That's something I don't think I've really come to grips with. In college I touched on it a bit because once I learned what annulment meant I thought it was ridiculous. I said, 'How can I not exist? If the marriage didn't exist, who am I? What am I?'" She paused. "But I never really investigated it."

I noticed that when Katy approached such a question, she would pause, peer over the edge at the difficult issue that threw the validity of her faith or her father's goodness into question, and back up, frowning. She held the two sides of her life—her family experience and her faith—together only by not focusing too much on the tensions between them.

Feeling God's Presence Outside a Faith Community

Other children of divorce discover and embrace a life-affirming spirituality that connects them to a source of meaning and to other people but which does not necessarily happen within a faith community. Daniel grew up the Jewish son of German immigrants who divorced when he was seven years old. A young medical resident at a busy urban hospital, he's now married with two small children of his own. Daniel remembers learning about God from his mother when he was a child and deciding that he sounded "like a pretty cool guy."

As a lonely, sometimes frightened boy, Daniel found God helpful. He recalled: "I remember talking to God as a little kid. You know, 'I'm afraid and this and that.'" Daniel talked to God "as if

God was somebody that was sort of watching over me. I pictured God as this caring entity."

Daniel's divorced parents supported him and his brothers in their early religious education, although they didn't sit together at his bar mitzvah. At some point, though, Daniel lost interest in being part of a faith community and his relationship with God began to take a different shape. "I don't have one-on-one talks with God anymore," he said. "That changed when I was thirteen or fourteen. I haven't actually sat down and talked to God in many, many years. I don't go to synagogue and pray to God either."

But Daniel then repeated a story he'd told me earlier, about the awe he felt delivering a baby for the first time: "There's a Jewish prayer for the first time something happens. You praise God for arriving at something for the first time. That something's so new. And I felt I had to say it."

Daniel does think often about God. "In the Bible it says that we're made in the image of God. In my mind our capacity for caring and compassion and love and all that kind of stuff is what the image of God really is. And I feel God is involved in the moral aspect of things. I believe that God is upset when mass atrocities take place. If I'm going to believe in a God I have to believe in a God that has that quality."

Daniel also feels that, through love and right action, God is present in his life today. With a fingertip he slowly traced a bit of graffiti etched into the school desk where he sat. "God is present if I do the right things," he reflected. "If I take pleasure in my family and in my work and in good relationships with friends, that's having God around."

Spiritual but Not Religious

Young adults from divorced families are less likely overall to feel *religious*. We feel just as *spiritual* as people from intact families—a similar majority in the national survey say they are "very" or "fairly" spiritual—but young people from divorced families are more likely to say that institutional religion is not relevant to them. Thirty-seven percent of them agree, "Religion doesn't seem to address the important issues in my life," compared to 29 percent of the people from intact families. Similarly, 46 percent agree, "I believe I can find ultimate truth without help from a religion," compared to 36 percent of the people from intact families.

Even a cursory look at our childhood involvement in faith communities turns up striking differences. Young people from intact families are much more likely to say that they attended religious services regularly as children, with almost three-quarters saying they attended every week or almost every week compared to just over half of children of divorce. People from divorced families are only half as likely as those from intact families to say that they attended services frequently throughout their childhood.

One reason we grow up to be less religious is that our parents too are less likely to be religious; overall, people who divorce are less religious than people who do not. But even if our parents did practice a faith while married, the complicated logistics of divorce could spell an end to our ties to a faith community.

Alicia's practice of a faith dropped off dramatically after her parents' divorce. Her parents split up when she was seven years old and each of them remarried within a year. "My mother's family was real Methodist and helped build the Methodist church, so she was really into it. I remember being real young and going to church a lot." She squinted at the bright sun shining through the window. "The funny thing is I don't remember ever going to church with my dad on those every-other-weekends that we visited." Alicia did have some exposure to a different background through her stepfather's family. "I remember going to the Presbyterian church with them a couple times and not liking it," she recalled. "They didn't sing the same hymns, they didn't do the same doxology, and the people were a bit more stuffy. I remember coming home and saying to my mom, 'I don't want to do that again.'" After that, she doesn't remember being involved in the church until college.

For whatever reason—less interest in religion or the lack of closeness with parents who have split—children of divorce are much less likely to recall finding sources of religious and spiritual guidance in our families. We are far less likely to say that our parents encouraged us to practice a religious faith. Just over half of children of divorce, versus almost four-fifths of people from intact families, agree, "My mother encouraged me to practice a religious faith." That very large difference is even greater when it comes to fathers, with about one-third of us saying our fathers encouraged us to practice a religious faith, compared to about two-thirds of people from intact families.

The national survey also turned up similar, striking differences in the area of prayer. Just 41 percent of children of divorce but 69 percent of people from intact families agree, "My mother taught me how to pray." Slightly more than one-third of children of divorce but a little over half of people from intact families said that they often prayed with their mothers. Similarly, only 17 percent of children of divorce but 47 percent of people from intact families said their fathers taught them how to pray, and fewer than a fifth of us versus well over a third of people from intact families said they often prayed with their fathers.

In perhaps the most poignant finding of the study, of those young adults who were regularly attending a church or synagogue at the time of their parents' divorce, two-thirds say that no one—neither from the clergy nor from the congregation—reached out to them during that critical time in their lives, while only one-quarter remember either a member of the clergy or a person from the congregation doing so.

It is not surprising, then, that when children of divorce reach adulthood they feel less religious on the whole and are less likely to be involved in the regular practice of a faith. One important study found that Catholic and moderate Protestant children of divorce are more than twice as likely to leave religious practice altogether, and conservative Protestants are more than three times as likely to do so. In the national study conducted by Professor Glenn and me, 68 percent of people from intact families, compared to 55 percent of children of divorce, say they are very or fairly religious, and 35 percent of people from intact families currently attend religious services at least almost every week, compared to 24 percent of people from divorced families. There is also a large difference in church membership. Almost two-thirds of people from intact families compared to just under half of children of divorce say they are currently a member at a house of worship.

Although it is a minority overall, the national survey also showed that children of divorce are also at least twice as likely to say that we doubt the sincerity of our parents' religious beliefs—a feeling that not only indicates the skepticism some of us have about our parents' religious beliefs but also hints at a deep lack of respect some of us have for our parents. Nineteen percent of children of divorce, compared to 9 percent of their peers from intact families, feel this way about their mothers, and 27 percent of children of divorce, compared to 14 percent of people from intact families, say the same thing about their fathers.

What Childhood Divorce Does to Religious Identity

Yet this overall picture masks important differences. Some of us from divorced families eventually become much more religious in the wake of our parents' divorce, while some become much less. And as young adults we are surprisingly likely to feel that we are more religious now than our parents ever were—twice as likely as people from intact families to feel that way about our mothers and also much more likely to feel that way about our fathers.

If we are religious there are also important differences in the identities we choose. A similar percentage of young people, one-third, from divorced and intact families describe themselves as Protestant. But while people from intact families are more likely to be Catholic, people from divorced families are more likely to be evangelical.

Twenty-six percent of those from intact families are Catholic compared to 19 percent of people from divorced families. In some ways this difference is not surprising. Because Catholics are somewhat less likely to divorce, one would expect to find fewer children of divorce among them. But there could be other explanations as well. The stricter Catholic theology on divorce can make some Catholic children of divorce feel unwelcome at church. As one young man said, "It seemed pretty clear that if you're from a divorced family, you can't be Catholic anymore." It is not true that Catholic children of divorce can no longer be Catholic, but the misconception is not uncommon.

Forty-one percent of young people from divorced families describe themselves as a born-again or evangelical Christian, compared to 37 percent from intact families. The difference is not all that large—4 percent—but as children of divorce are on the whole less religious, it is significant.

Why might children of divorce be more likely to be evangelical? Overall, people who identify as evangelical have a higher divorce rate than secular non-church-goers (although evangelicals who attend church regularly have a lower divorce rate than their secular counterparts). It is possible that slightly more children of divorce grew up with one or both parents who considered themselves evangelical and they share that identity. At the same time, evangelical churches are typically more willing than mainline Protestant churches to talk about divorce and consider it a problem—or even a sin. But they are also more likely to have active, welcoming ministries for separated and divorced people. In a culture that is too often unwilling to acknowledge what children of divorce have been through, perhaps the willingness of evangelical churches to openly discuss the problems with divorce while also welcoming divorced people is appealing.

Another reason why children of divorce might find evangelical churches more appealing is how they think about God. Evangelical theology emphasizes the central, saving role of a father God, and young people from divorced families are much more likely to say that they think of God as the father or parent they never had.

God as a Parent

Many children of divorce find thoughts about God painful. Looking at how ideas about God are presented to children and young people, it is easy to see why. I recently came across a small book of readings for children in which the authors introduced the idea of people being created in God's image by asking the reader, "Do people ever tell you that you have your dad's smile or his eyes? Or are you shy, or cheerful, or smart like your mom?"

For children from intact families, questions like these might sound natural. How better to get children thinking about their spiritual creation than by citing the two people who created them? But such questions are anything but lighthearted for children of divorce. To wonder whether we have our dad's smile or if we are shy like our mom evokes all kinds of anxious feelings for us. This seemingly innocuous comparison brings up deep and painful feelings of which the authors of this book of readings are apparently unaware. Unfortunately, many faith communities continue to teach children that God is like a parent without considering how children might hear and respond to such an idea.

I asked young adults from divorced and intact families to reflect on the idea of God as a parent. The responses of the children of divorce revealed a great deal about what they thought of their parents as well as what they thought of God. Will was mystified by the question. He had been angry at his father for years because of the way he treated Will's mother. When I asked Will if God is like a father or parent he looked puzzled. "Yeah, I think a father is somebody who is your last string of hope," he said slowly. "He'll watch over you, make sure everything is going to be okay." Then his voice faltered and he looked down at his hands in his lap. "I'm drawing a blank," he said. "I'm just drawing a blank."

Kimberly said that God is like a parent because God "is trying to test you . . . In life you're going to have many challenges. And the challenges come from somewhere."

"Do they come from God?" I asked.

"Yeah, I think they do," she said. In Kimberly's unusual perspective, the role of her parents and of God was to confront her with challenges. In the national survey, 22 percent of children of divorce agreed with her that "the hardships in my life come from God," compared to 17 percent of people from intact families.

Rochelle said that God is like a parent because God "supplies things I need." She emphasized, "Like you're *supposed* to be able to ask your parents for things and they're *supposed* to take care of you." Her father rarely supplied her needs when she was growing up, she said, even when she specifically asked.

Others said that God did *not* seem like a parent. Allison said that thinking of God as a parent "would be a negative relationship for me." Alicia said God is "like a mentor, an older, wiser person . . . not like a parent," revealing a lot about how she saw her parents. One young woman said that God is not like a parent because God is "something smarter" than us. Another said that parents are supposed to be nurturing and comforting but to her God seems "like a manager, keeping tabs on things."

Daniel cited the book *The Color of Water* by James McBride, in which the author, who grew up the child of a black father and a white mother, took comfort in his mother's assurance that God was neither black nor white but "the color of water." Daniel speculated that, similarly, God is neither father nor mother but the color of water, which felt liberating to him. Melissa said she thought of God not as a parent but as "authority, control, and safety." She told me that she didn't experience "full, untainted love" in her family so she didn't think of God as being "part of the family."

Prodigal Parents

Since young people from divorced families seem to have so many unexpected reactions to the idea of God as a parent, I decided to ask them about a well-known story that portrays God as a kind and loving father. In the story of the prodigal son, a son decides to leave home and asks his father for his share of his inheritance. He then travels far away, squandering his father's money. When he hits rock bottom, he returns home hoping only that his father might allow him to be a servant in the house. Instead, his father welcomes him with open arms and throws a party to celebrate his return. The story is often said to illustrate that God welcomes us like a loving father, happy to forgive when we acknowledge our mistakes and come home.

Some young people from intact families do not find this story very interesting or relevant to their lives, but others respond to it quite warmly. They see themselves as the prodigal son or daughter—or some said their sister or brother was—because they had disappointed their parents by getting bad grades, dropping out of college, doing drugs, wasting money, or making career choices that their parents hadn't liked. Yet their parents continued to love them and welcomed them home when they were ready to return.

Jennifer, a thirty-one-year-old scientist whose parents have been married for thirty-five years, said eagerly, "I can tell you a story about it." Years ago, when she was attending college out west, she "met this guy." "He was not in school and he wanted me to go traveling around the country with him, and he was very exciting," Jennifer remembered. "So I didn't call my parents and ask them, I just called and implied that I was thinking about it. Their reaction was violently no. They asked me, 'What are you talking about? You can't drop out of college.' All the things that a parent would say. And I just didn't listen to any of it.

"So we bought this old Volvo station wagon that we were going to live in. We got all this stuff together, a futon, and enough rice and beans for twenty years. I called my parents from Utah and said, 'Hi, guess what? I wanted to let you know that I'm okay, but I did drop out of school.' And they just said, 'Are you okay? Please keep calling us.'" She laughed sadly. "I remember I mailed them a letter that said, 'I know what I'm doing and I'm just being an individual and blah blah blah. I love you very much but you have to understand that now I'm an adult. And we're really in love.'"

Seven months later, things had changed. Jennifer found herself in the deep South with a broken-down car, a boyfriend she didn't like much anymore, and a nagging conscience about all the school she was missing, as well as a deep longing to see her parents.

"I realized that I'd made the wrong decision, and I decided I was going to leave him," she said. She got a bus ticket and headed toward home in Richmond, Virginia. "I didn't call my parents to say I was coming. And I was absolutely terrified. I came up to the front door and I was in all my hippie glory, with the hair and whatever I was wearing. And they just gave me the biggest hug. Both of them started crying and said, 'We're so glad to see you!' I was so embarrassed by my behavior and how stupid I'd been, and the way they welcomed me back was just incredible."

Like Jennifer, when people from intact families hear the story of the prodigal son they tend to focus on the end of the story, when the son finds himself loved in spite of his mistakes. But children of divorce often think about the beginning of the story instead. The idea of someone leaving home resonates for us, though not necessarily the idea of a *child* who leaves home. Rather, some of us are reminded of being home alone while our divorced parents were working or socializing, or of the departure that caused the divorce in the first place. In our understanding of the story, the roles are reversed: the story is about not the prodigal son but the prodigal parents.

Joanna said that when she heard the story of the prodigal son in church when she was growing up it always made her think, "Well, maybe my father will decide to come back one of these days." After her parents' divorce when she was five years old, her father lived in the same town but saw Joanna and her brothers only once a year. During the Christmas holidays he would pick the children up and take them out to breakfast for a couple of hours. When he dropped them off afterward he would say—"like clockwork," Joanna recalled—"Yeah, I'll come around and see you one of these Saturdays," but he never did. Joanna would run to her room crying after these visits. She always wondered why her father would spend far more time being a dad to the five children his second wife brought to their marriage than to his own three children.

Joanna says she has given her father many chances to come

back. She is wary and cautious with him, but she wants him to know her and especially her baby. She even said to him, "I'll make the effort, but I have to see you making the effort. And I don't mean like you come once and disappear for another year." In the story of the prodigal son it is the father who is willing to give his son a second chance despite his mistakes. Yet this story reminds Joanna of her own willingness to continue hoping—despite the constant rejections as a child—that her father will start showing interest in her life.

Other children of divorce also think of their parents leaving when they hear the story. Alicia's parents divorced when she was seven years old. Each remarried within a year after that, and both later divorced again. When I asked her if the story had any relevance to her life she said, "Well, I don't really see anybody going away and coming back and being welcomed, you know?" She laughed bitterly. "In my life people have either gone away and done something else or gone away and stayed away."

Other children of divorce interpret the story slightly differently. They think about the son coming home but say that even if they had rebelled and left home there would not have been a stable home for them to come back to. Instead, they see themselves as the one who stayed put while their parents came and went, or themselves as the ones who traveled back and forth to keep their families connected.

Melissa thought about the story and said, "I thought it was a nice idea if it would ever really work . . . to actually believe that you could just leave and the fact that love would always be constant. For me it was like, if they love me then why do they live so far away? Or why are they always going out with boyfriends?" As a child of divorce, she said, "you're always staying put in one place and trying your hardest to make something stable."

Melissa concluded, "I figured if I left and went away, when I came back my house would be gone."

Another young woman from a divorced family who I interviewed for an earlier project said she had friends for whom the story of the prodigal son meant a great deal. "They feel like they've gone away and rejected their families and came back," she said. But in her family "I was always kind of the dutiful one—the one traveling distances to be sure I saw my mother, traveling distances to be sure I saw my father. My family didn't even give me anything to reject! There wasn't a stable enough thing to go away from or come back to."

Honor Your Father and Mother

The reactions of children of divorce to the story of the prodigal son were so moving that I decided to ask them about one of the Ten Commandments, the one to honor your father and mother. Because of the way the Ten Commandments have shaped Western religious, cultural, and legal traditions, many people, even those who do not consider themselves especially religious, take them seriously—especially those that deal with everyday morality.

Young adults whose parents are still married often respond to the honor commandment by talking about what their parents have done for them. This realization, they say, only grows stronger as they and their parents age. One man said, "When you're a kid you think life's real easy. I criticized my parents a lot growing up. And then as you grow up you realize life is pretty complex. The older I get the nicer I get to my parents." Another said that he "totally believes" the commandment because his parents "have given me so much, sacrificed so much. I respect them." One woman said that in adolescence she questioned everything about her parents but now it is easy for her to honor them because "I've had rock star parents. . . . I think the world of them. We've had our ups and downs but I had a pretty spectacular childhood compared to a lot of people."

Another young woman said, "My father and mother have done so much for me and sacrificed so much that not to honor them would be the ultimate disrespect." For her honor means to "keep them comfortable when they get older, to take care of their daily needs and also their emotional needs. To have a relationship with them." Like her, another young woman also said that honoring is about "being in relationship" with her parents. She said, "When I think of honor I think of being in relationship with them. . . . That's how we're honoring our parents, that we're able to show our love for them now by giving them things and paying them back for all the things they've given to us."

Not all young adults from intact families respond warmly to the commandment. Some had troubled relationships with their parents. One man from a high-conflict intact family said that observing the commandment to honor his parents has "been very difficult. In fact, my wife and I have talked about what that means." One thing he has realized, he said, is that "just nodding your head and saying, 'Oh, that's great,' to everything they do, that's not honoring them either."

While children of married parents say they struggle with the commandment only if there have been significant problems in their family, children of divorce typically find the commandment challenging. One problem is that the commandment implies that parents are a unit, while theirs were not. But the problems go much deeper.

Some children of divorce say they honor a parent who sacrificed a great deal for them—often a single mother who faced great odds and succeeded at raising her kids well. But when they thought of one of their parents as sacrificial it was often because the other parent had failed badly. They tended to focus on the failed parent, saying they struggled with how to understand the honor commandment in light of that parent's mistakes. Still other children of divorce thought that neither parent sacrificed much for them, and they were the ones who struggled with the commandment the most.

Infidelity and abandonment created a huge dilemma for some children of divorce when it came to honoring their parents. Joanna said she wondered how she could honor her father when she knew that he had had an affair and left her mother. Will said that he honors his mother but that given his father's infidelity and "the pain he's caused my mother and me, I guess I couldn't honor him right now." Eric said he has come to respect and honor his mother now, but it has not always been the case. Her affair with a boyfriend ended his parents' marriage and he lost respect for his mother for many years.

Others struggled with a lack of trust in one of their parents. Kimberly fought often with her mother when she was growing up. She said that as a child she would have responded to the commandment by asking, "Why? Why honor my mother if she's not able to show love or honor for me?" Ashley had a similarly troubled relationship with her mother and said that she now sees the commandment as "Honor my father, deal with my mother." To "deal" with her mother meant to maintain the pretense of a bond—to be sure to give her gifts on Mother's Day and her birthday, for example—but otherwise to keep her distance.

Samantha said, "To honor your parents is a good idea, maybe to a certain age, until you learn about the world for yourself."

I asked her, "At what age did you learn about the world for yourself?"

She rubbed a tight muscle in her neck and replied, "I think I learned early because of my mom's second marriage when I was ten years old. I learned that I don't necessarily agree with everything that she's doing. So the honor commandment becomes 'Honor, but use your best judgment.'"

For some children of divorce their relationships with both parents are so thin or painful that fulfilling the honor commandment seems mysterious or impossible. Melissa shooed her cat off her lap and said she does not honor her parents because "I don't think they thought about the children as much as they should have. When you have a child they're helpless and you're supposed to give your full life to them. . . . It never occurred to me to have unending honor for them because they never had it for me."

Alicia, who talked easily about other spiritual issues, was stumped by the honor commandment. "What does that mean exactly? Honor their wishes? I don't know what that means." She frowned. "Everybody's honor is different, isn't it? How do you honor?"

Although some had given up on the honor commandment, other children of divorce—especially those who were actively growing in a faith—spoke of how it called them into a relationship with their parents. An awareness of the commandment was what kept these young people working at a relationship that had hurt or disappointed them, rather than abandoning it altogether now that they were independent and grown.

Katy said the commandment is "very much a supporting theme" in her life, because "through thick and thin that would hold me to honor both of them." In fact, she recalled that a sense of needing to honor her father partly explained why she continued to make the effort to visit him routinely even after she left home.

Anthony said he thought about the commandment a lot growing up. He recalled his father's hurt when Anthony and his brother were teenagers and did not want to visit him often. His father said, "The Bible says honor your father, and I don't feel you're honoring me." Anthony recalls arguing with his father, saying that the Bible also says that parents should honor their children, which he felt his father had not done.

As an adult Anthony has resolved the problem by deciding, "The commandments are things we do for God, so honor your father because God told you to do it—that is how you honor God." Today he does not honor his father so much as feel sorry for him: "With regard to honoring him, I've not ever wanted to just completely leave him and not have anything to do with him. Because I feel sorry that he doesn't have people that really love him and are attached to him as a father."

Rochelle had been deeply disappointed by her father. She searched her heart, prayed, and talked to her father about her feelings. She has reached a point where she can "care for him now in a way he never did for me," in part because of her awareness of this commandment.

Tammy described a similar experience of forgiving her father as part of her spiritual growth and said that today, "Even when I'm mad at my father I don't ever want to do anything that makes God upset."

When I asked Steve about the honor commandment he said heatedly, "I have struggled with that commandment from the point at which I became a believer to this day. . . . It's only because of my faith that I would even approach that as something I need to be doing. If it weren't for that I would probably have written off my mom; the same with my dad. . . . But I can't honor God if I'm not honoring my mother and my father."

Michael recalled that after his conversion to Christianity as a teenager he often reflected on this commandment and what it meant for his faith and his relationship with his parents. Honoring his mother was easy, he said, but with regard to his father he concluded, "Okay, I'll respect him, but it doesn't mean that I always have to like him."

Coming Home

Faith traditions can seem alienating or irrelevant to children of divorce, especially when they are interpreted in ways that ignore our experience. But these same traditions also harbor moving stories that can name our experience in new ways. One of them is the story of the exile. In the Judeo-Christian tradition, the story of the exile is a central theme in some of the prophetic books of the Hebrew Bible and in the history of Judaism, and exile is a formative theme for the Christian faith.

We children of divorce who stay in touch with both parents are travelers on the move. We often felt far away from home and uncertain where we belonged. Our experience is not unlike the biblical story of the exile. We were not usually sent away—although this happened to a small number of us. Rather, we had to go away because of forces beyond our control. Often it was a custody decision, rather than the wishes of our parents, that kept us on the move.

As children of divorce, we experienced a kind of exile in two ways. We lost our original family: We might still have had a mother and a father in our lives, but that life was never the same. The experience of having a mother and father as a unit, the home in which

we lived, the neighborhood and the friends that were there, the larger network of relationships in which the marriage existed—some or all of this was lost.

The second experience of exile stretched throughout our childhoods as we journeyed between our parents. There is an elemental wholeness that children feel in the company of both parents, a wholeness that can only be compared to the closeness and security we seek in intimate relationships when we are adults. Yet once our parents became individuals and not a married unit, we never experienced that elemental wholeness again. For children of divorce, to gain one parent *always* means to lose the other. Over time we became divided, torn between two worlds. Exile is a spiritual name for our feeling of inner division. It helps explain our sense of being fragmented, spread out, scattered.

But exile is not the end of the story. In the Judeo-Christian tradition the faithful are assured they can come home to God. Like Katy and Michael, some find that a spiritual journey in the context of a faith community is both possible and healing. They discover a single identity and life story that help them make sense of their shifting and complex family histories.

I continue to struggle with these questions. For now, I find peace and hope in my growing family and in my writing. I discovered years ago that I could find a calm in the storm by trying to name the storm itself, to capture it in words. When I'd finish writing, a certain peace would descend—a sense of order, even beauty restored.

Writing this book has been a spiritual practice: an exercise in deep questioning, a search for meaning, a discovery of connection with others, an affirmation that I am not alone. Through research for this book I concluded that my parents' divorce does not define me—that all of us are much too complex to be explained by any one event in our lives. Still, even when we do not feel that our parents' breakup defines us, the divorce is central to understanding who we are.

8

Getting Honest About Children of Divorce

This book chronicles my attempt to discover the truth about divorce, a journey that began in my mid-twenties and comes to an end now, when I am almost thirty-four years old. I'll admit that at the beginning of this journey I was angry. I was tired of all the wrongheaded assumptions about my life. Too many people thought that because my parents loved me and didn't fight, or because their divorce took place before I could remember it, or because I had managed to grow up and become a reasonably functional person, then the divorce must not have been a big deal. I felt that my parents and the culture at large had very little understanding of my real experience.

I still sometimes get frustrated with my parents, as anyone does, but I don't feel angry with them anymore. The decision they made was a very long time ago, when they were only twenty-one years old. When they split up, leading experts assured parents that as long as they found happiness their children would be happy too. Some experts even insisted that parents in unhappy marriages had a duty to divorce or they would irrevocably damage their children. More nuanced ideas about happiness—that there are degrees of unhappiness in marriages, that marital happiness can go in cycles, that divorce doesn't necessarily make adults happy, that children's natural inclination is not to worry about their parents' happiness so much as their own—did not have much influence in the early seventies.

Today when I look at my mother and father and my stepmother of almost fifteen years, what stands out is how they have supported my journey in writing this book, how proud they are of my accomplishments, how they have welcomed my husband, and how wonderful they are as grandparents. I'm grateful to them.

But I am still angry at the culture. It's five years and counting into the new millennium. We've seen the effects of widespread divorce unfold for over three decades. Some big studies have been done and the first generation of children of divorce has grown up and started to speak out. Yet in the debate about divorce, our culture is still turning its back on children. For the generation who raised us and for divorced parents today, the story told in this book is a new one.

Compare the story in this book with what the culture continues to say:

- The real problem with divorce lies with parents who can't stop battling. If parents can achieve a "good divorce," then the children will be fine.

- Children of divorce who do not end up damaged are fine and no one needs to worry about them.

- Divorced families are just one of many family types. We should embrace family diversity and stop making divorced parents feel bad.

- It doesn't matter whether a child's mother and father are married and living together. All that matters is that children have a loving family.

Upbeat language about divorce—call it "divorce happy talk"—is all around us. Such talk can be well-intended. Divorced parents are vulnerable and worried about their kids. Experts want to offer them reassurance and helpful advice. But when divorce happy talk minimizes, distorts, or ignores the pain felt by children of divorce, it crosses over into the realm of harm.

These glib, overly optimistic assumptions about divorce hurt my generation as we grew up and they are harming a new generation growing up now. My question is this: Can our culture get honest about children of divorce?

The Myth of the "Good Divorce"

The idea of the "good divorce" bears little resemblance to children's reality. In even a "good divorce," half of us say we always felt like adults, even as little kids. Half say our family lives were stressful. More than half say we experienced many losses. Close to half say our parents' household rules were different. Almost a third say our parents' versions of the truth were different. A third say we were alone a lot as children. Aiming for a "good divorce" might help adults feel better about their decision to divorce, or about the divorce that has been thrust upon them, but the stories of children of divorce show that it is wrong and misleading to describe our experience as "good."

Rebecca Walker, author of *Black, White, and Jewish,* is a product of a "good divorce." She kept in close contact with both her parents; her parents got along reasonably well with each other. Yet to be close to her parents Rebecca had to take on the burden of traveling routinely between their worlds, never knowing where she really belonged or where the boundaries of her "shifting self" might begin and end.

Walker writes that when her parents divorced, "[They] decide I will spend two years, alternately, with each of them. I don't know how they come up with that. . . . What their decision means is that every year I will move, change schools, shift. . . . Now as I move from place to place, from Jewish to black, from D.C. to San Francisco, from status quo middle class to radical artist bohemia, it is less like jumping from station to station on the same radio dial and more like moving from planet to planet between universes that never overlap. I move through days, weeks, people, places, growing attached and then letting go, meeting people and then saying good-bye. Holding on makes it harder to be adaptable, harder to meet the demands of a new place. It is easier to forget, to wipe the slate clean, to watch the world go by like a film on a screen, without letting anything stick."

Some might say that for divorced parents to live on opposite coasts and expect their child to alternate homes every two years is not really a "good divorce" at all. Of course young Rebecca was overwhelmed. But it is just as tough, perhaps even more so, when parents live in the same town and the children travel back and forth frequently. Even some strong advocates of the "good divorce" concede that these travels are hard for kids, but this observation is apparently not compelling enough to make them rethink their idea.

In *The Good Divorce*, Constance Ahrons acknowledges that "no matter how cooperative parents are, children have to make adjustments as they cross from one parent—and one home—to the other." She offers the example of Janet and Sybil, two little girls, ages four and seven, who spend half the week at their mother's house and half at their father's. Ahrons includes their family as one of four model examples of well-functioning families. In other words, Janet and Sybil are growing up in one of Ahrons' *best* "good divorce" scenarios.

She writes: "It's not unusual for children to be angry or clingy or distant for a few hours, or even a day, before they adjust [to a different home]. . . . On the days they changed homes, Janet, the younger child, regressed. She sucked her thumb more, became whiny, clung to her mother. Sybil acted very differently. She'd start to let go even before she left. She'd be more independent and somewhat ornery."

Ahrons shares the girls' reactions matter-of-factly, as some of the small details that have to be addressed in the larger task of managing a "binuclear" family. When I read her book I was shocked that she apparently did not think the children's clear suffering undermined her confident portrayal of this model "binuclear" family.

These girls exhibited such distressing responses—a four-year-old girl regressing, sucking her thumb, and clinging to her mother; a seven-year-old girl "letting go before she even left"—twice a week, every week, even though theirs was cited as an ideal "good divorce" family. I couldn't help but wonder how the children in her study fared who lacked such apparently highly functioning divorced parents.

Advocates of the "good divorce" refuse to recognize that our childhoods were dominated by frequent sad departures. Most children with married parents could not imagine being routinely separated from their mother or father for months at a time. Yet as children of "good divorces" we lived apart from our mother, and then our father, for days, weeks, months, or years at a time.

Once we felt so much loss, so many times, many of us grew numb to it. I learned to bottle up my longing for my father and did my best to ignore how much I missed my mother. Seven-year-old Sybil learned very quickly to "let go before she even left." Rebecca Walker decided, "It is easier to . . . watch the world go by like a film on a screen, without letting anything stick." As little children we were able to walk down an airplane jetway by ourselves, leaving our mother or father behind, with a matter-of-fact coolness that few children from intact families could approximate or imagine. To outsiders we looked improbably grown-up, even charmingly mature. But inside we struggled with feelings of detachment and division for years to come. Sure, a "good divorce" is better than a bad divorce—but it isn't good.

"Blended Families"

Some fear that the word *stepfamily* conjures up fairy-tale stories of wicked stepmothers and neglected children. They have popularized the term *blended family* to describe families created through remarriage. Remarried adults understandably like the term because they want to leave the past behind and create a new life for themselves that feels whole, and many therapists have embraced what they see as its positive connotations. But while the phrase *blended family* may name the experience or hopes of the adults, when it is used to describe children's lives it is just another form of happy talk. Our experience was anything but blended.

I never hear children of divorce use the term *blended family* when they talk about the families they grew up in. Instead they use a vocabulary of divorce, remarriage, stepparents, parents' boyfriends and girlfriends, step- and half-brothers and -sisters, and quite often subsequent divorces or breakups. However blended our parents might have felt or hoped to become in their new marriages, as children we always had two families, quite often with members who did not even know each other. After a divorce and remarriage our reality was *divided,* not blended. Saying we grew up in a "blended family" is dishonest and damaging—an attempt to redefine our experience with words intended to help the grown-ups feel better.

Given the bias in the term *blended family,* I was disappointed to learn that even the U.S. Census Bureau now uses it to describe any family that includes "at least one stepparent, stepsibling, and/or half-sibling."

Recently, too, the term *bonus family* has been proposed to describe stepfamilies. Like *blended family, bonus family* slaps an unambiguously positive label on a family type that children experience as divided, challenging, and too often full of loss.

"Bird Nesting"

Bird nesting is a recently coined term that refers to a situation in which two divorced parents, recognizing that traveling between two homes may be rough on their children, instead share one home where the children live all the time while the parents move in and out. Each parent spends the remainder of his or her time in a separate house or apartment nearby.

"Bird nesting" could be seen as a compassionate move on the part of divorced parents to provide one home for their child, as married parents do. But few manage to stick with it, because adults find it is extremely burdensome to travel between two homes. Of course, children of divorce travel between two homes all the time but our society tends to minimize how difficult this arrangement is. Like any "good divorce" arrangement, "bird nesting" is much more unstable than a married, intact family, and it's doubtful it could last more than a few years. If a parent starts dating or remarries, would the parent's new partner or spouse be willing to travel between two homes or live without his or her spouse for half the week? If a parent is offered a great job some distance away, would he or she turn it down to keep "bird nesting" with his ex?

"Bird nesting" also does not resolve one of the major losses of divorce: being with one parent always means *not* being with the other. In "bird nesting," Dad arrives, but Mom disappears, and vice versa. If you need Mom for something, well, you have to wait until Thursday. Bird nesting, like all "good divorce" arrangements, puts the children's needs on an adult timeline, while in a married, intact family the family functions much more often on the children's timeline.

In contrast to the term *blended families,* the term *bird nesting* is unlikely to come into widespread use because it describes a practice that is unlikely to become popular. Yet the choice of words is telling. The phrase sounds so cute and cuddly, conjuring up a picture of mommy and daddy birds alternately huddling with their babies in a warm nest.

Little could be further from the truth, which points to the dangerous temptation of most forms of divorce happy talk. It is unlikely that any parent in a stressed marriage would find their stress reduced by such a logistically complicated living situation. And despite the euphemistic language, the primary burden still falls on the kids to study and try to make sense of their parents' worlds.

Don't Fall Apart!

Divorce happy talk comes from adults. They generally use these terms with other adults or write books and articles intended for an adult audience. It filters down and shapes children's lives power-fully but indirectly. Yet there is a special genre of happy talk writ small and aimed directly at the children.

I've already written about *To & Fro, Fast & Slow*, a book that uses the organizing device of a child traveling between her divorced parents' homes to teach children about opposites. I wasn't sur-prised to find that its upbeat look at divorce is not lost on adults. As one reviewer wrote in the *New York Times*, "The pictures invite young readers to notice the specific differences between two life-styles while noting, also, that this child is really enjoying herself. It is possible, this book quietly asserts, that there may actually be riches gained and experiences broadened by something as theoret-ically troubling as a divorce." In his not-so-subtle conclusion, the reviewer implies that there is little need to pay attention to the actual facts about divorce. Let's just call the facts "theories" and find false comfort in a fictional child who thinks that life after divorce is terrific.

Other books aimed at children of divorce try to reassure them by explaining they are not alone—plenty of other children are also growing up with divorced parents. One example is *My Parents Are Divorced Too: A Book for Kids, by Kids*. Written for children ages nine to twelve, this book features children of divorce responding to questions asked by others like them, covering topics such as their parents' dating, sexuality, and more. Apparently the main idea is that the shock of witnessing your mother or father enter a sexual relationship with someone who is not your parent will be eased by knowing that other kids go through this too. Similarly, other books often deal fairly forthrightly with the losses and challenges of divorce while at the same time expressing great confidence that children will be comforted by knowing it's not just happening to them. Some of the more recent titles include *It's Not Your Fault, Koko Bear; My Parents Still Love Me Even Though They're Getting Divorced; Mommy and Daddy Bear's Divorce; I Don't Want to Talk About It*, and *Help! A Girl's Guide to Divorce and Stepfamilies*.

In a chapter titled "The Children's Story of Divorce," from her

1996 book *The Divorce Culture,* social critic and historian Barbara Dafoe Whitehead analyzed the then-current children's literature of divorce and concluded that these books, unlike resources aimed at divorcing adults, were at least more aware of children's concerns and fears. But she also notes that "the comforts of victimhood are small," that assuring children they are not the only ones going through divorce goes only so far to relieve their pain.

It is also true, as Whitehead writes, that some of these children's books seem more intent on regulating or managing children's emotions rather than giving free expression to them. A striking example is *Don't Fall Apart on Saturdays!: The Children's Divorce-Survival Book.* The cover alone is disturbing. A cartoon drawing of a young African American girl is set against a jagged yellow starburst centered on a hot pink background. Much like the girl on the cover of *To & Fro, Fast & Slow,* this child's arms and legs are widely flung open, as if she's being stretched on a rack. Yet this child's face is turned up toward the sky, her eyes are wide open, her mouth is turned down in cartoonish agony, and, strangely, every part of her body is segmented from the other, with open spaces between her upper arms, lower arms, hands, and so on with her entire body. Just above her head is the book's title, written in capital letters, with an exclamation point for good measure. She looks exhausted, dizzy, and scared. Every detail of the cover signals overwhelming emotion and a sense of inner fragmentation. Yet the title of the book tells her, actually screams at her, *not* to fall apart, even though she obviously already has.

Inside its pages, a psychologist discusses some of the toughest rites of passage for a child of divorce: a parent leaving home, choosing who to live with, watching your parents start to date, and more. Even if we acknowledge that some divorces have to happen and that a thoughtful book might be helpful for children, I have to wonder: Is this the way to do it? Will shouting "Don't fall apart on Saturdays!" give children any comfort when they are waiting for their dad to pick them up Saturday morning and, well, falling apart? And does it really help to spell out the gory aftermath of divorce for kids—the loss of their home, the choices between their parents, the knowledge that a parent is having sex with someone new, and more? Or are these efforts a quick salve applied by grown-ups that cannot even begin to heal the lifelong effects of divorce?

Divorce Happy Talk as Denial

In the end, divorce happy talk indicts itself. In the breathless portrayals of the upside of divorce, it is all too easy to spot a defensive awareness of the huge downsides. If they're honest, everyone knows that divorce hurts a lot. Even people who want to end their marriages find divorce wrenching and disorienting. Divorce routinely makes it to the top of the list of life's most stressful events that are likely to send a person spiraling into depression.

Yet few other events on the list inspire the endless books, magazine articles, websites, and talk shows devoted to looking at their upside. Why? Because unlike losing your job, or having your spouse die, or facing serious health problems, divorce is a *choice* that at least one adult in the marriage makes. Divorce happy talk is our culture's attempt to reconcile two competing desires: the desire to accept widespread divorce and the desire to raise happy, healthy children. These two desires are in direct conflict. To date, the culture's main way of confronting this conflict has been denial in the form of happy talk.

Happy talk misleads adults about the true nature of divorce. It portrays divorce as an orderly, perhaps even plannable event rather than a major upset that opens new, unexpected, and unwelcome doors. It minimizes the pain and chaos that often follow divorce and, in doing so, encourages parents who may be in troubled but salvageable marriages to split up.

The most serious problem with divorce happy talk is that it lies to children. Children of divorce typically experience painful losses, moral confusion, spiritual suffering, strained or broken relationships, and higher rates of all kinds of social problems. But divorce happy talk insists that children's experience is just the opposite. It declares that postdivorce family life is a fun challenge. It chirps about the new people who become part of one's family, the fresh unity of remarriages, the adventure of traveling between two worlds. When divorce happy talk does realistically confront the stresses of divorce, it pretends that just saying them out loud will make the pain go away. Either way, the misnaming of our actual experience makes it even more difficult to recognize and share our true feelings and eventually to heal.

Two Species of Kids

The lasting consequences of divorce happy talk are apparent when one compares our culture's attitudes about children in intact families with attitudes about children of divorce. People like to think that they treat all children the same way. But in truth our culture sustains two very different child-rearing philosophies—one that applies to children of married parents and one that applies to children of divorce.

I'll begin with babies. Believe it or not, there is an active debate about whether traveling constantly between divorced parents' homes is harmful for babies. Some experts say that babies of divorce are able to adjust just fine, while others find serious problems. One columnist argued recently in favor of increased overnight visitation for children under two years of age with their fathers. "Children become stressed by separations from either parent that last more than three or four days," she quotes researchers as saying. She urges family courts to move beyond the idea that children have one primary "psychological parent" (typically their mother) and recognize that children are attached to and need to see both parents. Otherwise, she concludes, it adds to their postdivorce stress.

Certainly children are attached to and need both parents. But what this columnist—and all those who favor a legal presumption of equal custody division, even for babies—seems to forget is that children of divorce *can see only one parent at a time*. Yes, as children we missed our father and needed to see him. But when we were with Daddy we missed Mommy. What should be done, then, about these findings that even babies "become stressed by separations from either parent that last more than three or four days"? Limit the baby's time with each parent to three days, so that within the period of one week the baby goes from Mom's house to Dad's and then back to Mom's again, only to repeat the same cycle the next week, and the next, and the next? Does anyone really think that being raised in a revolving door will be less stressful for children under two years old?

The two child-rearing philosophies I've alluded to quickly become apparent when we look at our culture's general attitude about babies. Umpteen parenting books and magazine articles tell us that babies are vulnerable and needy, requiring consistency and predictability. New parents fret about going out alone for a coffee date because the brief absence might upset the baby. They undertake decisions such as switching to a different brand of formula as if they were sending people up in the space shuttle.

But when our culture turns to children of divorce, everything people think about babies goes out the window. Babies need constant care from their mothers? Forget it. Babies who regularly go three days and nights without seeing their mothers do just fine! Babies need a predictable environment and love having the same routine? Forget it. They're happy to wake up anywhere! Households should be organized around the baby's needs? Forget it. Babies easily adapt to adult needs!

And babies are only the beginning. Our culture treats children of divorce who are beyond babyhood as if they are a separate species, more adaptable and resilient than other children. We routinely expect children of divorce to take in stride situations that children of married parents rarely, if ever, are expected to face.

How often do married parents send their child away from home for days, weeks, months, or years at a time? How often do married parents spend routine, non-work-related nights apart from their kids? How often do married parents put their children on airplanes by themselves? How often do married parents divide their financial responsibilities for their children down to the penny? How often do married parents take each other to court? How often do married parents sleep with someone besides the child's parent in the home when the child is present? How often do married parents read their children books that portray painful losses that the children might have experienced as fun adventures?

Certainly, married parents do not avoid doing all of these things, and divorced parents do not do all of them. But these actions are common among divorced parents, so common that no one thinks twice about them. It is almost unheard of for married parents to do any of them.

Yet the needs of children of married parents and children of divorced parents are the same. They are the same species. So why are children of divorce considered so resilient? *Because the adults need them to be that way.*

Conclusion

What Children of Divorce Want

One day this winter I dropped into a neighborhood bookstore to take one more look at books written for divorcing parents and their children. I was in a rush, so I approached the first clerk I saw, even though she looked harried and distracted.

"Excuse me," I said. "Can you tell me where to find the books about divorce?"

Her harried look melted away, quickly replaced by sympathy. It dawned on me that she thought *I* was getting divorced.

I looked down at myself. My large pregnant stomach protruded from my heavy coat. My hands were swelling, so I'd taken off my wedding ring weeks before. I'd stayed up late several nights in a row, working on a chapter after putting my toddler to bed, and probably looked wiped out. She must have thought I was in pretty bad shape—divorcing, pregnant, and falling apart.

I was about to explain but stopped. Maybe the kindness on her face was because she'd been through a divorce herself. Maybe my smiling protest—*Oh no, not me!*—would trade my discomfort for hers. I kept quiet and followed as she led me toward the back of the store, pointed out the books I needed, and left me alone. I didn't start flipping through the books right away, though. I sat on a wooden chair, thinking about what had happened.

For a moment I had felt the confusion, shame, and anger that a divorcing parent might feel. And I realized once again how much security my own marriage has given me as I wrote this book. I've been able to write from the child's perspective, not having to think about what I would do if my husband left me or if it turned out I'd married a jerk.

I spend most of my time thinking about divorce from a child's perspective, but it has never been my intention to accuse divorced parents. I meet divorced parents when I give talks, and the distress I see on many of their faces breaks my heart. I want to console them, to take them by the shoulders and say, "You're not the one I'm trying to convince. You already get it."

I'm trying to convince everyone else in our culture, especially married parents who might have unrealistic ideas about divorce. I want to shake loose those glaringly wrong assumptions: That divorce doesn't matter if the parents get along. That divorce doesn't matter if the kids don't look like damaged goods. That divorce doesn't matter as long as parents keep loving their children. I believe that all adults—whatever their own history—should be able to tolerate hearing the children's point of view.

The first generation to come of age in an era of widespread divorce has grown up. We know, because we lived it, that any kind of divorce thrusts upon us an enormous burden, one that shapes our moral and spiritual identities for years afterward. We know that a "good divorce" is not a panacea. We can speak for ourselves now.

This is what we want: a home, strong marriages, understanding of our true experience, and a secure world for our children—one world.

One True Home

On a practical level, divorce is the dividing of a home. When they grow up, children of divorce long for one true home and the sense of belonging that confers.

Many children of divorce seek to make a home with a lasting marriage of their own. Growing up, said Allison, nowhere felt like home, but home today is "with my husband and child. You walk in and it's a safe haven." Steve said, "My wife and I have been in our house for almost five years. It's the longest I've stayed put anywhere since 1980, so our house with our kids is our home. It's where we come to escape. It's, hopefully, peace."

Ashley recalled feeling at home for the first time only as an adult in the home she made for herself: "When I finally moved to my own apartment . . . all my stuff was with me, all that I really cared about, and I was like, 'Whoa, this is my house, this is me, this is my life.'" Ashley's new home was not just a roof over her head. It was her own place where she had her "stuff." Her new home gave firmer grounding to her life.

Daniel had only recently been struck by a strong, secure sense of home. It happened when he and his wife returned from a long vacation. His eyes glowed as he talked: "We'd been on a trip, and I knew the only place we belonged was when we pulled into the driveway. It just felt like I was home, for the first time. It was a very new feeling and I was very excited.

"I told my wife, 'You know what? I think for the first time in my life I know what home means.'

"She looked at me kind of sad and kind of real happy all at once.

"I said, 'I really feel like this is where I belong now.'"

When children of divorce grow up, we want one secure home for ourselves, and we want to raise our children with an unquestioned sense of home and security. All parents want the same thing for their children, but we feel this hope especially strongly. When we are able to give our children a loving home filled with predictable routines and a mother and father who are there for them every day, we feel deep gratitude and joy. When we face problems in our marriages, we agonize, knowing that if our marriages fail, a secure home would be the first thing our children would lose.

Since I am a child of divorce, people often ask me what kind of custody arrangements I think are best for children. If parents must divorce, where should the child's home be? There are no easy answers to this question. Everything I have discovered in my research and my life leads me to conclude that, overwhelmingly, the best possible scenario for children is to live in one home with their mother and father. Frequent, heated arguments or any kind of violence are very bad for children. If parents are having these kinds of problems, it is important for them to get help—and some might need to divorce. However, most marriages that end in divorce these days—two-thirds of them—are low-conflict. These troubled marriages offer the best hope for being saved and strengthened for the sake of the children.

If parents must divorce or are already divorced, they should know that no one custody arrangement is right for all children and families. Some children will do better living primarily with one parent, while some may adapt better to spending an equal amount of time with each parent.

Since most people realize that it is important for both parents to stay actively involved in the child's life, many assume that joint physical custody is the best arrangement for children. Only in this arrangement does the child spend substantial amounts of time living in each parent's home. For some children and families, such an arrangement may be the best decision. But, increasingly, some groups are pressing states to make a *presumption* of joint physical custody the law of the land. They don't want this option to be one among many; they want all family court judges to start from the assumption that joint physical custody is best for *every* child. Even in the absence of such a legal presumption, increasing numbers of judges, parents, and experts assume that joint physical custody is the best way to prevent one of the parents from losing out on a relationship with the child.

I find this trend extremely disturbing. When parents advocate for joint physical custody, they usually emphasize the parents' rights to their children. Fathers have a right to equal access to their children, fathers' rights groups argue. And mothers and their advocates predictably retort that mothers should have equal if not greater rights. The debate is tragic. Of course, divorced parents are devastated when they lose the right to have their children in their home all the time, and no one should be surprised that they are angry, grieving, and resentful. But to base custody decisions on adult rights to their children is the absolute worst thing we can do to children of divorce.

Children are not property. They can't be divided like a time-share or a set of heirloom dishes. They are vulnerable, evolving people with specific needs. Among those needs are love, stability, consistent moral guidance, and affirmation of their budding spiritual lives.

As this book has shown, these needs are much less often met when they lack one home with a married mother and father. Divorce requires children to travel between their two parents' worlds. Joint physical custody, in particular, forces them to be almost constantly on the move between those worlds. If anything, a "good divorce" featuring joint physical custody burdens children even more than other types of custody arrangements.

Joint physical custody also demands a great deal of cooperation between parents. The biggest risk may be that forcing all kinds of divorcing parents—even those who are at each other's throats—to attempt joint physical custody will increase animosity and lead to even more very bad divorces, with horrible outcomes for children.

I believe it is wrong and dangerous for any state to pass legislation that forces judges to assume joint physical custody is best for every child and family. Judges and parents should continue to have wide discretion in determining what kind of custody agreement might work best for a particular child's needs. I would also caution divorcing parents to avoid trying to divide their child's time rigidly and equally between their two homes unless the child is old enough to request that arrangement and really mean it.

In this book I have written about children of divorce who stay in touch with both parents, mainly because this situation is what many people envision as the "best case" for children. But this focus has prompted some people to ask me whether the stress I have discovered in children when they travel between their parents' two worlds means that it is better for children of divorce to stay in one world instead. Are those children who lose all contact with a divorced parent, or who very rarely see their other parent, better off?

I might examine this question in the future. For now, I suspect that on average it is no better, and probably much worse, for children of divorce to lose contact completely with a parent—often the father. The deep loss and sense of rejection that comes from feeling abandoned by a father lasts a lifetime. It is a fate I would wish on no one and it is certainly not an alternative that I would recommend for children of divorce.

When we ask whether children of divorce are better off traveling between two worlds or losing one parent altogether, we enter the realm of rating and comparing childhood pain—a sad exercise that yields no sense of victory. Unfortunately, when it comes to the arrangement of postdivorce family life there are no easy answers. What is clear is that most people recognize the deep loss children feel when growing up without a father or mother. Instead of trying to choose among these various, deeply flawed scenarios, we need to focus more energy on the larger question: How can fewer children grow up in divorced families and more children grow up in one secure home?

Strong Marriages

Providing a secure home for our children requires strong, lasting marriages. Having parents who live together is not the same as having married parents. Three-quarters of cohabiting parents break up before their child's sixteenth birthday, so the children of cohabiting parents are in especially unstable situations.

Children of divorce approach marriage with complex, sometimes dissonant emotions—from hope to fear to cynicism. When we achieve a happy marriage, we are thankful for it every day. But at the first sign of conflict, we become numb with anxiety. Many people note that children of divorce have a higher divorce rate themselves, and it is true. But in a divorce culture such as ours, everyone's marriage is made less stable by the presence of widespread divorce.

For years the most-asked question about children of divorce was this: Should unhappily married parents get divorced or stay put for the sake of the children? This is no longer the right question. For one thing, a marriage that is unhappy now might not be unhappy a few years later. For another, divorce is not a sure remedy for unhappiness.

One study showed, for instance, that only a minority of people who are unhappy in their marriages today still feel that way even five years later. Unhappy marriages can and often are turned around when couples learn better communication skills or get helpful counseling, or even when they just stick it out and wait for the stresses that are preying on their marriage to subside. And divorce often brings new, unexpected stresses. The divorce rate for remarriages is quite a bit higher than for first marriages.

If our society is to find a balance, one that recognizes the need for divorce while supporting healthy marriages, we need to make sweeping changes to our thinking about marriage. Currently many people across the country are involved in a growing grassroots "marriage movement" to do just that.

Those of us who are children of divorce are plagued by a legacy that makes it harder to succeed in our own marriages. Yet we also know instinctively that divorce should be a last resort, that even a "good divorce" is far worse than what some call a "good enough" marriage. Barring very serious problems in our marriages, we know from experience that our best chance at happiness, for ourselves and for our children, is to reach out for help when needed and try to stick with the person we fell in love with, forever.

Facing the Truth Squarely

The search for belonging can be especially trying for children of divorce. Both those of us who are now grown and those who are still young would be helped greatly in healing and finding wholeness if the people around us — our families, friends, and colleagues; our teachers, clergy, and counselors; social leaders and policy makers — understood our true experience.

This is the truth about us: Some of us, many more than those from intact families, struggle with serious problems. Our parents' divorce is linked to our higher rates of depression, suicidal attempts and thoughts, health problems, childhood sexual abuse, school drop-out, failure to attend college, arrests, addiction, teen pregnancy, and more. Some of us were practically abandoned to raise our-selves in the wake of our parents' divorce and turned to drugs or alcohol or thrill seeking to numb our pain. Some of us were abused by new adults who came into the house when one of our parents left. Some of us continue to struggle with the scars left from our parents' divorce: we have a harder time finishing school, getting and keeping jobs, maintaining relationships, and having lasting marriages. Though we are suffering, we might seem invisible. We end up living on the margins, struggling with our pain, while our friends and neighbors move on with their lives.

Yet those who are visibly suffering are not the entire story. They're the tip of the iceberg. The others, the ones without seri-ously disabling problems, are everywhere—at your workplace, at school, at church. We don't look much different from anyone else. We might seem a bit more guarded, a bit slower to make new friends, a bit more anxious about life in general. But we do manage to make friends, fall in love, accomplish goals, succeed at work; some of us do quite well.

If you ask any of us about our lives, though, you'll discover that our parents' divorce is central to the story of our childhoods and to who we are today. We grew up too soon. We were not sure where we belonged. We often missed our parents terribly when we were not with them. Some of us longed to be like our parents and yet ago-nized if we resembled one of them too closely. We had to figure things out for ourselves—what is right and wrong, what to believe, whether there is a God. We never knew we could ask for help if we needed it. When we faced struggles, we thought it was up to us alone to make sense of it, because the silence about our childhoods seemed to leave us little other choice.

Those of us who are successful have more in common with the visibly suffering children of divorce than you might think. The fact that we managed to come through it, get jobs, maybe go to college and build careers—these accomplishments do not necessarily imply that our parents handled the divorce better than others. Some children survive devastating experiences and ultimately become stronger for it. Others are broken by the same crises and remain tormented. To look at any of us who survived childhood divorce and conclude that our childhood and the divorce itself must have been "fine" shows little understanding of the enormous losses in our lives or of the capacity of the human spirit to survive and flourish despite adversity.

Those of us who are children of divorce are not all falling apart, but neither are we willing to be held up as proof—convenient proof—that kids don't really need both parents. We needed our mothers and fathers, living together, married to each other, preferably getting along well.

If our parents could not stay together, we needed and deserved to grow up in a society that faced up squarely to our loss, that refused to engage in happy talk, that resisted the temptation to call children resilient in order to defend adult decisions.

We now know what divorce does to children. Let's give the children what they need.

One Secure World

I met Allison at a downtown café on a cool, overcast day. She had just come from caring for her daughter and would soon be off to teach a class at a suburban university. She spent a couple of hours telling me about growing up with divorced parents, losing touch with her father as an adult, then reconnecting with him only weeks before he died in surgery. She told me how much she loved her husband, how he understood her, and how he admired and teased her for being an "Academy Award–winning actress," always able to adapt to any situation.

Allison needed to prepare last-minute notes for class, and I had to travel across town for another interview. As we were wrapping up, I looked at her—a young, attractive woman so quiet and in control, friendly but not bubbly—and thought about the warmth and excitement that rose to the surface whenever she talked about her baby.

"How do you want to raise your daughter?" I asked.

Allison leaned forward, looked me in the eye, and spoke passionately: "I just want her to be a kid. I don't want her to feel responsible for me or my husband." Her voice rose and strengthened as the words poured out. "I want her to feel like she can wake up, and she's in a secure family, and she never has to worry about being bounced around between parents."

Many of us dream of a whole family, unbroken by divorce—a family where our children never even think about the concept of home because they blessedly take it for granted. Where our children stand firmly rooted in our family and look out, with awe and wonder and a little enticing fear, at the world outside.

As I complete this book my seventeen-month-old daughter is toddling around downstairs, chattering happily with her babysitter in tow. I'm weeks away from having our second baby, who they tell us is a boy. My husband of almost eight years has turned out to be a wonderful father, as I never doubted he would be. In my early twenties I wasn't able to imagine a future for myself, but now I see a future bright with hope.

This book is a chance for my generation to tell its story. But even more, it is written with the hope that the children now growing up will benefit from a stronger awareness—among their parents and the culture at large—that it's not enough to love our children. As hard as I know it can be, we parents must also do our best to love and forgive *each other,* every day. We do this so that our children can have what so many of us did not have—a mother and father at home, stability and wholeness as well as love. We do this so that we can sustain unbroken families that last a lifetime, not just for the sake of our own happiness, but for theirs.

Appendix A

**COMPARISON OF "GOOD" AND "BAD" DIVORCES WITH
HAPPY, UNHAPPY AND LOW-CONFLICT, AND UNHAPPY
AND HIGH-CONFLICT MARRIAGES[1]**

| Marriage Was: | PARENTS' MARRIAGE INTACT[2] | | | CHILDREN OF DIVORCE[3] | |
	Very Happy, Low-Conflict	Un-Happy,[4] Low-Conflict	Un-Happy,[4] High-Conflict	"Good" Divorce[5]	"Bad" Divorce[5]
Very happy	72.7	47.8	41.7	57.1	51.1
Very satisfied with life as whole	73.1	56.2	50.0	62.3	54.3
Never divorced (of those ever married)	89.9	86.7	81.8	76.3	82.6
Agreed: Most people can be trusted.	62.7	51.2	39.6	53.2	44.5

Marriage Was:	PARENTS' MARRIAGE INTACT[2]			CHILDREN OF DIVORCE[3]	
	Very Happy, Low-Conflict	Un-Happy,[4] Low-Conflict	Un-Happy,[4] High-Conflict	"Good" Divorce[5]	"Bad" Divorce[5]
Agreed: I don't feel that anyone really understands me.	7.2	17.5	29.2	14.6	30.0
Agreed: I have experienced many losses in my life.	37.0	42.0	52.1	53.2	61.0
Agreed: In my family relationships my own needs have to come first.	16.8	21.0	25.0	20.2	30.9
Agreed: When I have conflict with someone I usually feel it can only get worse, not better.	6.0	11.7	10.7	8.6	20.0
Agreed: I think my understanding of right and wrong is cloudy.	5.2	7.2	8.3	6.1	10.6
Agreed: My parents protected me from their worries.	88.2	81.7	35.4	77.7	45.4

Marriage Was:	PARENTS' MARRIAGE INTACT[2]			CHILDREN OF DIVORCE[3]	
	Very Happy, Low-Conflict	Un-Happy,[4] Low-Conflict	Un-Happy,[4] High-Conflict	"Good" Divorce[5]	"Bad" Divorce[5]
Agreed: My mother's household rules and my father's household rules were the same.	93.7	81.1	60.5	57.7	32.4
Agreed: What my mother said was true and what my father said was true were often two different things.	12.1	24.1	56.5	29.3	78.4
Agreed: At times I felt like an outsider in my home.	6.9	21.8	52.1	19.2	44.6
Agreed: I felt like a different person with each of my parents.	12.4	26.1	47.9	28.7	59.9
Agreed: It was stressful in my family.	6.3	35.2	93.6	51.7	82.3
Agreed: My childhood was filled with playing.	94.8	90.3	77.1	81.2	70.4

Marriage Was:	PARENTS' MARRIAGE INTACT[2]			CHILDREN OF DIVORCE[3]	
	Very Happy, Low-Conflict	Un-Happy,[4] Low-Conflict	Un-Happy,[4] High-Conflict	"Good" Divorce[5]	"Bad" Divorce[5]
Agreed: I always felt like an adult, even when I was a little kid.	36.1	38.6	50.0	50.5	70.2
Agreed: My family was in the habit of sharing a daily meal together.	96.8	89.4	83.3	70.9	64.3
Agreed: Christmas or Hanukkah was a stressful time in my family.	7.5	19.2	26.2	22.3	54.0
Agreed: I often heard stories about my birth.	74.1	61.7	64.6	60.8	58.4
Agreed: I often missed my mother.	15.1	30.8	39.1	25.7	38.0
Agreed: I often missed my father.	31.2	37.6	34.0	55.6	67.8

Marriage Was:	PARENTS' MARRIAGE INTACT[2]			CHILDREN OF DIVORCE[3]	
	Very Happy, Low-Conflict	Un-Happy,[4] Low-Conflict	Un-Happy,[4] High-Conflict	"Good" Divorce[5]	"Bad" Divorce[5]
Agreed: I felt the need to protect my mother emotionally.	23.1	36.4	68.7	44.0	65.8
Agreed: I felt the need to protect my father emotionally.	12.4	17.2	35.4	20.1	42.0
Felt too responsible for taking care of mother	7.7	8.0	39.6	14.7	34.5
Felt too responsible for taking care of father	0.9	4.9	10.4	3.3	16.4
Felt too responsible for taking care of a brother or sister	5.2	17.2	37.5	24.7	40.6
Agreed: I generally felt physically safe.	98.5	96.6	87.5	94.3	83.3
Agreed: I generally felt emotionally safe.	98.9	93.1	60.4	81.9	57.8

Marriage Was:	PARENTS' MARRIAGE INTACT[2]			CHILDREN OF DIVORCE[3]	
	Very Happy, Low-Conflict	Un-Happy,[4] Low-Conflict	Un-Happy,[4] High-Conflict	"Good" Divorce[5]	"Bad" Divorce[5]
Agreed: Children were the center of my family.	93.7	86.5	79.2	77.1	57.8
Agreed: I was alone a lot as a child.	4.9	20.6	41.6	30.2	59.9
Agreed: Sometimes I felt like I didn't have a home.	0.0	5.7	20.9	8.9	29.4
Agreed: At times I feared being homeless.	1.2	5.7	14.6	4.7	5.1

1. Cases with "don't know" and "no response" codes are omitted from the base for the percentages. Measures used to determine parental marital situation were reported retrospectively by the adult child respondent.
2. When the respondent was age fourteen.
3. People who did not see both parents at least once a year after the parents separated until the people were age eighteen or left home are excluded from the study.
4. Parental marriages not reported to be "very happy" are considered unhappy.
5. If the respondent reported "a lot" of postdivorce parental conflict, being kidnapped by a parent, being told he or she might be kidnapped, parental requests to keep secrets from the other parent, and/or having to take sides in parental conflict, the divorce is classified as "bad." All other divorces are classified as "good."

Appendix B

FULL SURVEY DATA

All numbers are percentages.

1. Taking all things together, how would you say things are these days? Would you say you're

	DIVORCED FAMILY	INTACT FAMILY
Very happy	53.5	58.9
Pretty happy	42.1	37.5
Not too happy	3.6	3.2
Don't know/refused	0.8	0.4

2. How satisfied are you with your life as a whole? Would you say you are

	DIVORCED FAMILY	INTACT FAMILY
Very satisfied	58.3	63.8
Somewhat satisfied	36.6	33.8
Somewhat dissatisfied	4.2	1.9
Very dissatisfied	0.7	0.5
Don't know/refused	0.3	0.0

Questions 3–17, 45–55, and 102–10 were phrased "after the divorce" for those from a divorced family.

3. My parents protected me from their worries.

	DIVORCED FAMILY	INTACT FAMILY
Strongly agree	31.1	51.1
Somewhat agree	31.8	30.3
Somewhat disagree	22.0	12.1
Strongly disagree	14.7	6.4
Don't know/refused	0.4	0.1

4. My parents seemed like polar opposites of each other.

	DIVORCED FAMILY	INTACT FAMILY
Strongly agree	41.6	11.7
Somewhat agree	24.6	22.6
Somewhat disagree	18.0	22.4
Strongly disagree	15.2	42.6
Don't know/refused	0.5	0.7

5. At times one of my parents would ask me to keep important secrets from the other parent.

	DIVORCED FAMILY	INTACT FAMILY
Strongly agree	12.8	4.0
Somewhat agree	14.3	5.6
Somewhat disagree	11.1	6.4
Strongly disagree	60.8	83.8
Don't know/refused	0.9	0.3

6. It would upset me if one parent said I looked or acted like the other parent.

	DIVORCED FAMILY	INTACT FAMILY
Strongly agree	15.2	4.4
Somewhat agree	12.5	10.5
Somewhat disagree	14.7	15.9
Strongly disagree	54.8	67.9
Don't know/refused	2.8	1.3

7. At times I felt like an outsider in my home.

	DIVORCED FAMILY	INTACT FAMILY
Strongly agree	14.0	4.0
Somewhat agree	16.4	12.8
Somewhat disagree	13.0	13.0
Strongly disagree	56.2	70.1
Don't know/refused	0.4	0.1

8. What my mother said was true and what my father said was true were often two different things.

	DIVORCED FAMILY	INTACT FAMILY
Strongly agree	26.8	5.4
Somewhat agree	24.5	14.6
Somewhat disagree	17.9	20.4
Strongly disagree	28.9	58.3
Don't know/refused	2.0	1.3

9. I felt like a different person with each of my parents.

	DIVORCED FAMILY	INTACT FAMILY
Strongly agree	20.4	7.5
Somewhat agree	22.6	13.5
Somewhat disagree	19.3	18.9
Strongly disagree	36.6	58.9
Don't know/refused	1.1	1.1

10. It was stressful in my family.

	DIVORCED FAMILY	INTACT FAMILY
Strongly agree	33.8	6.5
Somewhat agree	30.6	18.9
Somewhat disagree	16.7	18.0
Strongly disagree	17.9	56.3
Don't know/refused	1.1	0.3

11. I always felt like an adult, even when I was a little kid.

	DIVORCED FAMILY	INTACT FAMILY
Strongly agree	32.2	16.3
Somewhat agree	26.2	21.6
Somewhat disagree	17.2	21.7
Strongly disagree	24.0	39.3
Don't know/refused	0.4	1.1

12. My childhood was filled with playing.

	DIVORCED FAMILY	INTACT FAMILY
Strongly agree	43.0	69.8
Somewhat agree	32.1	21.7
Somewhat disagree	13.0	4.5
Strongly disagree	10.3	4.0
Don't know/refused	1.6	0.0

13. My mother's household rules and my father's household rules were the same.

	DIVORCED FAMILY	INTACT FAMILY
Strongly agree	19.3	63.6
Somewhat agree	24.8	21.7
Somewhat disagree	21.7	8.1
Strongly disagree	32.2	6.4
Don't know/refused	2.0	0.3

14. I had to take sides in my parents' conflicts.

	DIVORCED FAMILY	INTACT FAMILY
Strongly agree	14.3	3.4
Somewhat agree	17.4	7.9
Somewhat disagree	16.6	9.5
Strongly disagree	51.4	78.5
Don't know/refused	0.4	0.5

15. When my parents had conflicts I always knew they would get over it.

	DIVORCED FAMILY	INTACT FAMILY
Strongly agree	26.6	74.2
Somewhat agree	31.1	17.6
Somewhat disagree	18.9	4.2
Strongly disagree	18.3	3.2
Don't know/refused	5.0	0.8

16. I felt the need to protect my mother emotionally.

	DIVORCED FAMILY	INTACT FAMILY
Strongly agree	23.3	12.3
Somewhat agree	29.0	20.3
Somewhat disagree	18.5	17.1
Strongly disagree	28.1	49.9
Don't know/refused	1.1	0.4

17. I felt the need to protect my father emotionally.

	DIVORCED FAMILY	INTACT FAMILY
Strongly agree	11.3	6.9
Somewhat agree	18.3	11.0
Somewhat disagree	19.1	14.6
Strongly disagree	50.6	67.0
Don't know/refused	0.8	0.5

18. When you were growing up, did you feel too responsible for taking care of your mother?

	DIVORCED FAMILY	INTACT FAMILY
Yes	23.7	6.9
No	76.3	93.0
Don't know/refused	0.0	0.1

19. When you were growing up, did you feel too responsible for taking care of your father?

	DIVORCED FAMILY	INTACT FAMILY
Yes	8.9	3.0
No	91.1	96.6
Don't know/refused	0.0	0.4

20. When you were growing up, did you feel too responsible for taking care of your brother or sister?

	DIVORCED FAMILY	INTACT FAMILY
Yes	29.8	12.7
No	63.7	85.2
I am the only child	6.2	2.0
Don't know/refused	0.3	0.1

21. My mother and I share similar moral values.

	DIVORCED FAMILY	INTACT FAMILY
Strongly agree	55.1	70.1
Somewhat agree	27.4	23.7
Somewhat disagree	10.2	4.5
Strongly disagree	7.0	1.7
Don't know/refused	0.3	0.0

22. My mother is a good person.

	DIVORCED FAMILY	INTACT FAMILY
Strongly agree	83.3	95.6
Somewhat agree	13.4	4.1
Somewhat disagree	1.7	0.1
Strongly disagree	1.3	0.1
Don't know/refused	0.3	0.0

23. My mother taught me clearly the difference between right and wrong.

	DIVORCED FAMILY	INTACT FAMILY
Strongly agree	68.9	89.1
Somewhat agree	18.8	9.5
Somewhat disagree	7.2	0.7
Strongly disagree	4.8	0.7
Don't know/refused	0.4	0.0

24. I love my mother but I don't respect her.

	DIVORCED FAMILY	INTACT FAMILY
Strongly agree	5.7	1.7
Somewhat agree	13.2	4.5
Somewhat disagree	8.9	4.2
Strongly disagree	71.8	88.6
Don't know/refused	0.4	0.9

25. My father and I share similar moral values.

	DIVORCED FAMILY	INTACT FAMILY
Strongly agree	45.0	68.7
Somewhat agree	29.7	24.4
Somewhat disagree	12.2	5.0
Strongly disagree	12.1	1.7
Don't know/refused	1.1	0.1

26. My father is a good person.

	DIVORCED FAMILY	INTACT FAMILY
Strongly agree	70.9	92.2
Somewhat agree	22.1	7.5
Somewhat disagree	3.2	0.0
Strongly disagree	3.3	0.1
Don't know/refused	0.5	0.1

27. My father taught me clearly the difference
    between right and wrong.

	DIVORCED FAMILY	INTACT FAMILY
Strongly agree	52.3	85.0
Somewhat agree	24.6	11.7
Somewhat disagree	12.6	2.4
Strongly disagree	10.2	0.7
Don't know/refused	0.3	0.3

28. I love my father but I don't respect him.

	DIVORCED FAMILY	INTACT FAMILY
Strongly agree	11.5	2.0
Somewhat agree	14.0	4.6
Somewhat disagree	12.1	4.6
Strongly disagree	61.3	87.4
Don't know/refused	1.1	1.3

29. When I have a conflict with someone I usually feel
    it can only get worse, not better.

	DIVORCED FAMILY	INTACT FAMILY
Strongly agree	3.4	1.5
Somewhat agree	10.2	7.4
Somewhat disagree	20.4	20.7
Strongly disagree	65.6	70.1
Don't know/refused	0.4	0.4

30. I think my understanding of right and wrong is cloudy.

	DIVORCED FAMILY	INTACT FAMILY
Strongly agree	3.2	2.5
Somewhat agree	4.6	4.0
Somewhat disagree	10.2	9.4
Strongly disagree	81.9	83.8
Don't know/refused	0.1	0.3

31. In family relationships my own needs have to come first.

	DIVORCED FAMILY	INTACT FAMILY
Strongly agree	7.0	4.5
Somewhat agree	17.1	14.4
Somewhat disagree	26.5	26.1
Strongly disagree	49.1	54.2
Don't know/refused	0.3	0.8

32. At any time in the years after the divorce were you asked to choose which parent to live with?

	DIVORCED FAMILY
Yes	33.6
No	65.7
Don't know/refused	0.7

33. If you answered No to question 32: At any time in the years after the divorce did you want to have the choice about which parent to live with?

	DIVORCED FAMILY
Yes	34.5
No	64.1
Don't know/refused	1.4

34. What religion, if any, were you raised in?

	DIVORCED FAMILY	INTACT FAMILY
Protestant	36.0	37.6
Catholic	26.1	31.7
Jewish	2.0	1.7
Muslim/Islam	1.6	1.2
Mormon	2.1	2.5
Orthodox Church	0.1	0.3
Other Christian religion	16.3	12.7
Other religion (not Christian)	0.3	2.6
None/no preference	13.9	8.9
Atheist/agnostic	0.7	0.7
Don't know/refused	0.9	0.1

35. Did you attend religious services when you were a child?

	DIVORCED FAMILY	INTACT FAMILY
Yes	85.7	88.9
No	13.8	11.1
Don't know/refused	0.5	0.0

If you answered Yes to 35:

36. Thinking about the period in your childhood when you attended religious services most often, how often did you attend?

	DIVORCED FAMILY	INTACT FAMILY
Almost never	5.7	1.6
Occasionally but less than once a month	15.9	9.1
One to three times per month	22.3	15.8
Every week/almost every week	55.8	73.5
Don't know/refused	0.3	0.0

37. What was the period during childhood when you attended religious services most frequently?

	DIVORCED FAMILY	INTACT FAMILY
Before age 7	19.2	14.2
Ages 8 to 11	40.2	27.4
Age 12 or older	20.9	16.4
I attended frequently throughout my childhood	19.0	41.3
Don't know/refused	0.8	0.7

38. What is your religious preference today?

	DIVORCED FAMILY	INTACT FAMILY
Protestant	32.2	32.7
Catholic	19.2	25.7
Jewish	1.7	1.5
Muslim/Islam	0.8	1.1
Mormon	1.5	2.5
Orthodox Church	0.5	0.3
Other Christian religion	18.0	13.5
Other religion (not Christian)	1.6	2.6
None/no preference	18.7	14.7
Atheist/agnostic	4.0	3.8
Don't know/refused	1.9	1.6

39. Would you describe yourself as a "born-again"
    or evangelical Christian, or not?

	DIVORCED FAMILY	INTACT FAMILY
Yes	41.3	36.8
No	54.6	60.0
Don't know/refused	4.2	3.2

40. How religious do you currently consider yourself to be?

	DIVORCED FAMILY	INTACT FAMILY
Very religious	19.7	27.2
Fairly religious	35.4	40.3
Slightly religious	30.9	21.9
Not religious at all	13.2	9.8
Don't know/refused	0.8	0.8

41. How spiritual do you currently consider yourself to be?

	DIVORCED FAMILY	INTACT FAMILY
Very spiritual	30.9	33.2
Fairly spiritual	39.3	39.9
Slightly spiritual	22.0	20.8
Not spiritual at all	7.3	5.3
Don't know/refused	0.5	0.8

42. Aside from weddings and funerals, how often
    do you attend religious services?

	DIVORCED FAMILY	INTACT FAMILY
Never or almost never	29.9	21.3
Occasionally but less than once a month	29.8	25.2
One to three times per month	15.9	18.0
Every week/almost every week	24.2	35.4
Don't know/refused	0.1	0.1

43. Are you currently a member at a place of worship?

	DIVORCED FAMILY	INTACT FAMILY
Yes	48.7	62.6
No	50.7	36.7
I do not have a place of worship	0.4	0.4
Don't know/refused	0.1	0.3

44. Do you hold any leadership positions at a place of worship?

	DIVORCED FAMILY	INTACT FAMILY
Yes	10.2	14.6
No	89.3	85.2
I do not have a place of worship	0.5	0.3

45. My family was in the habit of sharing a daily meal together.

	DIVORCED FAMILY	INTACT FAMILY
Strongly agree	42.6	77.9
Somewhat agree	24.8	14.4
Somewhat disagree	10.1	3.7
Strongly disagree	21.7	3.8
Don't know/refused	0.8	0.1

46. Christmas or Hanukkah was a stressful time in my family.

	DIVORCED FAMILY	INTACT FAMILY
Strongly agree	18.1	6.0
Somewhat agree	18.1	8.6
Somewhat disagree	14.6	13.4
Strongly disagree	48.9	70.7
Don't know/refused	0.3	1.3

47. I often heard stories about my birth.

	DIVORCED FAMILY	INTACT FAMILY
Strongly agree	25.7	38.4
Somewhat agree	33.8	28.9
Somewhat disagree	15.8	15.2
Strongly disagree	24.6	17.1
Don't know/refused	0.1	0.4

48. I often missed my mother.

	DIVORCED FAMILY	INTACT FAMILY
Strongly agree	15.1	12.8
Somewhat agree	16.6	15.5
Somewhat disagree	12.3	11.3
Strongly disagree	55.4	59.1
Don't know/refused	0.7	1.3

49. I often missed my father.

	DIVORCED FAMILY	INTACT FAMILY
Strongly agree	28.1	14.0
Somewhat agree	33.0	20.1
Somewhat disagree	14.0	16.7
Strongly disagree	24.4	47.9
Don't know/refused	0.5	1.2

50. My mother encouraged me to practice a religious faith.

	DIVORCED FAMILY	INTACT FAMILY
Strongly agree	33.0	54.7
Somewhat agree	23.8	23.3
Somewhat disagree	13.5	7.9
Strongly disagree	29.4	14.0
Don't know/refused	0.3	0.0

51. My father encouraged me to practice a religious faith.

	DIVORCED FAMILY	INTACT FAMILY
Strongly agree	16.2	40.5
Somewhat agree	14.8	23.0
Somewhat disagree	13.5	13.6
Strongly disagree	54.7	22.6
Don't know/refused	0.8	0.1

52. My mother taught me how to pray.

	DIVORCED FAMILY	INTACT FAMILY
Strongly agree	22.5	40.1
Somewhat agree	18.5	29.3
Somewhat disagree	14.4	11.1
Strongly disagree	42.8	18.5
Don't know/refused	1.7	0.9

53. My father taught me how to pray.

	DIVORCED FAMILY	INTACT FAMILY
Strongly agree	7.4	23.4
Somewhat agree	9.8	23.2
Somewhat disagree	12.3	17.6
Strongly disagree	68.9	35.1
Don't know/refused	1.6	0.7

54. I often prayed with my mother.

	DIVORCED FAMILY	INTACT FAMILY
Strongly agree	13.5	26.0
Somewhat agree	22.0	27.5
Somewhat disagree	15.2	16.4
Strongly disaqree	49.0	29.8
Don't know/refused	0.3	0.3

55. I often prayed with my father.

	DIVORCED FAMILY	INTACT FAMILY
Strongly agree	6.2	18.1
Somewhat agree	9.8	22.3
Somewhat disagree	12.6	18.8
Strongly disagree	71.0	40.5
Don't know/refused	0.4	0.3

56. I worry about what will happen to me when I die.

	DIVORCED FAMILY	INTACT FAMILY
Strongly agree	9.3	7.3
Somewhat agree	17.6	17.7
Somewhat disagree	17.2	15.1
Strongly disagree	55.4	59.5
Don't know/refused	0.5	0.4

57. I feel that I can depend on my friends more than my family.

	DIVORCED FAMILY	INTACT FAMILY
Strongly agree	9.4	3.7
Somewhat agree	13.9	8.7
Somewhat disagree	23.7	21.1
Strongly disagree	52.3	65.8
Don't know/refused	0.7	0.7

58. My parents have told me they got married too young.

	DIVORCED FAMILY	INTACT FAMILY
Strongly agree	25.4	5.0
Somewhat agree	13.9	6.8
Somewhat disagree	10.2	7.7
Strongly disagree	48.9	80.4
Don't know/refused	1.6	0.1

59. My parents have told me that my or my sibling's birth
    was an accident or a surprise.

	DIVORCED FAMILY	INTACT FAMILY
Strongly agree	18.7	10.1
Somewhat agree	8.9	8.6
Somewhat disagree	5.6	4.0
Strongly disagree	66.1	77.1
Don't know/refused	0.8	0.3

60. I have experienced many losses in my life.

	DIVORCED FAMILY	INTACT FAMILY
Strongly agree	24.0	15.4
Somewhat agree	32.6	24.5
Somewhat disagree	22.4	24.0
Strongly disagree	20.9	35.9
Don't know/refused	0.1	0.3

61. Religion doesn't seem to address the important issues in my life.

	DIVORCED FAMILY	INTACT FAMILY
Strongly agree	15.0	10.9
Somewhat agree	22.1	18.4
Somewhat disagree	20.4	21.7
Strongly disagree	41.3	48.2
Don't know/refused	1.2	0.8

62. I don't feel that anyone really understands me.

	DIVORCED FAMILY	INTACT FAMILY
Strongly agree	6.1	2.4
Somewhat agree	15.9	11.1
Somewhat disagree	22.1	23.3
Strongly disagree	55.6	63.0
Don't know/refused	0.3	0.1

63. My spirituality has been strengthened by adversity in my life.

	DIVORCED FAMILY	INTACT FAMILY
Strongly agree	43.7	37.5
Somewhat agree	30.5	34.3
Somewhat disagree	12.7	12.5
Strongly disagree	11.7	14.6
Don't know/refused	1.5	1.2

64. I believe I can find ultimate truth without help from a religion.

	DIVORCED FAMILY	INTACT FAMILY
Strongly agree	23.3	16.4
Somewhat agree	22.5	19.3
Somewhat disagree	18.7	19.3
Strongly disagree	34.4	44.0
Don't know/refused	1.1	0.9

65. I think I am more religious now than my mother ever was.

	DIVORCED FAMILY	INTACT FAMILY
Strongly agree	15.1	6.9
Somewhat agree	16.3	8.3
Somewhat disagree	21.3	21.9
Strongly disagree	46.1	61.5
Don't know/refused	1.2	1.5

66. I doubt the sincerity of my mother's religious beliefs.

	DIVORCED FAMILY	INTACT FAMILY
Strongly agree	7.7	2.6
Somewhat agree	11.0	6.6
Somewhat disagree	17.9	12.8
Strongly disagree	60.7	76.6
Don't know/refused	2.8	1.3

67. There are things my mother has done that I find hard to forgive.

	DIVORCED FAMILY	INTACT FAMILY
Strongly agree	19.9	3.3
Somewhat agree	17.7	9.5
Somewhat disagree	14.8	10.9
Strongly disagree	47.5	76.2
Don't know/refused	0.0	0.1

68. I think I am more religious now than my father ever was.

	DIVORCED FAMILY	INTACT FAMILY
Strongly agree	29.9	13.5
Somewhat agree	17.0	15.0
Somewhat disagree	19.5	20.9
Strongly disagree	31.5	48.9
Don't know/refused	2.1	1.7

69. I doubt the sincerity of my father's religious beliefs.

	DIVORCED FAMILY	INTACT FAMILY
Strongly agree	12.5	3.4
Somewhat agree	14.6	10.2
Somewhat disagree	19.9	15.9
Strongly disagree	48.2	68.9
Don't know/refused	4.9	1.6

70. There are things my father has done that I find hard to forgive.

	DIVORCED FAMILY	INTACT FAMILY
Strongly agree	26.4	6.2
Somewhat agree	24.5	10.6
Somewhat disagree	14.4	11.7
Strongly disagree	34.6	71.4
Don't know/refused	0.1	0.1

71. In general, would you say most people can be trusted or you can't be too careful in life?

	DIVORCED FAMILY	INTACT FAMILY
Most people can be trusted	48.7	54.8
Can't be too careful	48.9	42.3
Other, depends	1.7	1.3
Don't know/refused	0.7	1.6

72. In thinking back on your childhood (or childhood after the divorce), when you needed comfort, what did you do?

	DIVORCED FAMILY	INTACT FAMILY
Went to my mom	22.0	27.9
Went to my parents	7.8	37.6
Went to my dad	3.2	3.0
Other	8.5	3.4
Went to my siblings	9.7	2.3
Went to my friends	11.5	4.2
Went to my grandparents	6.8	1.3
Prayed	4.2	3.7
Went to family (unspecified)	0.9	1.6
Went to pets	1.2	0.5
Dealt with it myself/ alone/nothing	5.6	3.4

	DIVORCED FAMILY	INTACT FAMILY
Played sports/games/ with toys	3.3	1.9
Read books/listened to music	3.6	1.7
Cried	0.9	0.5
Don't know/refused	10.9	6.8

73. Would you say God is all-powerful?

	DIVORCED FAMILY	INTACT FAMILY
Strongly agree	72.8	75.0
Somewhat agree	14.4	14.4
Somewhat disagree	2.9	5.4
Strongly disagree	6.6	3.4
Don't know/refused	3.2	1.7

74. Would you say God is caring?

	DIVORCED FAMILY	INTACT FAMILY
Strongly agree	79.1	82.3
Somewhat agree	12.6	11.5
Somewhat disagree	1.9	1.7
Strongly disagree	3.4	2.4
Don't know/refused	3.0	2.1

75. Would you say God loves us unconditionally?

	DIVORCED FAMILY	INTACT FAMILY
Strongly agree	78.8	79.7
Somewhat agree	11.8	11.7
Somewhat disagree	1.5	2.9
Strongly disagree	4.5	2.9
Don't know/refused	3.4	2.8

76. Would you say God does not exist?

	DIVORCED FAMILY	INTACT FAMILY
Strongly agree	4.4	3.6
Somewhat agree	5.7	3.4
Somewhat disagree	8.7	8.7
Strongly disagree	78.7	82.1
Don't know/refused	2.5	2.1

77. Would you say God is angry?

	DIVORCED FAMILY	INTACT FAMILY
Strongly agree	5.0	3.8
Somewhat agree	12.6	11.0
Somewhat disagree	17.0	17.5
Strongly disagree	62.1	65.3
Don't know/refused	3.3	2.4

78. Would you say God is just?

	DIVORCED FAMILY	INTACT FAMILY
Strongly agree	65.4	69.8
Somewhat agree	19.3	17.7
Somewhat disagree	4.5	4.5
Strongly disagree	6.0	3.7
Don't know/refused	4.8	4.2

79. Would you say God is absent?

	DIVORCED FAMILY	INTACT FAMILY
Strongly agree	5.7	4.8
Somewhat agree	11.8	7.7
Somewhat disagree	11.9	12.8
Strongly disagree	67.2	72.2
Don't know/refused	3.4	2.5

80. Would you say God is conniving?

	DIVORCED FAMILY	INTACT FAMILY
Strongly agree	1.7	0.8
Somewhat agree	2.6	2.3
Somewhat disagree	7.4	6.8
Strongly disagree	83.7	86.2
Don't know/refused	4.5	4.0

81. Would you say God is compassionate?

	DIVORCED FAMILY	INTACT FAMILY
Strongly agree	74.7	79.5
Somewhat agree	16.0	13.6
Somewhat disagree	2.3	2.1
Strongly disagree	4.0	2.3
Don't know/refused	3.0	2.5

82. Would you say God is like a friend?

	DIVORCED FAMILY	INTACT FAMILY
Strongly agree	64.9	66.1
Somewhat agree	21.1	19.9
Somewhat disagree	5.0	6.5
Strongly disagree	5.8	5.3
Don't know/refused	3.2	2.3

83. Would you say God is like a father?

	DIVORCED FAMILY	INTACT FAMILY
Strongly agree	56.3	60.7
Somewhat agree	24.6	22.4
Somewhat disagree	6.5	6.9
Strongly disagree	9.4	7.8
Don't know/refused	3.2	2.3

84. Would you say God is like a mother?

	DIVORCED FAMILY	INTACT FAMILY
Strongly agree	39.5	41.9
Somewhat agree	30.7	28.9
Somewhat disagree	11.3	12.6
Strongly disagree	14.2	13.6
Don't know/refused	4.4	3.0

85. Would you say God is forgiving?

	DIVORCED FAMILY	INTACT FAMILY
Strongly agree	79.9	82.5
Somewhat agree	11.3	12.1
Somewhat disagree	1.9	0.9
Strongly disagree	3.6	2.6
Don't know/refused	3.4	1.9

86. Because there is so much suffering in the world
    I find it hard to believe in God.

	DIVORCED FAMILY	INTACT FAMILY
Strongly agree	4.8	3.7
Somewhat agree	12.7	10.5
Somewhat disagree	14.6	11.5
Strongly disagree	66.1	73.4
Don't know/refused	1.9	0.9

87. I sometimes feel the presence of God.

	DIVORCED FAMILY	INTACT FAMILY
Strongly agree	45.2	46.5
Somewhat agree	33.6	32.1
Somewhat disagree	9.7	9.8
Strongly disagree	9.7	9.8
Don't know/refused	1.9	1.9

88. I think of God as the loving father or parent I never had in real life.

	DIVORCED FAMILY	INTACT FAMILY
Strongly agree	18.1	9.8
Somewhat agree	20.1	12.6
Somewhat disagree	22.8	21.5
Strongly disagree	35.2	52.5
Don't know/refused	3.7	3.7

89. When I think about bad things that have happened in my life I find it hard to believe in a God who cares.

	DIVORCED FAMILY	INTACT FAMILY
Strongly agree	5.3	3.3
Somewhat agree	14.4	10.1
Somewhat disagree	12.3	16.0
Strongly disagree	65.7	69.0
Don't know/refused	2.3	1.6

90. I feel like a member of God's family.

	DIVORCED FAMILY	INTACT FAMILY
Strongly agree	56.7	60.8
Somewhat agree	26.8	24.1
Somewhat disagree	6.1	6.1
Strongly disagree	8.2	6.8
Don't know/refused	2.3	2.3

91. The hardships in my life come from God.

	DIVORCED FAMILY	INTACT FAMILY
Strongly agree	7.7	6.0
Somewhat agree	14.6	11.1
Somewhat disagree	13.2	15.9
Strongly disagree	61.7	65.7
Don't know/refused	2.8	1.3

92. When I have needed help God has been there for me.

	DIVORCED FAMILY	INTACT FAMILY
Strongly agree	53.6	56.0
Somewhat agree	27.7	28.1
Somewhat disagree	7.4	7.9
Strongly disagree	8.1	6.0
Don't know/refused	3.2	2.0

Answer 93–94 only if you responded "One to three times a month" or "Every week/almost every week" to 36.

93. When your parents were going through a divorce, did a member of the clergy—such as a priest, pastor or rabbi—reach out to you?

	DIVORCED FAMILY
Yes	23.4
No	66.3
I was too young to know	8.5
Don't know/refused	1.8

94. When your parents were going through a divorce, did someone from the congregation reach out to you?

	DIVORCED FAMILY
Yes	25.0
No	65.1
I was too young to know	7.3
Don't know/refused	2.6

95. After your parents' divorce your attendance at a place of worship was

	DIVORCED FAMILY
More frequent	21.6
Less frequent	19.9
Stayed the same	54.0
I never attended a place of worship at all	1.5
I was too young to remember	2.6
Don't know/refused	0.4

96. When you were a teenager did you become

	DIVORCED FAMILY	INTACT FAMILY
More religious	20.7	19.1
Less religious	37.6	35.5
Stayed the same	40.5	44.8
I was never religious at all	0.8	0.5
Don't know/refused	0.4	0.1

97. Looking back, do you think your parents' divorce made you

	DIVORCED FAMILY
More religious	10.7
Less religious	6.0
Neither more nor less religious	81.9
I was never religious at all	0.3
I was too young to remember	0.9
Don't know/refused	0.3

98. Did you pray when you were a child?

	DIVORCED FAMILY	INTACT FAMILY
Yes	81.9	86.1
No	16.4	13.6
Don't know/refused	1.7	0.3

Answer 99–100 only if you responded Yes to 98.

99. Thinking about the period in your childhood when you prayed most often, how often did you pray?

	DIVORCED FAMILY	INTACT FAMILY
Every day	52.1	59.1
Once or twice a week	28.5	28.9
A few times a month	13.4	9.1
Hardly ever	5.2	2.5
Don't know/refused	0.8	0.5

100. Which of the following best describes your practice
of prayer as a child?

	DIVORCED FAMILY	INTACT FAMILY
It was an obligation	14.7	20.3
It was a source of comfort	54.7	50.5
None of these	29.3	28.0
Don't know/refused	1.3	1.2

101. In your life now, which of the following best describes
your practice of prayer?

	DIVORCED FAMILY	INTACT FAMILY
Prayer is a regular part of my life	48.2	52.7
I usually pray in times of stress or need but rarely any other time	29.1	24.5
I usually pray in formal ceremonies	7.7	11.0
I never pray	13.6	10.6
Don't know/refused	1.3	1.2

102. I generally felt physically safe.

	DIVORCED FAMILY	INTACT FAMILY
Strongly agree	73.4	89.0
Somewhat agree	15.8	7.8
Somewhat disagree	6.0	1.2
Strongly disagree	4.6	1.9
Don't know/refused	0.3	0.1

103. Children were at the center of my family.

	DIVORCED FAMILY	INTACT FAMILY
Strongly agree	33.6	63.4
Somewhat agree	32.6	26.0
Somewhat disagree	16.2	6.2
Strongly disagree	14.4	3.6
Don't know/refused	3.2	0.8

104. I was alone a lot as a child.

	DIVORCED FAMILY	INTACT FAMILY
Strongly agree	21.2	3.3
Somewhat agree	22.9	11.1
Somewhat disagree	11.9	8.6
Strongly disagree	43.7	77.0
Don't know/refused	0.3	0.0

105. Sometimes I felt like I didn't have a home.

	DIVORCED FAMILY	INTACT FAMILY
Strongly agree	5.6	0.7
Somewhat agree	12.5	3.4
Somewhat disagree	9.3	3.4
Strongly disagree	72.2	92.5
Don't know/refused	0.5	0.0

106. At times one of my parents suggested my other parent might try to kidnap me or my sibling.

	DIVORCED FAMILY	INTACT FAMILY
Strongly agree	2.8	0.3
Somewhat agree	3.7	0.0
Somewhat disagree	3.4	0.9
Strongly disagree	89.7	98.8
Don't know/refused	0.4	0.0

107. I generally felt emotionally safe.

	DIVORCED FAMILY	INTACT FAMILY
Strongly agree	43.6	78.8
Somewhat agree	27.8	15.0
Somewhat disagree	17.4	4.2
Strongly disagree	10.9	2.0
Don't know/refused	0.4	0.0

108. At times I feared being homeless.

	DIVORCED FAMILY	INTACT FAMILY
Strongly agree	3.0	1.2
Somewhat agree	6.1	2.9
Somewhat disagree	6.1	3.0
Strongly disagree	84.2	92.8
Don't know/refused	0.5	0.0

109. I felt like I had two families.

	DIVORCED FAMILY
Strongly agree	35.5
Somewhat agree	27.4
Somewhat disagree	12.1
Strongly disagree	24.6
Don't know/refused	0.4

110. I felt like I had two homes.

	DIVORCED FAMILY
Strongly agree	38.0
Somewhat agree	20.3
Somewhat disagree	12.8
Strongly disagree	28.5
Don't know/refused	0.4

111. Before you and your siblings reached the age of 18, was there ever a time in which you lived in separate households?

	DIVORCED FAMILY
Yes	44.5
No	49.1
I was the only child	6.1
Don't know/refused	0.3

112. When you were growing up did you ever run away from home?

	DIVORCED FAMILY	INTACT FAMILY
Yes	16.8	12.6
No	82.9	87.4
Don't know/refused	0.3	0.0

113. When you were growing up were you ever kicked out of the house?

	DIVORCED FAMILY	INTACT FAMILY
Yes	13.6	3.6
No	86.2	96.4
Don't know/refused	0.1	0.0

114. When you were growing up were you ever kidnapped or abducted by one of your parents?

	DIVORCED FAMILY	INTACT FAMILY
Yes	2.9	0.4
No	96.8	99.6
Don't know/refused	0.3	0.0

115. After the divorce, which place felt like home for you?

	DIVORCED FAMILY
Your mother's home	53.8
Your father's home	11.9
Both your mother's and your father's homes	26.9
Somewhere else	3.4
Nowhere felt like home	3.4
Don't know/refused	0.5

116. Before your parents' divorce, how would you have rated their marriage overall?

	DIVORCED FAMILY
Very happy	5.6
Pretty happy	28.5
Not too happy	43.7
I was too young to remember	14.6
Don't know/refused	7.7

117. In the year or so before your parents separated, how much conflict did they have?

	DIVORCED FAMILY
A lot	30.6
Some	26.4
Not much	7.3
Almost none	12.6
I was too young to remember	20.0
Don't know/refused	3.2

118. In the two or three years after your parents divorced, how much conflict did they have?

	DIVORCED FAMILY
A lot	20.3
Some	28.3
Not much	19.2
Almost none	25.7
I was too young to remember	4.4
Don't know/refused	2.1

119. After your parents' divorce, did you

	DIVORCED FAMILY
Live primarily with your mother	72.5
Live primarily with your father	13.2
Spend about the same amount of time living with both parents	11.1
Have another living arrangement	2.8
Don't know/refused	0.4

120. How would you rate your parents' marriage overall during the years that you lived with them?

	INTACT FAMILY
Very happy	46.9
Pretty happy	45.3
Not too happy	7.4
Don't know/refused	0.4

121. When you were living at home with your parents, how much conflict did they have? Take into account such things as quarreling, shouting, and physically fighting.

	INTACT FAMILY
A lot	6.9
Some	24.4
Not much	26.5
Almost none	41.9
I was too young to remember	0.1
Don't know/refused	0.3

122. Did you ever think that your parents might separate or divorce?

	INTACT FAMILY
Yes	27.5
No	72.1
Don't know/refused	0.4

Appendix B

123. What is your marital status?

	DIVORCED FAMILY	INTACT FAMILY
Married	57.9	62.5
Living with a partner	6.4	3.8
Single/never married	26.5	29.3
Divorced	7.2	3.4
Separated	1.5	0.8
Widowed	0.1	0.1
Don't know/refused	0.5	0.0

If you answered "married" to 123:

124. Taking all things together, how would you describe your marriage?

	DIVORCED FAMILY	INTACT FAMILY
Very happy	71.6	66.9
Pretty happy	26.8	31.4
Not too happy	1.6	1.3
Don't know/refused	0.0	0.4

125. Have you ever been divorced?

	DIVORCED FAMILY	INTACT FAMILY
Yes	11.6	7.7
No	87.6	91.9
Don't know/refused	0.8	0.4

Demographic data and detailed information on survey methodology and analysis available by visiting www.betweentwoworlds.org.

Notes

Introduction

2   **Project on the Moral and Spiritual Lives:** Study participants from divorced families were required to have seen both parents a minimum
of once a year in the years following the divorce, but often they had
much more contact than that. None of the participants had experienced the death of a parent before they themselves were eighteen
years old, nor were any of them adopted. "Intact" family means the
participant's parents got married before he or she was born, stayed
married, and are still married today, unless one or both died after the
participant turned eighteen. We did not recruit those whose parents
divorced after the participant turned fourteen because our intent was
to study those who spent at least some of their childhood years in a
postdivorce family.

Because so many studies focus on the question of how many children of divorce have obvious, serious problems, and in order to test
whether divorce influences the lives of all children, even those who
appear to be "fine," we recruited "successful" children of divorce—that
is to say, college graduates—for the in-person interview portion of the
study. In this way we sought to obtain a qualitative sample of young
people with divorced parents who appeared to be doing well and who
were less likely to have experienced other hardships besides divorce.

In recruiting for the national survey sample of fifteen hundred
young people we did not require participants to be college graduates
(i.e., "successful"). This way the national survey data cited in the book
tell us about *all* children of divorce who stay in touch with both parents (and not just the ones who end up "fine"), while the in-person

interviews, from which the stories and anecdotes in this book are drawn, were conducted with the children of divorce who appear to be "fine." Note that young people who lost all (or virtually all) contact with a parent after the divorce were *not* studied and their experience is not reflected in any of the survey data or in-person interviews reported in this book.

2   **an advisory committee:** The researchers who formed an advisory committee for this project are Norval Glenn of the University of Texas in Austin, who was also co-investigator of the project's national survey; Judith Wallerstein of the Center for the Family in Transition and lead author of *The Unexpected Legacy of Divorce: A 25 Year Landmark Study;* Don Browning of the University of Chicago Divinity School and founder of the Religion, Culture, and Family Project; and Barbara Dafoe Whitehead, co-founder of the National Marriage Project and author of *The Divorce Culture*.

2   **the first nationally representative survey:** Other studies have used samples from various regions of the country. This is the first nationally representative sample of people who grew up in divorced families (with a similar-size control group of young people from intact families) that has been conducted in the United States.

2   **seventy-one in-person interviews:** These seventy-one young adults were randomly recruited by the firm SRBI, Inc., in New York City from selected zip codes in Atlanta; Chicago; Arlington, Virginia; and suburban Philadelphia. I contacted each recruit and scheduled a time and place in their area to meet for our audiotape-recorded interview, which typically lasted at least two hours. The interviews were then transcribed.

3   **One major national study:** Paul R. Amato and Alan Booth, *A Generation at Risk: Growing Up in an Era of Family Upheaval* (Cambridge: Harvard University Press, 1997), 220.

4   **children do better:** Life may not become easy for children after their parents' high-conflict marriage ends, but it does on average become better. We should not let a reasonable defense of divorces that end high-conflict marriages blind us to the difficulties that can persist in these children's lives. Too often the assumption is that if the parents *had* to divorce then the child's subsequent experiences are irrelevant.

4   **resources they may not know about:** For couples who wish to save or strengthen their marriages or who wish to head off potential problems through premarital education, see www.smartmarriages.com for resources in your area.

5   **Among the people:** The names and identifying details of all study participants have been changed to protect their confidentiality.

1: Growing Up Divorced

9   **the studies I read:** Some of these studies include Frank F. Furstenberg Jr. and Andrew J. Cherlin, *Divided Families: What Happens to Children When Parents Part* (Cambridge: Harvard University Press, 1991); Sara McLanahan and Gary Sandefur, *Growing Up with a Single Parent. What Hurts, What Helps* (Cambridge: Harvard University Press, 1994); and Amato and Booth, *A Generation at Risk.*

9   **E. Mavis Hetherington:** E. Mavis Hetherington and John Kelly, *For Better or for Worse: Divorce Reconsidered* (New York: W. W. Norton and Company, 2002).

9   **divorce has a "sleeper effect":** Judith Wallerstein, Julia Lewis, and Sandra Blakeslee, *The Unexpected Legacy of Divorce: A 25 Year Landmark Study* (New York: Hyperion, 2000).

10   **one-quarter of all young adults:** The statistic on the percentage of young adults who are children of divorce was compiled by Professor Norval Glenn, using the 2000 General Social Survey and the 2000 Census.

10   **Among those accounts:** Ava Chin, ed., *Split: Stories from a Generation Raised on Divorce* (New York: Contemporary Books, 2002); Stephanie Staal, *The Love They Lost: Living with the Legacy of Our Parents' Divorce* (New York: Delacorte Press, 2000); Jen Abbas, *Generation Ex: Adult Children of Divorce and the Healing of Our Pain* (Colorado Springs, CO: WaterBrook Press, 2004).

10   **For Walker, whose parents divorced:** Rebecca Walker, *Black, White, and Jewish: Autobiography of a Shifting Self* (New York: Riverhead Books, 2001).

11   **"I don't remember things.":** Walker, *Black, White, and Jewish,* 1–2.

11   **"I remember airports. . . .":** Walker, *Black, White, and Jewish,* 3.

14   **A therapist is quoted:** Anita Miller, director of divorce education at the nonprofit Storefront Group in Minneapolis, quoted in, "The Kids' Schedule? See the Website," *Christian Science Monitor,* July 2, 2003, Web edition.

14   **"more humane divorce":** Scott Coltrane and Michele Adams, "The Social Construction of the Divorce 'Problem': Morality, Child Victims, and the Politics of Gender," *Family Relations* 52, 4 (October 2003): 371.

14   **"The problem is not so much":** Michael G. Lawler, review of Hetherington and Kelly, *For Better or for Worse, INTAMS Review* 9 (2003): 136.

14 **"more than the divorce itself"**: Julie Schelfo, "Happy Divorce," *Newsweek,* December 6, 2004, 43 (emphasis in the original).

14 **A November 2002 cover story**: Bob Thompson, "Is This Any Way to Run a Divorce?" *Washington Post Magazine,* November 24, 2002, 14–20, 25–28.

15 **"a screaming match"**: Jennifer Frey, "For Families of Divorce, an Online Link to Sanity," *Washington Post,* July 29, 2003, C1.

15 **The term was first coined**: Constance Ahrons, *The Good Divorce: Keeping Your Family Together When Your Marriage Comes Apart* (New York: HarperCollins, 1994).

16 **"it matters not"**: Cited in William J. Doherty, *Take Back Your Marriage: Sticking Together in a World That Pulls You Apart* (New York: Guilford Press, 2001), 4.

16 **a "good divorce" is far worse**: See table in Appendix A for comparison of "good" and "bad" divorces with happy and unhappy marriages.

17 **Even the great works**: The literature on children's moral and spiritual development has a tremendous gap when it comes to children of divorce: No attention is given to the question of family structure and how growing up in a different kind of family, such as a divorced family, might influence children's moral and spiritual development. Some of the primary authors on children's moral development include Jean Piaget, Erik Erikson, Lawrence Kohlberg, Robert Coles, and Carol Gilligan. The field of children's religious or spiritual development is more diffuse but can include people from Sigmund Freud and Carl Jung to James Fowler and, again, Robert Coles, as well as other, less well-known scholars.

The theorists of moral development are often required reading in degree programs that train professionals who work with children and young people. Yet in this field, with the exception of Coles and Gilligan, the major works are decades old. Most were writing when one could assume that most children grew up living with their married mother and father. Even contemporary authors who write on moral or spiritual issues continue at least implicitly to assume that children have an intact family experience, often focusing instead on other sites of socialization such as schools, peers, or faith communities. While these sources of influence are certainly important, none is as primary and formative in a child's experience as the family.

2: Divided Selves

19 ***To & Fro, Fast & Slow:*** Durga Bernhard, *To & Fro, Fast & Slow* (New York: Walker and Company, 2001).

21 **almost two-thirds of children of divorce:** Unless otherwise noted, all statistics cited in this book, including this one, are from the National Survey on the Moral and Spiritual Lives of Children of Divorce, for which
Dr. Norval Glenn and I served as co-investigators.

27 **Litigation and conflict:** Joseph Hopper has a fascinating body of work
that explains how divorce polarizes couples. He writes, for example,
"The profound value attached to marriage engenders an important
problem of meaning when couples go through divorce. Namely,
because most people get married with the belief that marriage is forever, they face a difficult interpretive problem in explaining why theirs
is ending. To resolve the problem, they undo the previous meanings of
their marriages: initiators of divorce come to see their marriages as
having not been true marriages from the start, so efforts to preserve
their marriages seem absurd; noninitiating partners come to see their
spouses as having deceived them, so efforts to negotiate a divorce
seem rife with lies. In short, the solutions thus formulated effectively
resolve the interpretive problems posed, but they put the partners
dramatically at odds with one another." In "The Symbolic Origins of
Divorce," *Journal of Marriage and the Family* 63, 2 (2001): 431. See also
his "The Rhetoric of Motives in Divorce," *Journal of Marriage and the
Family* 55, 4 (1993): 810.

27 **harmful for children:** See for instance Andrew Cherlin, *Marriage,
Divorce, and Remarriage* (Cambridge: Harvard University Press, 1992):
79; Paul R. Amato, "Children's Adjustment to Divorce: Theories,
Hypotheses, and Empirical Support," *Journal of Marriage and the Family* 55, 1 (1993): 35; and Marsha Kline, Janet R. Johnston, and Jean M.
Tschann, "The Long Shadow of Marital Conflict: A Model for Children's Postdivorce Adjustment," *Journal of Marriage and the Family* 53,
2 (1991): 307.

28 **out of each other's way:** At least three studies, two of them rigorous and
large, confirm that many if not most divorced parents keep conflict to
a minimum basically by communicating only very rarely, if at all.
E. Mavis Hetherington found that 50 percent of the divorced parents
in her large study fell into the category she called "Parallel Co-
Parenting." She writes, "Basically, the 50 percent of divorced parents
who adopted this arrangement simply ignored each other. The former
husband didn't interfere with the former wife's parenting, and vice
versa, and no effort was made to coordinate their parenting strate-
gies. . . . Each parent did his or her 'own thing,' and while sometimes
the things they did were very different, parallel parenting arrangements

often contained minimum overt or persistent conflict." Hetherington and Kelly, *For Better or for Worse*, 139.

In their large and substantial study of divorced parents Eleanor E. Maccoby and Robert H. Mnookin concluded that "the avoidance of communication is a widespread phenomenon—one that does not lessen, but instead increases, with the passage of time." In each time period in which they assessed divorced couples an ever-smaller proportion were communicating regularly. "At Time 1," they write, "two-fifths of the couples talked with each other about aspects of the children's lives more than once a week; by Time 2, this proportion had declined to one-sixth. . . . At Time 2, one parent or both were reported to be attempting to limit communication between the parents in half of the families, and the proportion had increased to nearly three-fifths by Time 3." Eleanor E. Maccoby and Robert H. Mnookin, *Dividing the Child: Social and Legal Dilemmas of Child Custody* (Cambridge: Harvard University Press, 1992), 219.

Similarly, in her smaller study of ninety-eight divorced couples, Constance Ahrons found that only 12 percent of her sample were "high interactors—high communicators" (what she calls "Perfect Pals") and 38 percent were "moderate interactors-high communicators" ("Cooperative Colleagues"). The rest were Angry Associates, Fiery Foes, and Dissolved Duos. Ahrons, *The Good Divorce*, 52–59.

30 **confident they will get over it:** In our national survey, 92 percent of young adults from intact families, compared to 58 percent of young adults from divorced families, agreed, "When my parents had conflicts I always knew they would get over it." Most people from intact families (74 percent) strongly agreed with this statement, while only a small minority of children of divorce (27 percent) strongly agreed. This question, like most in the survey, was posed to the young adults from divorced families as "after your parents' divorce." They are reporting how they viewed their parents' conflicts *after* the divorce, not before it.

31 **upbeat guides on how to divorce:** There are many books that offer advice to divorcing parents. Just a few: Robert E. Emery, *The Truth About Children and Divorce: Dealing with the Emotions So You and Your Children Can Thrive* (New York: Viking, 2004); Susan Allison, *Conscious Divorce: Ending a Marriage with Integrity* (New York: Three Rivers Press, 2001); Edward Teyber, *Helping Children Cope with Divorce*, 2nd ed. (San Francisco: Jossey-Bass, 2001); Isolina Ricci, *Mom's House, Dad's House: A Complete Guide for Parents Who are Separated, Divorced, or Remarried*, 2nd ed. (New York: Fireside, 1997); Vicki Lansky, *Vicki Lansky's Divorce*

Book for Parents (Minnetonka, MN: Book Peddlers, 2003); Matthew McKay et al., *The Divorce Book* (Oakland, CA: New Harbinger Publishers, 1999); James Friedman, *The Divorce Handbook: Your Basic Guide to Divorce* (New York: Random House, 1999); Diana Mercer and Marsha Kline Pruett, *Your Divorce Advisor* (New York: Fireside, 2001); Sharon Naylor, *The Unofficial Guide to Divorce* (New York: Wiley, 1998).

3: Little Adults

36   **a script for divorcing parents:** See for instance: Emery, *The Truth About Children and Divorce*, 97–133; Allison, *Conscious Divorce*, 182; McKay et al., *The Divorce Book*, 179–85; Friedman, *The Divorce Handbook*, 29–30; Mercer and Pruett, *Your Divorce Advisor*, 177–81; Naylor, *The Unofficial Guide to Divorce*, 27–30. Parenting magazines routinely feature articles instructing parents how to tell their children they are divorcing, and there are many websites offering this kind of advice, such as www. divorcesource.com and www.betterdivorce.com.

38   **Those of us who grew up:** See table in Appendix A. A description of how we calculated the "good" divorce is found in note 5 to that table. By our not-too-stringent calculation half of our respondents grew up in "good" divorces. This formulation is consistent with Constance Ahrons' study, in which she classified about half the divorced couples she studied as having "good" divorces. (She refers to such couples as Cooperative Colleagues and Perfect Pals.) Ahrons, *The Good Divorce*, 52. In contrast, E. Mavis Hetherington's more stringent definition of what well-functioning divorced parents should achieve led her to classify only a quarter of her large sample of couples as doing well. Under a subheading titled "The Benefits of Cooperative Co-Parenting" she writes, "Because of the adversarial nature of divorce, a cooperative co-parenting arrangement where parents put the well-being of their children first is often difficult to attain. . . . Only about a quarter of our divorced parents achieved a cooperative relationship in which they talked over the children's problems, coordinated household rules and child-rearing practices, and adapted their schedules to fit their children's needs." Hetherington and Kelly, *For Better or for Worse*, 138.

49   **"what did you do?":** Respondents were not offered a series of choices; instead the question was open-ended and they were asked to provide one answer. Many of the responses fell into a fairly short list of categories.

51   **divorcing parents are commonly instructed:** See for instance Teyber, *Helping Children Cope with Divorce*, 55–56; Lansky, *Vicki Lansky's Divorce Book*, 76.

4: Home

60   **More than seventy reputable studies:** Robin Fretwell Wilson writes,
      "These studies of fractured families differ in their estimates of the
      percentage of girls molested during childhood. However, regardless of
      whether the precise number is 50% or even half that, the rate is stag-
      gering and suggests that girls are at much greater risk after divorce
      than we might have imagined." She continues, "Despite these studies,
      the idea that so many girls in fractured families report childhood sex-
      ual abuse strains credulity. Nevertheless, with more than seventy social
      science studies confirming the link between divorce and molestation,
      there is little doubt that the risk is indeed real. As difficult as it is to
      accept, a girl's sexual vulnerability skyrockets after divorce, with no
      indication that this risk will subside." In "Children at Risk: The Sexual
      Exploitation of Female Children after Divorce," *Cornell Law Review*
      86.2 (2001): 256.

61   **"reconstituted families":** Joseph H. Beitchman et al., "A Review of the
      Short-Term Effects of Child Sexual Abuse," *Child Abuse and Neglect* 15
      (1991): 550, cited in Wilson, "Children at Risk," note 9.

61   **"Living with a stepparent":** Martin Daly and Margot Wilson, "Evolution-
      ary Psychology and Marital Conflict: The Relevance of Stepchildren,"
      in *Sex, Power, Conflict: Evolutionary and Feminist Perspectives,* ed. David
      M. Buss and Neil M. Malamuth (Oxford: Oxford University Press,
      1996), 9–28, cited in Coalition for Marriage, Family and Couples Edu-
      cation and the Institute for American Values, *Why Marriage Matters:
      Twenty-One Conclusions from the Social Sciences,* (New York: Institute for
      American Values, 2002).

63   **Others speak respectfully:** For stepfamily support visit the Stepfamily
      Association of America at www.saafamilies.org.

68   **primarily with our mothers:** Thirteen percent lived primarily with their
      father. Eleven percent spent about the same amount of time with both
      parents. A few (3 percent) had another living arrangement.

75   **"For two miserable years":** Ahrons, *The Good Divorce,* 1–2.

75   **"ongoing escalations":** Ahrons, *The Good Divorce,* 58.

5: Early Moral Forgers

86   **It made a similar impression:** Young adults from divorced families are
      typically quite adept at talking about their parents' values. It is a sub-
      ject they have spent a lot of time thinking about. A couple of young
      men I interviewed, however, drew a complete blank when it came to
      describing their divorced fathers' values. This was true even though

they grew up with fathers who lived close by and who they saw routinely, eating dinner with them, attending sporting events with them, and more. But these sons simply could not think of anything that was overwhelmingly important or meaningful to their fathers. As one said, "We never really had those types of conversations."

In contrast, even people from intact families who had exceptionally busy fathers—those who ran their own businesses or were physicians, for example, and were rarely at home—could talk easily about their fathers' values. They may not have had frequent conversations with their dads either, but by sharing a home with them these young men observed the daily sacrifices their fathers made to keep their homes and families running. Children of married parents know that their parents' work outside the home benefits the family, but a divorced father's efforts typically happen beyond the scope of his child's daily life, making it that much more difficult for the child to discern his values.

106 **"like polar opposites":** Similarly, only 7 percent of the people from intact families said their parents conflicted a lot, but 34 percent of them saw their parents as polar opposites. When asked about conflict *before* the divorce, 31 percent of the children of divorce say that their parents conflicted a lot before the divorce. (Interestingly, a much larger, longitudinal study also found that only about one-third of divorces end high-conflict marriages. Amato and Booth, *A Generation at Risk,* 220.)

6: Secrets

114 **Experts discourage this practice:** There are many divorce books that urge parents not to keep secrets. See for instance Ricci, *Mom's House, Dad's House,* 142. I have been critical of the how-to-divorce books as a genre, but there is at least one book that I think is very sensitive and informative for parents who must divorce or those who are considering it. That book is Judith Wallerstein and Sandra Blakeslee, *What About the Kids? Raising Your Children Before, During, and After Divorce* (New York: Hyperion, 2003).

114 **Secrets, they say:** Secrets are viewed as a primary problem in family systems theory. Family secrets in the past continue to haunt subsequent generations, contributing to dysfunctional relationships in the children and grandchildren of those family members who first harbored the secret. Secrets also aid in the creation of "triangles," in which two family members keep secrets from a third, or share a secret

with a third member, as a way to draw that person in or exclude others from their relationship. Keeping secrets is said to impede the kind of communication and openness that is essential to healthy family functioning and the development of secure individuals. For a textbook review, see Carlfred B. Broderick, *Understanding Family Process: Basics of Family Systems Theory* (Newbury Park, CA: Sage Publications, 1993).

115   **While infidelity is a serious problem:** It is hard to come by solid numbers on how many marriages have experienced infidelity; studies vary quite widely in the numbers they find.

124   **Jen Robinson . . . writes:** Robinson, "Normal Abnormal," in Chin, ed., *Split: Stories from a Generation Raised on Divorce,* 15.

124   **"I made friends easily":** Robinson, "Normal Abnormal," 18.

130   **truth about their father:** Sometimes too, divorced parents may share other kinds of information with their children that married parents more often conceal. For instance, more children of divorce agree, "My parents have told me that my or my sibling's birth was an accident or a surprise" (27 versus 19 percent). Unfortunately, we did not ask the young adults *when* they learned this information. I suspect that the children of intact families were more likely to learn this information as adults, while the children of divorce may have been given this news earlier in life, sometimes as an explanation for why the parents got married (and subsequently got divorced).

132   **special episode about children of divorce:** *Oprah Winfrey Show,* transcript entitled "How to Protect Your Child's Emotions During Divorce," January 28, 2002, 7.

132   **"As I expected":** Ahrons, *The Good Divorce,* xii.

133   **revising their stories:** Hopper, "The Rhetoric of Motives in Divorce."

7: Child-Sized Old Souls

151   **Jesus says that a man:** Mark 10:2–12. Other New Testament passages on divorce are Luke 16:18, Matthew 5:31–32, and 1 Corinthians 7:10–13; 7:15. In the Gospel of Mark Jesus refers to what "Moses commanded," which is based on the divorce law in Deuteronomy 24:1–4.

153   **We feel just as *spiritual*:** Seventy percent of children of divorce say they are "very" or "fairly" spiritual, compared to 73 percent of people from intact families. Likewise, they report, at a surface level, very similar attitudes and experiences when it comes to having a relationship with God. Children of divorce and people from intact families look almost identical in their responses to items such as "I sometimes feel the presence of God" and "I feel like a member of God's family." There was

a difference of only two percentage points between the two groups in responding to "I worry about what will happen to me when I die" and only three percentage points in responding to "When I have needed help God has been there for me." When asked about their current frequency of prayer, they differed by only three percentage points. Similarly, there was only the slightest difference, perhaps not statistically significant, in their responses to items about God's qualities. The two groups differed by two to four percentage points when asked if God is "all-powerful," "caring," "loves us unconditionally," "does not exist," "angry," "just," "absent," "conniving," "compassionate," "like a friend," "like a father," "like a mother," and "forgiving."

However, these fairly similar responses could perhaps indicate that questions like these were too blunt. As noted earlier, a more precisely worded question yielded a much clearer difference: When presented with the statement "I think of God as the loving father or parent I never had in real life," 38 percent of children of divorce agreed versus 22 percent of their peers from intact families.

Although their feelings about being spiritual and their responses to some questions about God seem fairly similar, the spiritual lives of children of divorce *as children* differed a bit more. Again, in some cases the differences are slight. When asked, "Did you pray when you were a child?" 86 percent of people from intact families said yes, compared to 82 percent of children of divorce. When asked, "Thinking about the period in your childhood when you prayed most often, how often did you pray?" 59 percent of people from intact families said "every day," versus 52 percent of children of divorce. Interestingly, children of divorce were a little more likely to view prayer positively, perhaps because it was something they chose for themselves. When asked, "Which of the following best describes your practice of prayer as a child?" 20 percent of people from intact families, but 15 percent of children of divorce, viewed it as an "obligation." And 51 percent of people from intact families, but 55 percent of children of divorce, viewed it as a "source of comfort." The in-person interviews support the idea that when children of divorce were spiritual it was more likely to be something they turned to of their own volition and less likely to be something they engaged in with their parents or were made to do by their parents.

154   **only half as likely:** "I attended frequently throughout my childhood" was a voluntary response.

154   **people who divorce are less religious:** One set of researchers found that the "rate of marital dissolution [divorce] is 2.4 times higher among

couples where neither spouse attends [religious services] than among couples where each spouse attends religious services every week." Vaughn R. A. Call and Tim B. Heaton, "Religious Influence on Marital Stability," *Journal for the Scientific Study of Religion* 36 (1997): 382–92. These authors found that the positive effects of attendance are largely mediated through higher marital satisfaction and negative attitudes about extramarital sex. Likewise, other researchers found that those couples who "frequently attend religious services are only about half as likely to separate." Edward Laumann et al., *The Social Organization of Sexuality* (Chicago: University of Chicago Press, 1994), 501.

155 **Catholic and moderate Protestant children:** Leora E. Lawton and Regina Bures, "Parental Divorce and the 'Switching' of Religious Identity," *Journal for the Scientific Study of Religion,* March 2001, 106. They compared subjects' religious affiliation in adolescence (recalled) and now. "Moderate" and "conservative" are their terms.

156 **member at a house of worship:** Further, 15 percent of young adults from intact families say they currently hold a leadership position at a house of worship, compared to 10 percent of young adults from divorced families.

157 **the misconception is not uncommon:** The North American Conference of Separated and Divorced Catholics is a large national group working at the parish level to improve ministries to divorced people and their families. Their website can be found at www.nacsdc.org.

157 **people who identify as evangelical:** See W. Bradford Wilcox, "Conservative Protestants and the Family: Resisting, Engaging, or Accommodating Modernity?" in *A Public Faith: Evangelical Civic Engagement,* ed. Michael Cromartie (Lanham, MD: Rowman and Littlefield, 2003).

157 **Another reason why:** Some also might speculate that the lower socioeconomic status of children of divorce that most studies turn up is a factor, since evangelicals have a greater proportion of this income bracket among their members compared to comparatively well-off mainline Protestant denominations. But in our national survey of fifteen hundred individuals, the household income of young adult children of divorce and people from intact families was very similar. It is possible the two groups differed in net worth, which we did not ask about.

158 **a small book of readings:** Susan R. Garrett and Amy Plantinga Pauw, *Making Time for God: Daily Devotions for Children and Families to Share* (Grand Rapids, MI: Baker Books, 2002).

159 **"the color of water":** James McBride, *The Color of Water: A Black Man's Tribute to His White Mother* (New York: Riverhead Books, 1996).

159 **the story of the prodigal son:** Luke 15:11–32.

162 **Another young woman ... who I interviewed:** Elizabeth Marquardt, "Children of Divorce: Stories of Exile," *Christian Century* 118, 6 (2001): 26–29.

8: Getting Honest About Children of Divorce

171 **"[They] decide I will spend":** Walker, *Black, White, and Jewish*, 116–17.

172 **the example of Janet and Sybil:** Ahrons, *The Good Divorce*, 156.

173 **I couldn't help but wonder:** Constance Ahrons' newest book is *We're Still Family: What Grown Children Have to Say About Their Parents' Divorce* (New York: HarperCollins, 2004). For this book she located 173 of the now-grown children from her earlier study, using assistants to conduct telephone interviews. The anecdotes these young people shared are often quite moving, even disturbing, but what is more disturbing is that Ahrons wraps their experience in a thesis that denies that experience entirely. For instance, she asks them what was "positive" about their parents' divorce. Some replied their parents' divorce taught them that they want to work hard on their marriages and never divorce because they don't want to "do that" to their kids. Ahrons uses responses like these to support her thesis that children of divorce have many positive things to say about their parents' divorce which the culture doesn't hear because no one asks them if anything good came out of the divorce. Another major problem with her study is that the numbers are small and it has no control group, so although she speculates that the young people in her sample don't differ developmentally from their peers from intact families, she offers no data to back up that claim. For my review of her book, see Elizabeth Marquardt, "The Bad Divorce," *First Things: A Monthly Journal of Religion and Public Life*, February 2005, 24–27.

173 **families created through remarriage:** Just a few of the titles among hundreds of books on "blended families" include: *Stepcoupling: Creating and Sustaining a Strong Marriage in Today's Blended Family; The Blended Family Sourcebook: A Guide to Negotiating Change; And the Two Became One Plus: An Upfront Look at Today's Blended Family; The Stepparent's Survival Guide: A Workbook for Creating a Happy Blended Family; Step-by-Step-Parenting: A Guide to Successful Living with a Blended Family; Blended Families: Creating Harmony as You Build a New Home Life.*

174 **the U.S. Census Bureau now uses:** To see an example of U.S. Census Bureau use of the term *blended family*, see Jason Fields, "Living Arrangements of Children 1996," Current Population Reports P70–74,

and Stacy Furukawa, "The Diverse Living Arrangements of Children 1991," Current Population Reports, P70–38, U.S. Census Bureau, Washington, D.C., 1994, cited in *The Family Portrait: A Compilation of Data, Research and Public Opinion on the Family,* ed. Bridget Maher (Washington, D.C.: Family Research Council, 2002): 126.

174　**the term *bonus family*:** See www.bonusfamilies.com. This term is advocated by Jann Blackstone-Ford and Sharyl Jupe, authors of *Ex-Etiquette for Parents: Good Behavior After a Divorce or Separation* (Chicago: Chicago Review Press, 2004).

174　***Bird nesting* is a recently coined term:** See for instance Rachel Emma Silverman and Michelle Higgins, "When the Kids Get the House in a Divorce; To Ease the Disruption of Splits, Children Live in Family Home While Parents Alternate Stays," *Wall Street Journal,* Eastern edition, September 17, 2003, D1. This article was widely reproduced.

175　**conjuring up a picture of mommy and daddy birds:** Another problem with the choice of the term *bird nesting* is that it appropriates and distorts a biological phenomenon. In nature, birds don't decide they can't stand each other and set up a separate nest elsewhere, flying in and out to take care of their baby birds on alternate days. Adult birds leave the family nest briefly to get *food* for their baby birds.

176　**As one reviewer wrote:** David Small, "Passages," a review of *To & Fro, Fast & Slow* by Durga Bernhard, *New York Times,* November 18, 2001, online edition.

176　***My Parents Are Divorced, Too:*** Jan Blackstone-Ford et al., *My Parents Are Divorced, Too: A Book by Kids, for Kids* (Washington, D.C.: Magination, 1998).

177　**"the comforts of victimhood are small":** Whitehead, *The Divorce Culture,* 123.

177　**more intent on regulating . . . children's emotions:** Whitehead, *The Divorce Culture,* 123–24.

177　**A striking example:** Adolph Moser, *Don't Fall Apart on Saturdays!: The Children's Divorce-Survival Book* (Kansas City, MO: Landmark Editions, 2000).

178　**Divorce routinely makes it to the top:** The National Institute of Mental Health ranks divorce second on their list of triggers for depression. See www.nimh.nih.gov. Another typical list is (1) death of a spouse, (2) divorce, (3) marital separation, (4) jail term, (5) death of a close family member, (6) personal injury or illness, (7) marriage, (8) fired at work, (9) marital reconciliation, and (10) retirement. The latter can be found at www.crescentlife.com/wellness/stressors.htm.

179 **One columnist argued recently:** Bettina Arndt, "After Divorce, Kids Need Both Parents," *The Age* (Australia), August 29, 2003. Arndt cites research from the Australian Institute of Family Studies finding that in that country "only 38 percent of children up to two years old living with single mothers stay overnight with their fathers, compared to 60 percent of children aged 3 to 4." The researchers advocated increased visitation for these very young children. But another recent study, reported a couple of months later, found that "the majority of babies who live alternately with their divorced parents develop long-lasting psychological problems. . . . Such arrangements cause enduring 'disorganised attachment' in 60 percent of infants under 18 months, says a clinical psychologist and family therapist." From Lauren Martin, "Trouble Ahead for Babies of Divorce," *The Age* (Australia), October 21, 2003.

For a recent summary of some of the research in the United States regarding overnight stays for babies, from someone who favors the practice, see Richard A. Warshak, "Payoffs and Pitfalls of Listening to Children," *Family Relations* 52, 4 (2003): 379–80.

Conclusion

185 **some groups are pressing states:** Susan Dominus, "The Father's Crusade," *New York Times Magazine*, May 8, 2005, 26–33, 50, 56–58.

187 **Three-quarters of cohabiting parents:** "Fully three-quarters of children born to cohabiting parents will see their parents split up before they reach age sixteen, whereas only about a third of children born to married parents face a similar fate. One reason is that marriage rates for cohabiting couples have been plummeting. In the last decade, the proportion of cohabiting mothers who go on to eventually marry the child's father declined from 57% to 43%." From David Popenoe and Barbara Dafoe Whitehead, *Should We Live Together? What Young Adults Need to Know about Cohabitation Before Marriage*, 2nd ed. (Piscataway, NJ: National Marriage Project, 2002), 8. They cite Wendy Manning, "The Implications of Cohabitation for Children's Well-Being," in *Just Living Together: Implications for Children, Families, and Public Policy*, ed. Alan Booth and Ann C. Crouter (Hillsdale, NJ: Lawrence Erlbaum Associates, 2002).

187 **children of divorce have a higher divorce rate:** Our own data show that children of divorce are about 75 percent more likely to divorce than those from intact families are, and other, newer studies have produced similar results. About 43 percent of current first marriages are likely to

end in divorce, but that number takes into account people from all kinds of family backgrounds, including children of divorce. If the children of divorce are separated out, a realistic projection for their first-marriage divorce rate is about 60 to 65 percent. (Interestingly, this means their first-marriage divorce rate is similar to the 60 percent divorce rate for remarriages in the general population.) However, a hopeful note is that if a marriage survives the first four or five years, the probability of divorcing in any given year is fairly low, even for the children of divorce.

188 **only a minority of people:** Linda J. Waite et al., *Does Divorce Make People Happy? Findings from a Study of Unhappy Marriages* (New York: Institute for American Values, 2002); Linda J. Waite and Maggie Gallagher, *The Case for Marriage: Why Married People are Happier, Healthier, and Better Off Financially* (New York: Doubleday, 2000).

188 **Unhappy marriages can and often are turned around:** See Waite et al., *Does Divorce Make People Happy?* In focus groups the researchers found that many couples attributed the survival of their marriage to what the researchers called a "marital endurance ethic." The authors write, "Many spouses said that their marriages got happier, not because they and their partner resolved problems but because they stubbornly outlasted them. With time, they told us, many sources of conflict and distress eased" (p. 7). The divorce culture taught couples to attribute any unhappiness they felt to the marriage itself. The message was if you're unhappy, get out. But couples favoring the "marital endurance ethic" often find that it is outside stressors—job problems, meddling in-laws, health crises, even troublesome teenagers—that stress the marriage and make the partners unhappy. When these stressors subside—a new job is found, health problems become manageable or improve, the teenager grows up, etc.—the marriage may become happier.

188 **divorce often brings new, unexpected stresses:** On the question of whether divorce brings happiness, see Waite et al., *Does Divorce Make People Happy?*

188 **The divorce rate for remarriages:** The projected divorce rate for first marriages is 43 percent; for remarriages it is 60 percent. Remarriages face the extra challenges of bringing children from previous marriages, and possible new children as well, into a new family, as well as dealing with ex-spouses, budgets that are stretched between different households, emotional baggage, and more.

188 **a growing grassroots "marriage movement":** See "What Next for the Marriage Movement?" Institute for American Values, New York, 2004, and "The Marriage Movement: A Statement of Principles," Coalition for Marriage, Family and Couples Education, Institute for American Values, and the Religion, Culture, and Family Project at the University of Chicago Divinity School, 2000.

188 **would be helped greatly:** For some things that faith communities can do, see Marquardt, "Stories of Exile"; Elizabeth Marquardt, "Ministering to Children of Divorce Through the Life Cycle," *Circuit Rider,* May/June 2002, 20–23; and Elizabeth Marquardt, "The Prophetic Task of the Churches on Behalf of Children of Divorce," *Criterion—A Publication of the University of Chicago Divinity School* 40, 1 (2002): 16–19, 24. This last article is available at www.americanvalues.org. The Religion, Culture, and Family Project at the University of Chicago Divinity School has published numerous books and articles in recent years that offer ideas for a "critical familism" in the churches and the culture. See www.divinity.uchicago.edu/family/. A large national organization that has successfully helped clergy in many local communities organize to strengthen marriage and reduce their divorce rates is Marriage Savers. See www.marriagesavers.org. A new, high-quality church-based curriculum for young children of divorce is Divorce Care for Kids. See www.dc4k.org.

Acknowledgments

I first imagined writing this book more than eight years ago, but I could never have imagined all the people and institutions who would support this project, and me, in the years that followed.

My deepest thanks go to the Lilly Endowment and Dr. Craig Dykstra, its vice president for religion. The Lilly Endowment has been the sole and extremely generous funder for the project on which this book is based: a four-year-long adventure (that began in 2001) involving qualitative interviews, a national survey, data analysis, and manuscript writing and dissemination, known as the Project on the Moral and Spiritual Lives of Children of Divorce. They were willing to make a bet on an unusual project led by a newcomer to the field. I am very grateful to them for this opportunity.

I am also extremely indebted to the Institute for American Values and its president, David Blankenhorn. At the Institute I have been fortunate to find an extraordinary home: gatherings of some of the best scholars in the nation, lively debate, rigorous criticism of ideas, and friendship and emotional support through the ups and downs of this project and life in general. If there is anything solid and lasting in this book it is due in large part to the Institute, which routinely produces high-caliber, groundbreaking work.

Some of the scholars who give their time to the Institute served as advisors to my project. They are Judith Wallerstein, Norval Glenn, Barbara Dafoe Whitehead, and Don Browning. Each of them has been extraordinarily generous.

Judith Wallerstein, who for decades has led the way in the study of the inner lives of children of divorce, showered me with encouragement and brought a helpfully critical eye to the questions I asked and the conclusions I reached. Norval Glenn, a leading family scholar, partnered with me to co-investigate the nationally representative survey reported in this book, bringing a heft to the book that I could not have accomplished alone. In addition, the favorable reception he gave my ideas in our conversations over the years gave me much-needed courage. More than eight years ago, Barbara Dafoe Whitehead was the very first person to encourage me to write a book after I wrote telling her how personally moved I was by her important book, *The Divorce Culture*. After reading my eight-page, single-spaced letter she stunned me by calling and telling me I had a book in me. I think that without her push it would have taken me many more years to figure it out. Don Browning, now professor emeritus at the University of Chicago Divinity School, was my professor and thesis advisor when I first began formulating the questions that eventually led to this book. He became a great mentor who gave freely of his time and gave me a wonderful opportunity by bringing me on as an intern on the Religion, Culture, and Family Project. All four of these scholars have read multiple drafts of the book and Drs. Wallerstein and Glenn have contributed forewords. I will always be grateful to all of them.

Over the years many others have given critical support to this project. At the Institute, I would like to thank in particular Josephine Tramontano, Charity Navarette, Mary Schwarz, Sara Butler, and Bonnie Robbins. In addition, Deb Strubel brought an expert eye to the manuscript, suggesting many revisions throughout that ultimately made it tighter and clearer.

Other scholars have been instrumental to this project as well, especially Maggie Gallagher, who first brought my work to the attention of those at the Institute. Over the years she has given me cheerful encouragement, read many drafts, and helped me believe in what I was doing. Enola Aird attended early meetings and provided an important insight on the usefulness of this thesis for understanding what marriage does for children. Kay Hymowitz read an early draft of this manuscript and gave very helpful feedback. Brad Wilcox provided reassurance by giving an expert read to the chapter that reports the findings on religion.

I'd like to thank my fellow students in the M.Div. class of '99 at the University of Chicago Divinity School, especially Anna Lee, Amy Ziettlow, Sam Adams, and Alain Epp Weaver, and the then-director of the ministry program, Stephanie Paulsell, who all formed my first sounding board for these ideas. I'd also like to thank my fellow students who worked on the Religion, Culture, and Family Project, especially John Wall, M. Christian Green, and Melanie O'Hara, all of whom encouraged me with their enthusiasm and provided helpful resources and feedback.

I'm grateful to many who gave me logistical support, in particular by providing space and help for qualitative interviewing. Many thanks to Rick Rosengarten and Sandra Peppers at the University of Chicago Divinity School; John Witte at Emory University's Center for the Interdisciplinary Study of Religion; M. Christian Green, who was at that time at the Park Ridge Center for Health, Faith, and Ethics; and Mark Grady of the George Mason University School of Law. Students at Haverford College and St. Joseph's University graciously and enthusiastically helped with early field testing of the qualitative interview instrument. Thanks to Aliza and Steve Baron and Don and Carol Browning for giving me restful places to stay—and fun conversations—in Chicago and Atlanta.

Above all, I'd like to thank the seventy-one young adults from divorced and intact families who rearranged their schedules and opened their hearts to me. Each of their life stories could fill a book. Not only are they quoted extensively in this book but the patterns I observed in their lives helped inform questions that we asked later in a national survey. I still think often of them and thank them for their trust and generosity. I would also like to extend a special thanks to those from intact families who may not see as much of their story in these pages but whose participation was vital to the quality of this study and who taught me so much.

I would like to thank Chintan Turakhia and SRBI, Inc., in New York City for fielding the national survey so ably. Many thanks as well to others who have helped with questions or read drafts, including David Popenoe, Bridget Maher, Andrea Lemke, Linda Ranson-Jacobs, Tom Sylvester, and Diane Sollee. Thanks to Sherri Hauser for early support of this work. Thanks to Kevin Hsu for helping with the tables. Much gratitude to Jenna Paulson for keeping our baby daughter so happy while I wrote this manuscript.

With the help of these people, I was able to research and write a manuscript. A whole new set of very important people have turned it into a book. My deepest gratitude goes to Rachel Klayman, my editor at Crown Publishers, for seeing the merit in what I wrote. In our first conversation after she read my manuscript she restated my argument to me, saying it better than I could. I knew my work would be in safe hands. She has brought an extremely knowledgeable and literary eye to every word in this book, improved the writing, caught (I hope) at least most of the mistakes, and been a pleasure to work with in every way. My thanks as well to the whole team at Crown, especially Alex Douglas, who helped tremendously with the endnotes and other details, and Tina Constable, who, together with Darlene Faster, brought formidable energy and creativity to the publicity campaign for this book.

Very special thanks to my agent, Carol Mann, who helped this book find just the right home.

All of these people have helped this book become the best it can be. The shortcomings and mistakes that remain are my own.

Finally, the most important thanks of all—to my family.

With all my love, I would like to thank my parents. They were only twenty-one years old when they separated and later divorced. Few deserve to have their grown child so intensely analyze a decision made so young as I have theirs. Yet my mother and father not only tolerated this book project but actively and bravely supported it. As I write in these pages, this book is not about whether you love your parents. It's about something quite different. I thank them and my stepmother for all their support and hope I can match their example if my own children choose to write a book someday about me.

Almost nine years ago my family doubled in size when I married my husband, Jim. His family, especially his parents, have been kindly and enthusiastically supportive of this project and of me. I've always been grateful for marrying into such a wonderful family and for the son they produced.

I guess no book is easy to write. This one certainly wasn't. My intense scrutiny of childhood and divorce has been the elephant in our marriage from practically our first days together, too often stirring an emotional cauldron in me. This book exists today because, despite that, Jim has steadfastly supported my work in a million small ways. He's tolerated the weird writing schedule, the research trips, the self-absorption, and more. Through it all he's been my rock, the man I could always count on to hug me and say that everything really would be okay. I am lucky to have found him and our beautiful children are blessed to have the best daddy in the world. Whatever good may come of this book I dedicate to him.

Index

About the Author

ELIZABETH MARQUARDT is an affiliate scholar at the Institute for American Values, a nonpartisan think tank in New York City focused on children, families, and civil society. She is the co-author of a groundbreaking study on college women's attitudes about sex and dating on campus, titled "Hooking Up, Hanging Out, and Hoping for Mr. Right: College Women on Dating and Mating Today." She has appeared on such national television programs as NBC's *Today Show,* CNN's *Talk Back Live,* ABC's *World News Tonight with Peter Jennings,* Fox's *O'Reilly Factor,* and PBS's *Religion and Ethics Newsweekly,* and has been interviewed on dozens of radio programs, including National Public Radio's *All Things Considered.* Her writings have appeared in the *New York Times, Washington Post, Chicago Tribune, Philadelphia Inquirer,* and elsewhere. She holds a B.A. from Wake Forest University and both an M.Div. and an M.A. in international relations from the University of Chicago. She lives in Chicago with her husband, Jim, and their two children.